SECURITY AND EMBEDDED SYSTEMS

NATO Security through Science Series

This Series presents the results of scientific meetings supported under the NATO Programme for Security through Science (STS).

Meetings supported by the NATO STS Programme are in security-related priority areas of Defence Against Terrorism or Countering Other Threats to Security. The types of meeting supported are generally "Advanced Study Institutes" and "Advanced Research Workshops". The NATO STS Series collects together the results of these meetings. The meetings are co-organized by scientists from NATO countries and scientists from NATO's "Partner" or "Mediterranean Dialogue" countries. The observations and recommendations made at the meetings, as well as the contents of the volumes in the Series, reflect those of participants and contributors only; they should not necessarily be regarded as reflecting NATO views or policy.

Advanced Study Institutes (ASI) are high-level tutorial courses to convey the latest developments in a subject to an advanced-level audience

Advanced Research Workshops (ARW) are expert meetings where an intense but informal exchange of views at the frontiers of a subject aims at identifying directions for future action

Following a transformation of the programme in 2004 the Series has been re-named and re-organised. Recent volumes on topics not related to security, which result from meetings supported under the programme earlier, may be found in the NATO Science Series.

The Series is published by IOS Press, Amsterdam, and Springer Science and Business Media, Dordrecht, in conjunction with the NATO Public Diplomacy Division.

Sub-Series

A.	Chemistry and Biology	Springer Science and Business Media
B.	Physics and Biophysics	Springer Science and Business Media
C.	Environmental Security	Springer Science and Business Media
D.	Information and Communication Security	IOS Press
E.	Human and Societal Dynamics	IOS Press

http://www.nato.int/science
http://www.springeronline.nl
http://www.iospress.nl

Sub-Series D: Information and Communication Security – Vol. 2   ISSN: 1574-5589

Security and Embedded Systems

Edited by

Dimitrios N. Serpanos
University of Patras, Greece

and

Ran Giladi
Ben Gurion University, Israel

Press

Amsterdam • Berlin • Oxford • Tokyo • Washington, DC

Published in cooperation with NATO Public Diplomacy Division

Proceedings of the NATO Advanced Research Workshop on Security and Embedded Systems
Patras, Greece
22–26 August 2005

© 2006 IOS Press.

ISBN 1-58603-580-0
Library of Congress Control Number: 2005937976

Publisher
IOS Press
Nieuwe Hemweg 6B
1013 BG Amsterdam
Netherlands
fax: +31 20 687 0019
e-mail: order@iospress.nl

Distributor in the UK and Ireland
Gazelle Books
Falcon House
Queen Square
Lancaster LA1 1RN
United Kingdom
fax: +44 1524 63232

Distributor in the USA and Canada
IOS Press, Inc.
4502 Rachael Manor Drive
Fairfax, VA 22032
USA
fax: +1 703 323 3668
e-mail: iosbooks@iospress.com

To our families
  – D. Serpanos
  – R. Giladi

In memoriam
Yuri P. Shankin

Security and Embedded Systems
D.N. Serpanos and R. Giladi (Eds.)
IOS Press, 2006

Preface

Technological advances have led to wide deployment and use of embedded systems in an increasing range of applications, from mobile phones to car, plane and spacecraft and from digital id's to military systems in the field. Many of these applications place significant security requirements and have led to significant research activity in the area of security and embedded systems, due to the limited resources of conventional embedded systems. This emerging research area is of great importance to a large number of public and private organizations, due to their desire to deploy secure embedded systems in the field.

The NATO Advanced Research Workshop on "Security and Embedded Systems" constitutes one of the first international efforts to emphasize the importance of this emerging technical field and to provide a forum for presentations and participation of leading researchers in the field. Its objectives were to present the technologies and open problems of the emerging area of security and embedded systems, to present the latest research results in all aspects of security in embedded systems, and, finally, to provide a roadmap of the technology for the future. Considering the main directions of research in the field, we organized the workshop in 3 main areas: (i) foundations of security and embedded systems, (ii) secure embedded computing systems and (iii) telecommunications and network services. The program included 23 papers, covering all main areas with strong research and tutorial contributions from a wide range of participants from industry and academia. In these proceedings, we include all papers by the contributors to the workshop.

We thank the members of the Organizing Committee of the workshop: J. Dockal (University of Defence, Czech Republic), V. Gorodetsky (Russian Academy of Sciences, Russia), J. Henkel (University of Karlsruhe, Germany) and W. Wolf (Princeton University, USA). Their contributions and participation in this effort as well as their experience have led to a very successful program for the workshop, which was enjoyed by all participants. Finally, we thank Mr. Kyriakos Stefanidis for his invaluable help and support in the organization of the workshop.

Based on the results of the workshop and the interest of the attendants, we strongly believe that this effort should be followed up by additional workshops and conferences in the future, focusing on security and embedded systems.

D.N. Serpanos, University of Patras, Greece
R. Giladi, Ben Gurion University, Israel

Contents

Security and Embedded Systems
D.N. Serpanos and R. Giladi (Eds.)
IOS Press, 2006

Chaotic Routing as a Method of an Information Conversion

Y.P. SHANKIN

International Center for Informatics and Electronics, Moscow, Russia

Abstract. The information conversion method based on the nonlinear dynamic systems theory is proposed. It includes the initial open text transformation into hypersymbols of the symbolic dynamics. Under respective system states set Markov partition such an information conversion ensures strict one-to-one conformity with the initial text and can't be reduced to any traditional additive composition of information and random signals or block based encryption. The report includes a qualitative consideration of an information conversion method.

Keywords. Chaos, cryptography, symbolic dynamics, Markov partition

Introduction

There are a lot of coding algorithms for security insurance systems developed. In spite of it the elaboration of flexible effective high speed coding methods for information security is still an actual problem and gives rise to investigations of non-traditional approaches. At a present time there are some bases to speak about conceptional intersection of the nonlinear systems theory, which has the richest scientific potential (since Lyapunov's and Poincaré's works), and traditional cryptography, based on methods and tools of discrete mathematics, algebra and number theory. Complex behavior of chaotic systems "… may bears a cryptic relationship with the simple evolution laws which define them" [1]. Such a "simple complexity" based on nonlinear dynamics with floating point arithmetic gives rise to a possibility of its use for embedded systems security problems, as well as strict physical laws may promote traditional cryptography methods.

In spite of some inherent drawbacks of chaotic cryptosystems (such as low security or weakness in resistance against noise disturbances) investigations are going on in nonlinear community (for example, [2–4]). Hyperchaotic systems with many positive Lyapunov exponents (in particular spatiotemporal chaos) have been investigated widely for its excellent performance in spread spectrum communication [5].

Crypto-chaotic investigations are concentrated usually in fields of chaotic bit sequences generation for the stream cipher cryptography or block-based chaotic encryption (for example, [6,7]). Some new approach to an information conversion technique is considered in this report, which can't be reduced to an additive composition of information and random signals or block-based encryption.

1. Itinerary Formation

The theoretical background, upon which the fundamental relationship between properties of chaotic and cryptographic systems is based, includes discussions on chaos, ergodicity, complexity, randomness, unpredictability, incompressibility. In 1950 Shannon has mentioned the role of "stretching and shrinking" operation for data encryption [8]. About 50 years before Henri Poincare has found such a behavior in nonlinear dynamics [9]. He has proposed some special technology for the nonlinear dynamics investigation, now known as "Poincare mapping", that looks like discreet-time description of a physical processes and simplifies computer calculations (but it's not stroboscopic i.e. not equally spaced in time.)

Informational pithy symbolic sequences can be generated by nonequilibrium systems in a state of chaotic attractor (symbolic dynamics) [10] that can be considered as a text composed of hypersymbols. (In accordance with [11] the occurrence of chaos for the unimodal maps is related to the transcendence of the number defined by the corresponding symbolic dynamics). Under respective system states set Markov partition such a "text" can be one-to-one tied up with the chaotic dynamic system initial state.

Let us examine the case of one-dimensional partially smooth expanding (i.e. with Lyapunov's number $\alpha \geq const > 1$) mapping f of line segment $A = [P_0, P_k]$ of the length L on itself $(A \rightarrow A)$.

Let: $P_0 < P_1 < \ldots < P_k$, $A_\zeta = [P_{\zeta-1}, P_\zeta]$, $\zeta = 1, 2, \ldots, k$ – expanding partitioning of a given line segment (one-dimensional analogue of Markov partition). In this case [12]:

- every possible finite sequence $A_1 \ldots A_n$ equally corresponds to certain subsegment of line segment A of length:

$$\delta_n \leq \frac{L}{\alpha^{n-1}} \; ; \tag{1}$$

- every possible infinite sequence $A_1 A_2 A_3 \ldots$ corresponds to the single point x_0 of interval A, which generates chaotic orbit $f(f \ldots f(x) \ldots)$ (in the case, if symbolic sequence is not periodical).

So the initial information, which is contained in a digital representation of number $x_0 \in A$ (in general case – irrational), and sets initial state of iterative process:

$$x_{n+1} = f(x_n), n = 0, 1, 2, \ldots \tag{2}$$

can be equally converted into rout (or itinerary – symbolic sequence) $\overrightarrow{I} = \{A_{in}\}$, so that $f(x_n) \in A_{in}, i_n \in [1, k]$.

And vice verse. The initial information (so called "open text") may be originally considered as the given itinerary (if written with the Markov partition alphabet) and then transformed (under curtain conditions) to the start point of nonlinear mapping. Text restoration (i.e. itinerary formation on the receiving side) may be generated by direct nonlinear mapping with the present start point.

If assign $L = 1$, $\delta_n = 10^{-S_n}$, $\lambda = \ln \alpha$ (Lyapunov's index) then can be written:

$$S_n \geq \frac{(n-1)\lambda}{\ln 10}, \tag{3}$$

i.e. n symbols of the itinerary correspond to not less than S_n symbols of «decimal text», written at the initial state of dynamic system.

2. Text Restoration Problem

In fact, restoration of the text ($\overrightarrow{x}$) by means of a given itinerary $\overrightarrow{I}$ and mapping function f is possible by an itinerary reading both from the left to the right and from the right to the left, however algorithm of reading and it's main parameters (complexity and stability) are essentially diverse.

In the case of reverse ("Arabic" – i.e. from the right to the left) reading of $\overrightarrow{I}$, reverse mapping f^{-1} is drawn up, which ambiguity is eliminated by choice of its brunches in accordance to the given itinerary ($\overrightarrow{I}$).

Under "Latin" (from the left to the right) reading an itinerary ($\overrightarrow{I}$) in order to restore initial text ($\overrightarrow{x}$) in accordance with a given function f, the algorithm is more complex and consists of precise root calculations of the following iterative equations:

$$f(f \ldots f(x) \ldots) - x = 0 \tag{4}$$

with ultimate accuracy which is determined by precision of computing system used (in order to determine reliably boundaries of interval for search of equation (4) roots at the next iterations stage).

It can be proved that every disturbance of an itinerary leads to a complete loss of initial decimal text, corresponding to that part of an itinerary, which follows after introduced disturbance (even if it is completely identical to a corresponding part of an initial itinerary). Let $(N + 1)$'th symbol of the itinerary $\overrightarrow{I}$ is misrepresented (in a case of "Latin" type of reading). It means that on the $(N + 1)$'th step of iterations:

$$f^{N+1}(x_0) = \underbrace{f(f \ldots f(x_0) \ldots)}_{N+1}$$

a corresponding sub-element of initial line segment A is determined incorrectly. Preceding N «correct» symbols of the itinerary correspond, according to (1), to some interval of a length $\delta *$:

$$\delta^* \sim \frac{1}{\alpha^{N-1}},$$

which contains point x_0. At the same time the next choice of $(N + 1)$'th symbol of the itinerary corresponds to an incorrect choice of a segment on x-axis. And under further partitioning of this segment to shorter components the point x_0 do not belongs to any one more.

So, quantity δ^* can be considered as an initial system state determination inaccuracy under the disturbance of the itinerary at the $(N + 1)$'th step:

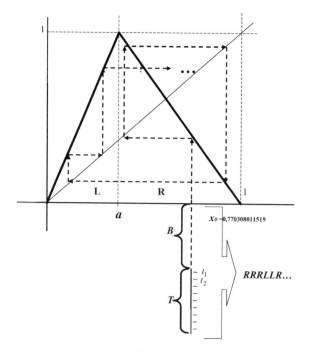

Figure 1.

$\Delta x_0 = \delta^*$.

On the other hand, divergence speed of dynamic systems trajectories is characterised by Lyapunov's index $\lambda = \ln \alpha$, and inaccuracy of state determination after M steps
can be written:

$$\Delta x_M = \Delta x_0 e^{\lambda M} = \delta^* e^{\lambda M} \approx e^{\lambda M - \lambda(N-1)}, \ (\lambda > 0)$$

Under $M > N$ inaccuracy Δx_M exceeds the length of initial interval, i.e. any correspondence of route segment with real initial state of the system is lost. This is an important fact for the initial "text"-restoring problem with a given symbolic one.

Let's simplify the problem by reducing initial Markov partition to the choice of the
right (R) or the left (L) subsegments of initial segment [0, 1] (Fig. 1, the «tent-map» is
shown as a nonlinear mapping f). Appearance of «buffer» (B) before the «text» part (T)
is caused by the necessity to bring the system to chaotic state (formation of a limit cycle). The buffer «size» (number of decimal positions) before information text determines the upper value of «key space» dimensionality of nonlinear transformation at
issue. A «key space» volume depends upon number of parametric clusters, assigned by
discretization threshold of the nonlinear mapping main parameters (under realisation of
«Markov partition» conditions). The text restoration is possible only in the case of
common parameter clusters for direct and invert information conversion. Number of
clusters N («key space») essentially depends on freedom degrees set (number of independent parameters – P of the system) and a «buffer length» (B):

$$N \leq 10^{PB}.$$

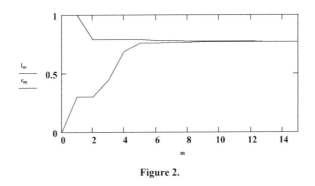

Figure 2.

The problem of unique restoration of an unknown function f with a help of a given initial data $\vec{x}$ and itinerary $\vec{I}$ (so called «an open text attack») is an ill-conditioned problem (in the sense of Hadamard) and has no correct solution unless some *a'priori* information about the type of mapping f is known.

3. Numerical Example

As an example let us consider the word «CHAOS», which decimal notation of initial state is given by:

$$x_0 = 0,770308011519. \tag{5}$$

Double-figure "77" plays a role of a buffer and the following digits are in accord with a sequential number of an English alphabet letters of the word «CHAOS». In the case of above mentioned mapping f of a «tent-map» type (Fig. 1) and parameter $a = 0,3$ the following itinerary corresponds to the initial value (5) of mapping (2):

$$\vec{I} = RRRLLRRRRRRRLRRRR \ldots \tag{6}$$

with a total length given by an evaluation (3). (The same type of the route (6) under different values of parameter «a» will be in accord with entirely different initial «texts»).

Figure 2 corresponds to a «Latin» reading of the itinerary (6). A sequential numbers of individual symbols of the itinerary (6) are laid on the abscissa axis. The Fig. 2 ordinates axis corresponds to an initial line segment [0, 1] of the Fig. 1 x-axis (the upper curve on the picture 2 corresponds to the upper boundary of subinterval, which contains initial value x_0 and the lower curve corresponds to the lower boundary of the same subinterval). As can be seen from the picture those boundaries consecutively converge under route reading, finally resulting in complete restoration of the initial value (5), and hence complete restoration of the initial word «CHAOS».

The more complicated type of mapping f (e.g., in the case of «tent-map» mapping with non-linear edges and increasing number of mapping «structural parameters») substantially complicates solving of inverse problem by outside person, who has no information about type of mapping f. At the same time, however, both the direct («Latin») and the reverse («Arabic») reading of the itinerary by a «proxy person» (i.e. under known function f) uniquely restores the initial text under compulsory realization of Markov partition conditions of initial segment [0, 1], which corresponds to the type of mapping f. In the case of Markov partition conditions violation rigorous solution of inverse problem remains formally possible, but it leads to numerical value of $\overline{x_0}$, which is different from initial value of x_0.

4. Conclusion

The information transformation method on the basis of initial text chaotic routing ensures rigorous equal (one-one) conformity:

$$(f, \vec{I}) \to x_0$$

$$(f, x_0) \to I$$

between elements of triad

$$(f / \{A\}, \vec{I}, x_0)$$

that includes namely the nonlinear mapping f with appropriate Markov partition $\{A\}$, itinerary vector $\vec{I}$ and initial state x_0.

Both the direct $(x_0 \to \vec{I})$ and the reverse $(\vec{I} \to x_0)$ transformations can be realised in digital or analogous form, at the same time the amount of the information transmitted in one act is determined by precision of computing system used or by precision accuracy of physical systems in case of analogous realisation of nonlinear mapping f.

Mappings $(x_0 \to \vec{I})$ and $(\vec{I} \to x_0)$ are sequential mappings with consequences, i.e. preceding elements of mapping essentially influence on formation of the consequent ones.

In the case of digital realisation of chaotic routing algorithm (under finite precision of data presentation) or taking into account limited instrument precision of the appropriate analogous physical systems it is possible to partition block-by-block the initial text to sub systems of finite length, that correspond to self-contained (independent) initial values of chaotic router.

The report includes a qualitative consideration of an information conversion method. Its actual characteristics depend upon many accompanying factors such as concrete type of a mapping, Lyapunov exponent maximum, Markov partition alphabet dimension etc. An engineering solution for practical realization of a proposed algorithm is an open problem.

References

[1] H. Gutowitz, Cryptography with Dynamical Systems, in: *Cellular Automata and Cooperative Phenomena*, Eds: E. Goles and N. Boccara, Kluwer Academic Press, 1993. (http://www.santafe.edu/~hag/crypto/crypto.html).

[2] Yu.V. Andreyev, A.A. Dmitriev, A Cryptosystem based on chaotic dynamics, *Proceedings SCS'2001*. Iasi. Romania (2001), 57–60.

[3] Shihong Wang, Weiping Ye, Huaping Lu, Jinyu Kuang, Jinghua Li, Yunlun Luo, Gang Hu, A Spatio-temporal-chaos-based Encryption Having Overall Properties Considerably Better Than Advanced Encryption Standard, *arXiv:nlin.CD/0303026* v1-**14**, Mar 2003.

[4] Xingang Wang, Meng Zhan, C.H. Lai "Error Function Attack of chaos synchronization based encryption schemes", *arXiv:nlin.PS/0305015* v1-**11**, May 2003.

[5] Xia Yongxiang, Shan Xiuming, Ren Yong, Yin Xunhe, Liu Feng, Correlation properties of binary spatiotemporal chaotic sequences and their application to multiple access communication, *Phys. Rev. E* **64**, (2001), 067201.

[6] Tohru Kohda, Akio Tsuneda, Chaotic bit sequences for stream cipher cryptography and their correlation functions, in *Chaotic Circuits for Communication, Proceedings of SPIE* **2612**, (1995), 86–97.

[7] J. Fridrich, Symmetric ciphers based on two-dimensional chaotic maps, *Int. J. Bifurcation and Chaos* **8**, N. 6, (1998), 1259–1284.

[8] C.E. Shannon, Communication theory of secrecy systems, *Bell SystemTechnical Journal* **28**, N. 4, (1949), 656–715.

[9] H. Poincare, *Les Methodes Nouvelles de la Mechaniqye Celecte*, Gauthier-Villars, Paris,1897.

[10] G. Nicolis, I. Prigogine, *Exploring Complexity: An Introduction*, W.H. Freeman & Co. NY, 1989.

[11] K. Karamanos, From symbolic dynamics to a digital approach, *Int. Journ. of Bifurcation and Chaos* **11**, N. 6, (2001), 1683–1694.

[12] K.T. Alligood, T.D. Sauer, I.A. Yorke, *CHAOS: an introduction to dynamical systems*, Springer, NY, 1996.

Security and Embedded Systems
D.N. Serpanos and R. Giladi (Eds.)
IOS Press, 2006

Combinatorial Game Models
for Security Systems

Edward POGOSSIAN

State Engineering University of Armenia, Computer Software Division
Academy of Science of Armenia, Institute for Informatics and Automation Problems
epogossi@aua.am

Abstract. An effective method of game based dynamic analysis of disturbances in security of systems and their preservation by elaboration of optimal strategies that can meet the requirements to embedded systems is presented. The results of preliminary experiments in strengthening intrusion protection strategies by expert knowledge and arguments in conceptual strategy knowledge simulation are discussed for further applications.

Keywords. Security, embedded systems, game model, strategy, knowledge based

1. Introduction

Embedded systems are intensively intervening in business, management, service, military and other applications and although their development meets, in general, common problems of system design, they require harder parameters for efficiency, especially, for high speed, low cost, simplicity of implementation and usage.

We aim to present an effective method of dynamic analysis of possible disturbances in security of systems and their preservation by elaboration of optimal strategies that can meet the above requirements to embedded systems. In the variety of problems we identify the class where *Space* of possible *Solutions* can be specified by combinatorial *Game Trees* (SSGT) and develop strategy formation algorithm – *Intermediate Goals At First* (IGAF).

The SSGT is a spacious class of problems with only a few following requirements to belong to:

- there are parties of interacting participants performing actions in identified moments of time
- the actions of parties comprised known finite sets
- there are identified benefits for all participants
- the situations where the parties act in and are transformed after actions have adequate models.

Many security and competition problems belong to SSGT class. Specifically, these are network Intrusion Protection (IP), Management in oligopoly competitions and Chess-like combinatorial problems. Many other security problems such as Computer Terrorism Countermeasures, Disaster Forecast and Prevention, Information Security, etc., announced by the NATO (http://www.nato.int/science/e/newinitiative.htm) as well as problems in [4,5,7,12] may be reduced to the SSGT class.

We prove an adequacy of game models for security problems by demonstrating their effectiveness compatible with system administrators [20,21].

The IGAF like algorithms were studied in [1,2,13] and in [22,24] where optimal strategy provision algorithms for chess and oligopoly market competitions were described. Suggested by Botvinnik the cutting-down tree algorithm for chess is based on the initial extraction of subgoals within a game tree, which allows to reduce sharply the searching tree as compared to the method of minimax [11]. The algorithm allows determination of moving trajectories of confronting parties in order to construct a zone around the extracted subgoal trajectory.

The IGAF algorithms were successfully probed in the network IP and management problems. For the IP problem the IGAF1 was outperformed system administrators and known standard protection systems in about 60% in experiments on fighting against 12 different types of known network attacks [20–22].

To increase the efficiency of the IGAF1 algorithm its more advanced version was suggested able to acquire a range of expert knowledge in form of goals or rules and to increase the efficiency of strategy formation with increasing the amount of expert knowledge available to the algorithm. A viability of the IGAF2 algorithm was tested against representatives of six classes of attacks [17].

In the consequent chapters we define the SSGT class and give two detailed examples how to represent different application problems as the game models. Then we describe the concept of optimal strategy and two on the-job-performance base criteria for measuring the quality of strategies – the min max and Testing Matrix Analysis. In Chapter 4, we concentrate on the security problems describing the IGAF method and evidence in its compatibility with advanced IP programs and experts. Then, we present the results of preliminary experiments in strengthening IP strategies by expert rules and goals, and argue why expert conceptual strategy knowledge can be simulated and how the adequacy of models has to be proved. Conclusions summarize the results and further plans.

2. Combinatorial Game Tree Models

2.1. SSGT problems are identified in a unified way by game tree constituents, which creates the base for a unified methodology of their resolution. The constituents include, particularly, the list of competing parties and their goals, their actions and contractions, states of trees and rules for their transformations.

For the above problems the GT constituents are determined as the following:

- The Chess OSP problem:
  - white and black players with checkmate as the goal,
  - chess piece moves as (contra)actions, and
  - composition of the chess pieces on the board as specific game states transformed by actions corresponding to chess rules.
- The MOSP problem for the Value War [3,23] model's interpretation:
  - a company competing against a few others with the goal to maximize Return-On-Investment,
  - changes of the product price and quality as the actions,

- tree states are determined by the scenario of competition (i.e., the competition template formed from the conceptual basis of management theory), the set of parameters of current competition with that scenario and actions of competitors,
- transformation rules are determined by general micro- and macro- economics laws, which applied to input states/market situations create new ones.
- The IP OSP problem:
  - network protection systems, e.g., system administrators or IP special software, combat against intruders or network disturbing forces (e.g., hackers or disturbances caused by technical casualties) to ensure that the network is kept in a safe and stable state,
  - network states are determined by the composition of current resources vulnerable to disturbances of the networks,
  - actions and (contra)actions are the means able to change resources and therefore transform states [20,21].

To bring SSGT problems to adequate game tree models the science and art have to be fused. Two fundamental issues of *correctness and attainability* of the models problem arise. *Correctness*, in general, answers whether the model is adequate to the corresponding reality of the world to an extent that its solution can be utilized in that world. *Attainability* – whether one can get the solution of the model problem at an acceptable computational cost. We refine these concepts as following: whether the model space of solutions includes the best solution of the problem and whether one can achieve that best solution in the model [22].

For example, both correctness and attainability take place in the computer chess problem if the optimality is understood as a superiority of the program over the best human chess player. Indeed, the correctness is evident due to the formal nature of chess. The corresponding game tree generated in a computer is a complete model for representing all possible chess strategies. The attainability of the problem is proved by convincing success of chess programs over chess champions in many announced tournaments.

The chess game tree model has a form of And/Or tree [11] and visualized chess strategies look as in Fig. 1. To unify concepts, algorithms, strategies, etc., game models for other SSGT problems are reduced to And/Or tree, as well.

In contrast to computer chess, accomplishing correctness for the MOSP needs special evidence. The MOSP problem includes, in particular, sub-models of markets, alternative strategies and competitions, evaluation and selection of strategies. Thus, the correctness of the MOSP is derivable from the adequacy of the market models and spaces of alternative strategies for the competitors. The attainability of the best solution is derivable, similar to chess, from strategy search and evaluation methods.

If an oligopoly competition is represented by a game tree, the correctness of the MOSP will depend on whether the market and the rules of its transformations can be described adequately.

Recalling that market models and rules are intensively used in business simulation games and have successful applications at least in business education we can argue about acceptable correctness of the MOSP game tree based models.

2.2. Let us consider how the MOST problem is reduced to game tree model. We assume that each competitor is identified by a corresponding deterministic program and

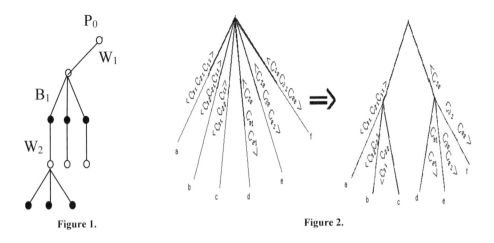

Figure 1.   Figure 2.

the competition in a market may be described by sets of situations, actions and strategies in discrete time periods.

Competitors make allowed actions, or *moves*, from corresponding sets **A1,..., Am**
simultaneously, step by step and in T periods. We name a vector of such actions as a
bundle of actions. Bundles of actions transform the initial situation S into sequences of
new situations (one period of actions on the left tree of Fig. 2).

We call a tree of all possible sequential bundles of actions of competitors from an
initial situation S in T periods a *S-game tree, or S-tree*.

In fact, S-tree is the sum of performances of all possible competitors' programs
started from S. The whole performance of the programs may be described by the forest
of such trees from different initial situations. To avoid technical complications we assume to have only one initial situation and all competitors have the same sets of allowed market moves.

We name the performance of the competitor C (i.e. the performance of corresponding program) in S-tree as a *(complete) S-strategy of C*.

A competition, or a game, of competitors C1, C2,..., Cm is determined by the
sample of corresponding programs and by the initial situation.

We evaluate the quality of a program by the forest of strategies generated by the
program from all possible initial situations. Thus, to evaluate a program we have to
consider all its possible games against all possible samples of other competitors in all
possible initial situations. The number of competitors in samples depends upon the
assessment objectives. For oligopoly competitions, for example, we have to consider
all possible combinations of competitors which are in the oligopoly.

Since each competitor is represented by a program and the performance of the
program in the S-tree is a S-strategy, in order to evaluate the quality of the program the
assessment criterion K must be applied to that S-strategy. We suppose that the value of
the criterion is determined by terminal nodes of the S-strategy. For example, we can
use the profit gained by S-strategy as a criterion and calculate by averaging the values
of the profit for all of its terminal nodes.

Given criteria F, we say that a *strategy G achieves the goal F* if criteria F satisfied
for the set of terminal nodes of G. The strategy G will be called *F-projected* if we are
interested in whether the terminal nodes of G satisfy criteria F or not. Any description
of an F-projected strategy G aimed to make a search of G more efficient is named *a*

Strategy Plan for *F*. A description of the problem under consideration and a description of the solving strategy itself constitute an extreme example of strategy plans. A
useful strategy plan would systematically identify the directions that are not promising
and eliminate them there for reducing the search space. Such a strategy plan would
have to be described in a high level language. *Strategy planning* is a process of nar-
rowing the search space for the target strategy which also reflects the specifics of the
planner such as knowledge of language, the system of values and methods of search.

Figure 2 illustrates reduction of an initial game tree model for competitors C1
against C2 and C3 to the AND/OR tree.

2.3. The game tree model for security problems in its IP application version is defined as follows [20,21].

It is a game between two playing in turn sides with opposite interests – the attacker
(A) and the defender (D), described by a set of states and a collection of conversion
procedures from one position to another defined as the following.

In particular, *system resources* are processor time, the size of TCP buffer, and a
number of incoming packages. Let $R = \{r\}$ be a non-empty set of the system resources
and Q be a set of resource parameters. Different measuring scales, such as seconds,
bytes, numbers of incorrect logins or incoming packages, etc., are used to measure different parameters. Each $r \in R$ is associated with a pair $<q; w>$ – a real system resource,
where $q \in Q$, $w \in W$ and W is a set of possible scales.

A *criterion function* is an arbitrary function f with the range of values $Z = [0, 1]$
and F is the set of such functions f.

A *local system resource state* on a non-empty set $R` \subseteq R$ is called the value $e \in Z$
of the criterion function $f \in F$ on this set: $e = f(r1, r2, ..., rk)$, where $R` = (r1, r2, ..., rk)$
& $\varnothing \neq R` \subseteq R$.

The *local state* is called *normal* if $e = 0$ and *critical* if $e = 1$, and L will denote the
set of local states e. Intuitively, by criterion functions are measuring "distance" of current states from those that are considered as normal. A system state on a non-empty set
$L` \subseteq L$ is called the value $s \in Z$ of the criterion function $g \in F$ on this set: $s = g(e1,
e2, ..., en)$, where $L` = (e1, e2, ..., en)$ & $\varnothing \neq L` \subseteq L$ The *state* is called *normal* if
$s = 0$ and *critical* if $s = 1$, and S will denote the set of states s.

The main goals of the attackers and defenders are to bring the system in the critical
states and avoid them, correspondingly.

Let us call an arbitrary function p(si, sj), the ranges of definition and values of
which are subsets of R, *a conversion procedure* of system from the state si to sj:

p(si, sj): $\{\{r1, r2, ..., rk\}\} \rightarrow \{\{r`1, r`2, ..., r`k\}\}$, where $\{r1, r2, ..., rk\} \subseteq R$ &
$\{r`1, r`2, ..., r`k\} \subseteq R$.

Let P is the set of conversion procedures, Pa and Pd are its subsets for the attacking
and the counteracting sides, pa(si, sj) $\in$ Pa and pd(si, sj) $\in$ Pd are the conversion procedures from the state si $\in$ S to sj $\in$ S for the attacking and the counteracting sides,
correspondingly.

The counteraction game model is represented by "AND/OR" tree G(S, P). At first
the attacker moves from the initial state s0 $\in$ S then the defender replies in turn. Thus,
the initial node s0 is an "AND" type. The terminal nodes correspond to the winning
states of the defender.

3. Game Model Security Strategies are Compatible with Experts

To prove correctness of the security game tree model strategies of the model were compared with the experts and existing contemporary security systems strategies by the following on – the-job performance testing methodology.

The quality of strategies, ideally, is determined by analysis of their on-the-job performance, i.e. the results of all possible interactions/competitions with all possible opponents/competitors. The results of competitions correspond to the values of terminal nodes of corresponding strategies on the game tree.

We use the following two concretizations of the on-the-job performance criteria:

- the Min max criterion, where the optimal strategy and corresponding best move is determined by raising up the values of terminal nodes,
- the Testing Matrix Analysis (TMA) criterion, where the vectors of terminal nodes of strategies comprise a matrix analyzed by voting-like methods [9,19].

We implement the Min max and TMA criteria through corresponding software. Although the Min max criterion is widely presented in strategy search studies and our software is following the state-of-the-art, we have developed original software for the TMA. The first tool aims to form the matrix of tests by results of on-the-job performance of strategies [17]; a current version of the tool is specialized for experiments with defense strategies to support IP Systems. The second package takes as input the matrix of tests and selects the best strategy by a variety of methods including voting ones [18]. It must be acknowledged that the Min max and TMA provide different criteria of optimality.

We demonstrate the correctness and attainability of the game model by its effectiveness for IP systems in a series of experiments on protection against attacks, such as Syn-Flood, Smurf, Fraggle, overflow of the buffer, IP-Hijacking, etc., where the model recommends decisions compatible with system administrators [20,21].

It was found that for making decisions compatible with experts it was enough to make an exhaustive, min max search in the game tree for depth in 3 "moves". The quality of decisions was permanently increasing when the depth of search was increasing and for depth in 5 "moves" the model was avoiding about 70% experts' false alarms. Unfortunately, the search time was increasing exponentially and for depth higher than 5 it became unacceptable.

The IGAF2 algorithm succeeds to reducing the burst of time in the strategy search and to achieve acceptable efficiency.

4. Empowering Security Strategies by Expert Knowledge

The IGAF2 algorithm is composed of the following operations [17]:

- it uses standard min max technique with alpha-beta pruning based on the range of critical/normal state values introduced as the goal. The current node is created and the value of its local state calculated. If the node is terminal, the local state value is compared with sibling nodes and their max (or min) value is sent to the parent node [20,21],
- it determines all suspicious resources,

- it builds the game subtree for suspicious resources starting from the root state of the tree and using the 4th group of rules it determines the trajectories of attacks,
- it calculates the values of the terminal states of the tree, it finds the values of others using the min-max procedure and determines the best min-max action from the root state,
- it determines the trajectories of attacks induced by the best action from the root of the tree to its critical states and it considers them as targets,
- it builds the zones of counteractions for the target trajectories using the 4th group of rules and the 5th rule; then, it calculates the values of the states of the corresponding subtree using min-max,
- it chooses the defender's action from the root as the one leading to the state with min value, i.e. to the most stable state estimated by min-max,
- it finishes the defense analysis and waits for the attacker's actions.

The IGAF2 algorithm is able to acquire a range of expert knowledge in the form of goals or rules and to increase the efficiency of strategy formation by increasing the amount of expert knowledge available to the algorithm. The following expert goals and rules have been embedded in the IGAF2 algorithm [17].
The goals are:

- the *critical vs. normal states* are determined by a range of values of the states of the system; for example, any state of the system with a value of corresponding criterion function, that is more or equal to some threshold, may be determined as a critical goal,
- the *suspicious vs. normal resources* are determined by a range of states of the classificators of the resources; combinations of values of the classificators identified as suspicious or normal induce signals for appropriate actions.

The rules are:

- identify the suspicious resources by the classifiers and narrow the search to the corresponding game subtree,
- avoid critical states and tend to the normal ones,
- normalize the state of the system; first, try such actions of the defender that influence on the resources that caused current change of its state; if they don't help, try other ones,
- when building the game subtree for suspicious resources, use
  - defending actions able to influence on such resources,
  - normal actions until there is no critical states,
  - if some defensive actions were used on previous steps decrease their usage priority.
- Balance the parameters of resources by keeping them in the given ranges of permitted changes.

IGAF2 was tested in experiments against six attacks with a depth of the game tree search up to 13 and the following controlled and measured criteria and parameters: distance to safety, productivity, working time and number of game tree nodes searched, new queue of incoming packages, TCP connection queue, number of processed packages, RAM, HD, unauthorized access to files and login into the system [17]. The results of the experiments show:

- Sampling means for Distance to Safety and Productivity of the IGAF2 and min-max algorithms are compatible.
- Number of nodes searched by the IGAF2 algorithm with all expert rules and subgoals are decreasing compared with the IGAF1 algorithm or the min-max one.
- Number of nodes searched by the IGAF2 algorithm with all expert rules and subgoals is the smallest compared with the IGAF1 algorithm or the min-max one when the depth of search is increasing up to 13.
- The time spent by the IGAF2 algorithm with all expert rules and subgoals is the smallest compared with the IGAF1 algorithm or the min-max one when the depth of search is increasing up to 13.

We plan to strengthen the IGAF2 algorithm through systematic enrichment of the knowledge base by new expert goals and rules. The question is whether it is possible to construct adequate models of strategy expert knowledge.

5. On Simulation of Strategy Expert Knowledge

We consider a comprehensive repository of *communicable* expert knowledge – concepts, descriptions, rules and other related texts, for a typical representative of the SSGT class – chess problem, in order to answer the following principal questions:

- Is it possible to find an adequate computer representation for an "alive" fragment of expert knowledge associated with solving problems of a target class?
- Is it possible to reproduce, or learn, procedurally with an acceptable computational complexity the expert knowledge associated with the problem?

In [16] the following statements were argued. Chess concepts identify configurations of elements of positions having winning by Zermelo [15] utility, which provides additional reasons to possibility of their computer simulation.

An uncertainty in representation of chess concepts is generic, caused by limited resources and individualized their learning by players. Despite concepts with the same name, which can have different interpretations by different players and coincide only in some "skeleton" parts, this does not create big casualties because of an intermediate usage of concepts for further deeper analysis of positions. Due a generic uncertainty in representation of concepts, it is worth to formulate the chess problem in a way allowing both forming concepts with strong common meaning and ones that exist in the forms individualized to the particular players. Correspondingly, adequacy of the models of concepts have to be examined taking into account those individualized representations of concepts.

6. Conclusion

The IGAF algorithms are consistent with strategy expert knowledge and can be applied to security problems have the following advantages:

- elaborate optimal defense strategies for any identified moment of decision making,

- counteracting a broad spectrum of disturbances and attacks that is possible to generate in the given alphabets of elementary attacks and defense actions,
- improvement of generated strategies by acquiring expert knowledge in the field,
- inheritance and development of achievements in combinatorial games, particularly chess, one of the most advanced studying in Computer Sciences.

Applied to the intrusion protection problem, the IGAF2 algorithm—for a range of types of knowledge in form of goals and rules—demonstrates strong tendency to increase the efficiency of strategy formation with an increase in the amount of knowledge available to the system. For further increase of the efficiency, new adequate models of expert knowledge are needed. For chess, a typical and representable game problem, it was argued that chess specifies in an individualized and quasi way the classes of winning by Zermelo positions, which provides important reasons to possibility of their computer simulation. By our preliminary analysis, the remaining chess knowledge repository—plans, ideas, attributes, etc.—specify additional tangible constructions of the game tree—the winning strategies—which can be simulated as well. Current experiments [18] aim to prove those assertions.

If experiments are successful, it can be expected that concepts and strategy knowledge of the SSGT problems can be computer simulated, because simulation of chess knowledge was induced by their reduction to constructions of the game tree and the game trees are the base for other SSGT problems, as well.

Chess conceptual and strategy knowledge simulation add arguments in favor of simulation of learnable knowledge not only for the SSGT problems but for a wider class of problems as well; this is, because, usually, the problems can be represented in form of games as well as to the power of prepositional form of simulation [10]. Finally, to fuse the high effectiveness of IGAF algorithms in embedded systems, it is necessary to estimate the computational resources in the context of embedded systems.

References

[1] Botvinnik M.M., About solving approximate problems, S. Radio, Moscow, 1979 (in Russian).
[2] Botvinnik, M.M., Computers in Chess: Solving Inexact Search Problems. Springer Series in Symbolic Computation, with Appendixes, Springer-Verlag: New York, 1984.
[3] Chussil M., Reibstein D. 1997 Putting the Lessons before the Test. In Wharton on to Analyse & Develop Competitive Strategies, John Wesley & Sons, 343–368.
[4] Chi, S.-D., Park, J.S., Jung, K.-C., Lee, J.-S.: Network Security Modeling and Cyber Attack Simulation Methodology. Lecture Notes in Computer Science, Vol. 2119 (2001).
[5] V. Gorodetski, I. Kotenko: Attacks against Computer Network: Formal Grammar Based Framework and Simulation Tool. Proc. of the 5 Intern. Conf. "Recent Advances in Intrusion Detection", Lecture Notes in Computer Science, v. 2516, Springer Verlag, pp. 219–238, 2002.
[6] Flavell J. The Develometal Psycology Of Jean Piaget, D. Vannostrand Company Inc., Princeton, NJ, 1962.
[7] I. Kotenko, A. Alexeev, E. Man'kov. Formal Framework for Modeling and Simulation of DDoS Attacks Based on Teamwork of Hackers-Agents. Proc. of 2003 IEEE/WIC Intern. Conf. on Intelligent Agent Technology, Halifax, Canada, Oct. 13–16, 2003, IEEE Computer Society. 2003, pp. 507–510.
[8] Kruchten P. The Rational Unified Process. An Introduction, Addison-Wesley, 2000.
[9] Moulin. H. Axioms of Cooperative Decision Making. Virginia Polytechnic & State University, 1988, ISBN-0-521-36055-2.
[10] Pylyshyn Z. Seeing and Visualizing: It's Not What You Think, An Essay On Vision And Visual Imagination, http://ruccs.rutgers.edu/faculty/pylyshyn.html.

[11] Russell S., Norvig. P. Artificial Intelligence: A Modern Approach. Prentice-Hall, Englew. Cliffs, NJ, 2002.
[12] Sheyner O., Wing J., Tools for Generating and Analyzing Attack Graphs, to appear in Proceed. of Formal Methods for Components and Objects, Lecture Notes in Computer Science, 2005.
[13] Stilman, B. Linguistic Geometry: From Search to Construction. Kluwer Academic Publishers. 2000.
[14] Winograd T., Flores F. 1986. Understanding Computers and Cognition (A new foundation for design).
[15] Zermelo E. Uber Eine Anwendung Der Mengenlehre Auf Die Theorie Des Schachspiels. Proceedings Of The Fifth International Conference Of Mathematicians, Cambridge, 1912, Cambridge Press, p. 501–504.
[16] Pogossian E. On Simulation of Strategy Conceptual Knowledge, CSIT2005, Yerevan, pp. 8.
[17] Pogossian E., Javadyan A., Ivanyan E. Effective Discovery Of Intrusion Protection Strategies. Lecture Notes In Computer Science, Ais-Adm-05: The International Workshop On Autonomous Intelligent Systems – Agents And Data Mining June 6–8, 2005, St. Petersburg, Russia http://space.iias.spb.su/ais05/, LNAI 3505, pp. 263–276, 2005.
[18] Karapetyan G., Vahradyan V., Pogossian E. Experiments in Simulation of Chess Conceptual Knowledge Proceedings of the CSIT2005, 5th International Conference in Computer Science and Information Technologies, Yerevan, 2005.
[19] Baghdasaryan T., Danielyan E., Pogossian E. Testing Oligopoly Strategy Plans By Their On The Job Performance Simulation, CSIT2005, Yerevan, 2005, pp. 7.
[20] Pogossian E. Javadyan A. A Game Model And Effective Counteraction Strategies Against Network Intrusion., CSIT2003, Yerevan, 2003, pp. 5.
[21] Pogossian E. Javadyan A. A Game Model For Effective Counteraction Against Computer Attacks In Intrusion Detection Systems, NATO ASI 2003, Data Fusion for Situation Monitoring, Incident Detection, Alert and Response Management, Tsahkadzor, Armenia, August 19–30, pp. 30.
[22] E. Pogossian Focusing Management Strategy Provision Simulation. CSIT2001, Yerevan, 2001.
[23] Pogossian E. Increasing Efficiency Of Management Skill Assessment. Proc. of the 26th annual conference of the Association for Business Simulation and Experiential Learning (ABSEL-99), Philadelphia, March.
[24] Pogossian E. The Adaptation of Combinatorial Algorithms. National Academy of Sciences of Armenia, Yerevan, 1983, pp. 290 (a book in Russian).

18

Security and Embedded Systems
D.N. Serpanos and R. Giladi (Eds.)
IOS Press, 2006

Architectural Enhancements for Secure Embedded Processing

Divya ARORA [a], Srivaths RAVI [b], Anand RAGHUNATHAN [b] and Niraj K. JHA [a]

[a] *Dept. of Electrical Engineering, Princeton University, Princeton*
[b] *NEC Laboratories America, Princeton*

Abstract. In this paper, we present architectural enhancements for ensuring secure execution of programs on embedded processors. The primary motivation behind this work is that software attacks often originate from unknown vulnerabilities in trusted programs. We propose two techniques to achieve secure program execution. They include (i) hardware-assisted monitoring of a trusted program's control flow to detect deviant control flow, and (ii) hardware-assisted validation of a program's data properties that may be violated in the event of an attack. Experiments show that the proposed architecture can be very effective in preventing a wide range of security threats.

1. Introduction

Various studies [1–3] indicate that software attacks today are not only increasing in number, but are also beginning to target a diverse range of electronic systems. Software attacks due to viruses, worms, and trojan horse applications have proliferated not only to personal computers, but also to embedded appliances such as cellphones and PDAs, automotive electronics, and networked sensors. This trend is attested to by the emergence of attacks on mobile phones such as the Skulls, Cabir, and Lasco viruses [4]. Given that embedded systems are ubiquitously deployed in several mission-critical and pervasive applications, it is not surprising that security of an embedded system is becoming a major and immediate concern to manufacturers and users, alike.

In the desktop and enterprise world, conventional software security solutions such as software certificates, software vulnerability patches, ant-virus software updates, *etc.* have achieved only limited success. This observation has led to the development of various architectural mechanisms to augment software security solutions, and many of these technologies are emerging today as commercial products/solutions. For example, processors from Intel and AMD now feature a non-executable bit that can be enabled to make selected regions of a program's address space non-executable [8]. This makes the programs that they execute less vulnerable against buffer overflow attacks. Similarly, chips designed for next-generation cellphones, such as TI's OMAP 2420 [6] and NEC's MP211 [7] systems-on-a-chip (SoCs) feature a wide range of security measures including secure bootstrapping, and protection of the code and data spaces associated with sensitive applications. Another recent technology applicable to embedded SoCs is ARM's TrustZone [5], which attempts to provide a secure execution environment for a selected set of applications called trusted applications. The basic objective is to provide protection for the code and data spaces of trusted applications against tamper by untrusted applications.

Our work also falls in the domain of architectural support for security. The objective is to provide higher security assurance when a trusted program executes, so that the system can be protected against software attacks that can even originate from a vulnerability in the trusted program. We have developed two techniques to address this objective, which include:

- *Hardware-assisted control flow monitoring:* Many attacks, such as stack-based buffer overflows, execute malicious code by exploiting vulnerabilities in a trusted program. Protecting against such attacks is, therefore, a critical objective. Our solution is based on a simple observation that the execution of malicious code will result in behavior or control flow that is different from the normal program behavior. In other words, if the trusted program can be characterized to have a normal execution behavior (in the absence of an attack), then any deviation from the said behavior can be flagged as an attack. We implement the proposed solution by designing a separate hardware monitor that models and enforces the characterized program behavior by monitoring the program's execution on the processor. The proposed framework shows that a program's function call graph, basic block control flow graph, *etc.* are invariants that can be statically derived, and enforced by the monitor at run-time, with minimum overheads, and in a minimally intrusive fashion.

- *Hardware-assisted validation of program's data properties:* Some attacks do not modify the control flow of a program, but only modify the data associated with a program in the program's stack or heap. Similar to control flow, a program's behavior with respect to data accesses can also be encoded and enforced as security policies during the program's execution. This led to the development of a HW/SW framework that can enforce various security policies. This framework is shown to be effective in preventing various kinds of software attacks, including heap-based and format string attacks.

The rest of this paper is organized as follows. Section 2 discusses related work. Sections 3 and 4 detail the two techniques. Section 5 presents experimental results, and Section 6 concludes the paper.

2. Related Work

Many techniques including code scan and review tools attempt to strengthen software security by eliminating vulnerabilities during the software design phase. Various solutions have been developed to address specific kinds of attacks such as stack-based buffer overflow attacks [9], heap overflow attacks [10], *etc.* Apart from such mechanisms, researchers have proposed a wide range of runtime monitoring techniques [11,12] to enforce various security policies. However, software-based runtime monitoring techniques suffer from various drawbacks including performance overheads, limited coverage of security vulnerabilities, *etc.*

More recently, researchers have focused on augmenting processor architectures for secure program execution. Examples of these works include enhanced processor architectures, such as XOM [13] and AEGIS [14], which attempt to provide code integrity and privacy in the presence of untrusted memory. However, these techniques do not safeguard an application from its own vulnerabilities. A more detailed survey of work related to this paper can be found in [15] and [16].

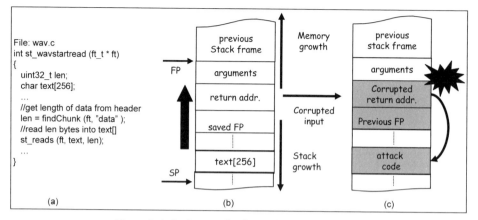

Figure 1. A simple example of a "stack smashing" attack.

3. Hardware-Assisted Control Flow Monitoring

We first present an example attack to motivate the proposed architecture, which we then describe in detail.

3.1. Example Attack

Figure 1(a) presents a code snippet from SoX (Sound eXchange), a popular audio conversion utility. The function *st_wavstartread()* reads *len* bytes from an input file into a local array *text[]*. Figure 1(b) shows the stack layout, when the function is called during program execution. An attacker creates an input *wav* file containing a payload of malicious code and *len* > *256*. This causes a buffer overflow for *text[]*, resulting in corruption of the local variables and function's return address stored on program stack. The input file can be constructed so that the corrupted return address points to the start of malicious code, which is executed when the function *st_wavstartread()* returns.

While the vulnerability in the above example could be easily addressed through input validation, bugs in large, complex programs can be much more subtle and elusive. In addition to software attacks, embedded systems are also susceptible to physical attacks that involve tampering with system properties such as voltage levels and memory contents. Irrespective of their origin, most attacks manifest as a subversion of "normal" program execution. Therefore, we concentrate our efforts on defining this behavior and monitoring execution to enforce it, using hardware support to make such extensive checking feasible.

3.2. Proposed Architecture

Figure 2(a) shows the block diagram of the proposed hardware-assisted monitoring architecture. The figure shows a 5-stage, in-order RISC processor pipeline that has been enhanced with a separate hardware unit or *monitor*. The monitor receives inputs from the program counter (PC), instruction register (IR) and the pipeline status from the pipeline control unit. The monitor's outputs include a *stall* signal and an *invalid* signal. When the monitor detects a violation of permissible behavior, it asserts the *invalid* signal resulting in a non-maskable interrupt to the processor. The *stall* signal is as-

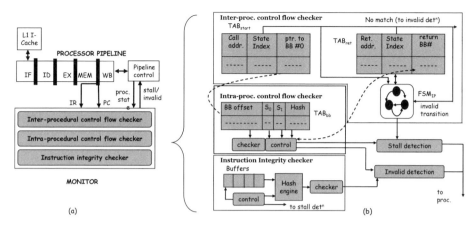

Figure 2. Hardware-assisted monitoring: (a) Block diagram, and (b) Detailed architecture.

serted if the monitor is unable to keep pace with the processor. This is handled as a normal processor stall, and the pipeline stages are "frozen" till the stall signal is de-asserted.

The monitor is composed of three sub-blocks, which check program properties at different granularities. The structure is hierarchical and follows from the natural structure of programs – the top-most level works at the application level and verifies that the *inter-procedural control flow* is in accordance with the program's static function call graph, the second level validates the *intra-procedural control flow* by validating each branch/jump instruction within a function and finally, the lowermost level verifies the *integrity of the instruction stream*. This hierarchical structure allows the designer to trade-off checking granularity and coverage for area and/or performance.

Figure 2(b) details the design of each of these sub-blocks. The call graph of the program is modeled as a finite state machine (FSM), with each function represented as a state and caller-callee relationships denoted by valid FSM transitions. The FSM monitors all call/return instructions and transitions to the next state accordingly. There is a common invalid state to which the FSM transitions if a function attempts to call or return to another function it was not permitted to. Tables TAB_{call} and TAB_{ret} maintain the mapping from program addresses to FSM state identifier and feed it to the FSM. Intra-procedural control flow is also modeled as an FSM with a state for each basic block in the control flow graph of the function. The information for a basic block b_i is represented as a tuple *(index, offset, S_0, S_1)* where *index* is its state identifier, *offset* is the address offset of b_i from function start, and S_0, S_1 are indices of basic blocks that are its possible successors. This FSM is stored in the table TAB_{bb} and the associated control/checking logic verifies that the branches and jumps made during execution correspond to the information stored in this table. The instruction integrity checker checks the integrity of executing instruction stream by computing a cryptographic hash of each basic block and comparing it against a pre-specified value. For this, the program loads the basic block hashes for a set of (sensitive) functions into the monitor before execution and the monitor verifies that the instructions are not modified during execution. This sub-block consists of a pipelined hashing unit and buffers to store the instructions while the hash of a previous basic block is being computed, so as to not stall the processor too frequently.

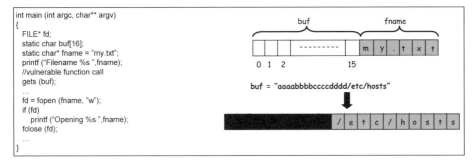

Figure 3. Program data corruption via heap overflow.

4. Hardware-Assisted Validation of Program Data Properties

We first use an example attack to motivate the proposed architecture, which we then describe in detail.

4.1. Example Attack

Figure 3 shows a typical heap overflow attack. The code contains two static variables, *buf[]* and *fname* on a program's heap. The program uses a vulnerable C function *gets()* to get input from the user and store it in *buf[]*. A malicious user can provide a long input that overflows *buf[]* and overwrites **fname*, tricking the program into writing to a completely different (sensitive) file. There are two points worth noting here: (i) it is possible to corrupt program data without altering its control flow behavior, and (ii) neither the OS nor the processor architecture provide any mechanism to prevent transgressions by one part of an application against another. We address these two limitations in this work in the context of program data protection. Data protection is significantly harder than protecting code, since unlike code (which is mostly known after compilation), data are highly dynamic, and may be allocated, initialized, and changed at run-time.

4.2. Proposed Architecture

Figure 4(a) shows the overall design flow for the proposed framework. We augment a program's abstract data state with a new field – SECTAG (SECurity TAG) that encodes its security-specific attributes. These attributes may be derived from application-specific policies, *e.g.*, allowing only some functions to access specified data structures, or they may be universally applicable, *e.g.*, disallowing writes to unallocated memory. The former require modification to application source code while the latter may be implemented with help from run-time libraries or the compiler. The flow produces an enhanced binary, which is run on the enhanced processor that has extra storage and control to manage SECTAGs of data and a dedicated hardware checker to check these SECTAGs and validate data accesses.

Figure 4(b) shows the details of the architecture with new/modified parts highlighted. We assume a cache configuration with unified L2 cache and split Instruction and Data L1 (I-L1 and D-L1) caches. Different design considerations guided this architecture. In L1 design, to minimize impact on L1 hit time, extra storage – $SECTAG_{L1}$ –

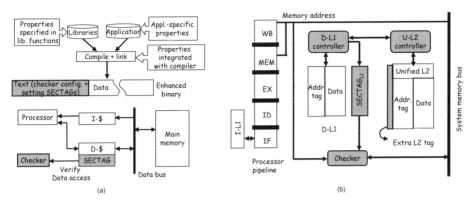

Figure 4. Run-time data validation: (a) Proposed framework (b) Architecture.

is added on-chip to store SECTAGs of data in D-L1. When the processor accesses a datum in D-L1, the checker accesses its SECTAG in parallel and verifies if the data access is allowed by the semantics of the SECTAG. For L2, a design similar to above is infeasible as most processors have large unified L2 caches, and having a separate tag area for each cache line would lead to large hardware overheads. Therefore, we designate lines in L2 to store SECTAGs of other L2 lines and modify cache tags to maintain bookkeeping information about where in L2 the SECTAGs of a particular data line are kept. Cache hit/miss handling policies are modified to fetch SECTAGs from memory and manage them during execution.

The checker is a programmer-visible peripheral that can be configured via registers. For example, the program can specify the address range of data to be checked, exact SECTAG value to be matched on every read/write, SECTAG bound to be compared against on every access, *etc*. Lastly, the instruction set is augmented with and extra instruction *(tsb $rs, $rt)* that sets the SECTAG of the address in *$rs* to the value in *$rt*. This framework is capable of supporting a wide range of security policies including preventing reads from uninitialized memory, segregating data into security levels and restricting access by functions belonging to different parts of a program, restricting access to stack variables of a function by its callees, *etc*.

5. Experiment and Results

To evaluate the proposed techniques, applications were selected from the embedded benchmark suites, Mediabench and Mibench benchmark suites. Cycle-accurate simulations were performed by modifying Simplescalar [17] to simulate the enhanced architectures.

5.1. Hardware-Assisted Control Flow Monitoring

We performed area estimation by synthesizing the monitors for several applications at different granularities. With a base case of ARM920T 32-bit processor core, the average area overheads for inter-procedural, intra-procedural and instruction integrity checking were 0.72%, 2.44%, and 5.59% respectively.

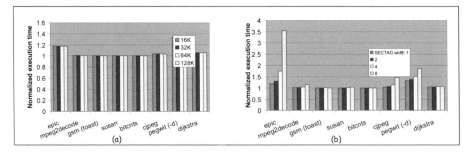

Figure 5. Performance penalty for checking heap accesses with (a) varying L2 sizes, and (b) varying SEC-TAG bit-widths.

Performance estimation also revealed minimal overheads – the penalty was <1% for inter-procedural checking, 1.77% for intra-procedural checking in *detection mode* (when the processor is allowed to continue while the monitor is checking and stalled only on a control instruction), and 4.94% for intra-procedural checking in *prevention mode* (no new instruction is permitted to commit before checking completes). Instruction integrity checking usually results in substantial overhead, but it can be virtually eliminated by using a pipelined hash engine.

5.2. Hardware-Assisted Validation of Program Data Properties

Figure 5(a) shows the performance impact for implementation of the policy: disallow reads/writes to unallocated memory. Library routines *malloc()* and *free()* are modified to maintain a 1-bit SECTAG for all allocated memory. This policy catches heap over-runs, access to freed memory, after it has been freed and exploits that operate by corrupting the *malloc* chunk header. The average and maximum execution time penalty for the default L2 cache size (64K) are 7.6% and 32.7%. Figure 5(b) shows the scalability of this approach in supporting higher bit-width SECTAGs. The incremental performance loss to go from a single-bit tag to widths of 2, 4 and 8 is 2.6%, 11.2% and 43.5% respectively.

6. Conclusions

Ensuring secure execution of software is a critical aspect of modern embedded systems. This paper presented two techniques for ensuring secure program execution. The techniques exploit a combination of hardware and software modifications to achieve this objective, by monitoring pre-defined control and data properties. Experimental results indicate that the proposed modifications are reasonable in terms of the overheads incurred, and ensure that a wide range of security attacks can be prevented.

References

[1] IBM, Global Business Security Index Report. http://www.ibm.com, 2005.
[2] P. Kocher, R. Lee, G. McGraw, A. Raghunathan and S. Ravi, "Security as a New Dimension in Embedded System Design," in *Proc. ACM/IEEE Design Automation Conference*, pp. 753–760, June 2004.

[3] S. Ravi, A. Raghunathan, P. Kocher, and S. Hattangady, "Security in embedded systems: Design challenges," in *ACM Trans. on Embedded Computing Sys*, pp. 461–491, Aug. 2004.

[4] Secure Mobile Systems, Mobile Threats. http://security.fb-4.com/mobilealerts.html.

[5] R. York, A New Foundation for CPU Systems Security, ARM Limited, 2003 (Available at http://www.arm.com/armtech/TrustZone?OpenDocument).

[6] Texas Instruments Inc., OMAP Platform (Available at http://focus.ti.com/omap/docs/omaphomepage.tsp).

[7] *MP21x mobile application processors*. NEC Electronics Corp. (Available at http://www.necel.com/en/techhighlights/application_processor/).

[8] M. Kanellos, *AMD, Intel put antivirus tech into chips*. CNET Networks Inc. (http://news.zdnet.com/2100–1009_22–5137832.html?tag=nl).

[9] C. Cowan et al., "Stackguard: Automatic adaptive detection and prevention of bufferoverflow attacks," in *Proc. USENIX Security Symp.*, Jan. 1998, pp. 63–77.

[10] W. Robertson, C. Kruegel, D. Mutz, and F. Valeur, "Run-time detection of heap-based overflows", in *Proc. USENIX Large Installation Systems Administration Conf.*, pp. 51–60, Oct. 2003.

[11] V. Kiriansky, D. Bruening, and S.P. Amarasinghe, "Secure execution via program shepherding," in *Proc. USENIX Security Symp.*, pp. 191–206, Aug. 2002.

[12] S.H. Yong and S. Horwitz, "Protecting C programs from attacks via invalid pointer dereferences," in *Proc. European Software Engineering Conf.*, pp. 307–316, Sept. 2003.

[13] D. Lie, C.A. Thekkath, M. Mitchell, P. Lincoln, D. Boneh, J.C. Mitchell, and M. Horowitz, "Architectural support for copy and tamper resistant software," in *Proc. Int. Conf. on Architectural Support for Programming Languages and Operating Systems*, pp. 168–177, Nov. 2000.

[14] G.E. Suh, D. Clarke, B. Gassend, M. van Dijk, and S. Devadas, "AEGIS: Architecture for tamper-evident and tamper-resistant processing," in *Proc. Int. Conf. on Supercomputing*, pp. 160–171, June 2003.

[15] D. Arora, S. Ravi, A. Raghunathan and N.K. Jha, "Secure Embedded Processing through Hardware-assisted Runtime Monitoring", *in Proc. ACM/IEEE Design, Automation, and Test in Europe (DATE)*, March 2005.

[16] D. Arora, A. Raghunathan, S. Ravi, and N.K. Jha, "Enhancing Security Through Hardware-assisted Run-time Validation of Program Data Properties", in *Proc. ACM/IEEE International Conference on Hardware Software Co-design and System Synthesis (CODES+ISSS)*, Sept. 2005.

[17] D. Burger and T.M. Austin, "The simplescalar toolset, Version 2.0," Comp. Sciences Dept, UW, Tech. Rep., June 1997.

26

Security and Embedded Systems
D.N. Serpanos and R. Giladi (Eds.)
IOS Press, 2006
© 2006 IOS Press. All rights reserved.

Computational Improvements to Differential Side Channel Analysis

David NACCACHE [a,b,1], Michael TUNSTALL [b,2] and Claire WHELAN [c,3]

[a] Gemplus Card International
[b] Royal Holloway, University of London
[c] Dublin City University

Abstract. The process of performing a Side Channel Attack is generally a computationally intensive task. By employing a number of simple optimisations the data analysis phase of the attack can be greatly improved. In this paper we will describe some of these improvements and show in the context of DES when attacked using Kocher's classic DPA [1], that a 97% reduction in data processing can be achieved.

Keywords. Side Channel Attacks, Differential Power Analysis, The Data Encryption Standard (DES)

1. Introduction

Side Channel Analysis (SCA) is an active area of research in the security community and in particular, the smart card industry today. The interest in these attacks is due to the fact that they are highly effective and difficult to defend against. The side channel acquired can be the power consumption of the chip, the electromagnetic emanations or even execution time. Differential SCA (DSCA) is a specific type of SCA in which the attacker captures numerous executions of the target device performing an operation of interest[4]. After acquiring the signals a data analysis phase follows, where statistical tools are applied. This ultimately results in the retrieval of sensitive data.

Vast efforts have been made to develop next generation SCA attacks, catering to the cryptosystem [1–3], or the device in question [4,5], or as a response to proposed countermeasures aiming to deter SCA [6–10]. However, to the authors' knowledge, the literature is devoid of addressing the computational complexity of these attacks. In actual fact the process of performing a differential attack is a lengthy process:

---

[1]David Naccache, Gemplus Card International, Applied Research and Security Centre, 34 rue Guynemer, Issy-les-Moulineaux, F-92447, France (phone: +33 616 598349, e-mail: david.naccache@gemplus.com).

[2]Michael Tunstall, Information Security Group, Royal Holloway, University of London, Egham, Surrey TW20 0EX, UK (phone: +44 1784 443093, e-mail: m.j.tunstall@rhul.ac.uk, david.naccache@rhul.ac.uk).

[3]Claire Whelan, School of Computing, Dublin City University, Ballymun, Dublin 9, Ireland (phone: +353-1-7005616, e-mail: cwhelan@computing.dcu.ie).

[4]This is limited to power consumption and electromagnetic acquisitions.

- Data capture can take a long period of time. This depends on a variety of practical factors, such as the duration of the monitored process, the oscilloscope→PC transfer rate, the equipment's sampling frequency, the number of curves necessary to overpower the target's signal to noise ratio *etc.*
- The processing of the captured information requires that the data is manipulated in various ways to derive information on the key used.

This is a tedious and time consuming process, that the present work seeks to improve on without affecting the attack's precision or probability of success. In this paper we will present a number of computational improvements to DSCA. These shortcuts will be described in terms of the notorious Differential Power Analysis (DPA) [1], which is most popular in the literature. The methods described are applicable to other forms of DSCA, such as Differential Electromagnetic Analysis (DEMA) [11,12], where once the acquisition stage of the attack is complete, the data analysis phase is exactly the same as DPA. As an illustrative example, assuming that a classic DPA (*i.e* as in [1]) of a given device requires $\simeq 64,000$ power curve operations. The techniques described in this paper would obtain exactly the same results by spending only 3% of the computational effort (namely $\simeq 2100$ operations).

The paper is organised as follows: Section 2 establishes the notations used throughout the paper. Section 3 recalls the general principles of differential side channel attacks. We will then evaluate the number of calculations that this involves, so as to establish a benchmark against which we will measure our optimisations. Section 4 contains the differential attack optimisations. Section 5 presents the results, and we conclude in Section 6.

2. Preliminaries and Notations

We introduce the following notation to track our plaintext segments through the S-boxes.

- The algorithm will be executed N times. This will produce N current consumption waveforms (also referred to as *power traces*) w_i and N plaintext-ciphertext pairs (P_i, C_i) where $1 \leq i \leq N$.
- The messages given to the algorithm are assumed to be random, unless otherwise stated.
- The algorithm is assumed to be a naive implementation that has no side-channel countermeasures, as a discussion on attack strategies is beyond the scope of this paper.
- We denote the S-boxes by ℓ_j where $1 \leq j \leq N_S$ and N_S is the number of S-boxes in the algorithm. For example, $N_S = 8$ for DES and 10 for AES.
- Each S-box will have as input, both subsets of P_i and the key K. For an m bit S-box, we denote the partial plaintext and partial key by $P_{i,j}$ and K_j where $P_{i,j}$ corresponds to the subset of P_i which is entered into S-box j and K_j corresponds to the key hypothesis $K_j = n$ for S-box j. Note that both $P_{i,j}$ and K_j can have the value n where $0 \leq n \leq 2^m - 1$.
- For each partial key K_j a hypothesis will be tested. In order to test this hypothesis, 2^m DPA waveforms will be created. We denote this set of waveforms by Δ_n where the nth key hypothesis produces the differential trace Δ_n.

- We will construct 'representative curves' W_n where there are 2^m possible curves of this form. We define W_n by

$$W_n = \sum_{i=1}^{N} \chi_i w_i \qquad \text{where} \qquad \chi_i = \begin{cases} 1 & \text{if } P_{i,j} = n \\ 0 & \text{otherwise} \end{cases}$$

W_n will be described further in Section 4.2.
- The operations on waveforms, such as the addition of two curves, are ordinary pointwise addition functions.

3. Generic Differential Power Analysis

DPA can be performed on any algorithm in which an intermediate operation of the form $\beta = S(\alpha \oplus k)$ is calculated, where α is known and k is the secret key (or some segment of the key). The function $S()$ is a non-linear function, usually a substitution table (referred to as an S-box), which produces an intermediate output value β.

The process of performing the attack initially involves running the target device N times with N random plaintext values P_i, where $1 \le i \le N$. The encryption of P_i under the secret key K to produce the corresponding ciphertext C_i, will result in N current consumption waveforms w_i. These waveforms are captured with an oscilloscope, and sent to a PC for analysis and processing.

To find a given partial key K_j, the output produced from the S-box ℓ_j when given K_j and all $P_{i,j}$ will be used to categorise the current consumption waveforms. A single output bit b from ℓ_j is used for this categorisation. For all possible hypotheses, *i.e.* $K_j = 0 \ldots K_j = 2^m - 1$, and each partial message $P_{i,j}$, b will classify whether waveform w_i is a member of one of two possible sets. The first set S_0 will contain all the waveforms where b is equal to zero, and the second set S_1 will contain all the remaining waveforms, *i.e.* where the output bit b is equal to one.

For each hypothesis, a differential trace Δ_n is calculated by finding the average of each set and then subtracting the resulting values from each other.

$$\Delta_n = \frac{\sum_{w_i \in S_0} w_i}{|S_0|} - \frac{\sum_{w_i \in S_1} w_i}{|S_1|} \qquad (1)$$

The DPA waveform with the highest peak will validate a hypothesis for K_j, *i.e.* $K_j = n$ corresponds to the Δ_n featuring a maximum amplitude. For a single DPA waveform this involves N additions (as there will be an average of $\frac{N}{2}$ elements in each set), two divisions and one subtraction, to create the differential Δ_n. Therefore, for all hypotheses the total number of operations to calculate all DPA waveforms for one S-box is $2^m \times (N+3)$.

4. Fast Differential Power Analysis

By introducing a number of basic pre-calculations we can accelerate DPA. We will optimise DPA in terms of the calculations performed in the statistical analysis phase of the attack, *i.e.* the calculation of the DPA waveforms. To calculate one differential Δ_n, the operations involved are basic pointwise addition, subtraction and division of curves. We target our optimisations in terms of minimising the number of additions of current consumption curves, as this is the most utilised operation. We will treat the division (calculation of mean) and subtraction operations as constant, as these are fundamental operations in the calculation of the differential Δ_n, and cannot be enhanced.

In the following section we will detail a number of optimisations which can greatly reduce the number of additions involved in performing a DPA. We will measure these optimisations in terms of the number of calculations required to calculate the differential traces Δ_n, for all hypotheses.

4.1. The Global Sum

The simplest optimisation involves the calculation of the global sum G. The global sum is nothing but the summation of all the current consumption waveforms that have been acquired.

$$G = \sum_{i=1}^{N} w_i$$

The calculation of the DPA waveform now only involves the summation of a single set, as opposed to two sets when using Eq. (1).

$$\Delta_n = \frac{G - S_{\text{least}}}{N - |S_{\text{least}}|} - \frac{S_{\text{least}}}{|S_{\text{least}}|} \tag{2}$$

S_{least} represents the set with the least number of elements, i.e:

$$S_{\text{least}} = \begin{cases} S_0 & \text{when } |S_0| \leq |S_1| \\ S_1 & \text{when } |S_0| > |S_1| \end{cases}$$

The expected number of additions required to generate S_{least} can be calculated using:

$$E(X) = \sum_{i=0}^{N} i \Pr[X = i]$$

$$= \sum_{i=0}^{\frac{N}{2}} i \binom{N}{i} \left(\frac{1}{2}\right)^N + \sum_{i=\frac{N}{2}+1}^{N} (N-i) \binom{N}{i} \left(\frac{1}{2}\right)^N$$

If, for example, 1000 acquisitions were taken this would result in an expected number of additions per hypothesis of 487. This is an improvement over the case where a set is chosen arbitrarily, when the expected number of additions will be 998.

The cost of precalculating G for a single hypothesis is obviously not worthwhile. However for 2^m hypotheses significant savings are realised, as the maximum number of operations to calculate all DPA waveforms for a single S-box is $(N-1) + 2^m \times (\frac{N}{2}+3)$.

Note, however, that separate pre-computation of G is not mandatory. The trick here consists in computing a first hypothesis just as in the original version of DPA and then summing the two resulting average curves to get G, thereby allowing the complexity of the next $2^m - 1$ hypotheses calculations to be reduced calculations at no extra cost.

In the remainder of this paper, S_{least} will no longer be used. This is due to the optimisation described in the following section, which will change the way in which the raw data is distributed. In subsequent sections the differential trace Δ_n will be calculated by subtracting either S_0 or S_1 from G, where the choice of S is completely arbitrary.

4.2. Formation of Waveform Equivalence Classes

The input to each S-box will consist of partial bits $P_{i,j}$ of the plaintext P_i and partial bits K_j of the key K. Concentrating on $P_{i,j}$, there are only 2^m possible values which can enter ℓ_j, yet we are dealing with N waveforms. Therefore, a number of the waveforms will have the same value for $P_{i,j}$ and thus can be treated in the same manner (*i.e.* they form an equivalence class[5]). We define W_n for ℓ_j as:

$$W_n = \sum_{i=1}^{N} \chi_i w_i \quad \text{where} \quad \chi_i = \begin{cases} 1 & \text{if } P_{i,j} = n \\ 0 & \text{otherwise} \end{cases}$$

This will produce 2^m representative curves. This can be calculated *on-the-fly*. The partitioning of the power curves according to the key hypothesis will now result in 2^{m-1} curves in each set. The differential trace will be calculated as

$$\Delta_n = \frac{G - S_0}{N - |S_0|} - \frac{S_0}{|S_0|}$$

where S_0 will now contain exactly 2^{m-1} elements[6]. To generate a single DPA waveform this will result in $2^{m-1} - 1$ additions. For all hypotheses a total of $2^m \times (2^{m-1} - 1)$ additions will be required to calculate all the DPA waveforms for one S-box. Pre-calculation involves the formation of the representative curves W_n and the global sum G. Since we can construct G as a function of W_n:

$$G = \sum_{n=1}^{2^m} W_n$$

The total number of operations that will be incurred in generating all DPA waveforms, is hence:

$$\text{Total Calculations} = 2^m \left(\frac{N}{2^m} - 1 \right) + (2^m - 1) + 2^m (2^{m-1} - 1)$$

$$= N - 1 + 2^m (2^{m-1} - 1)$$

---

[5]Note the curves form an equivalence class for each ℓ_j, *i.e.* for ℓ_0 the representative curves will be formed in a particular way, for ℓ_1 they will be formed in a different way, *etc.*

[6]If the case arises where a value for W_n does not occur, this may create a bias. This is the only situation where $|S_0| \neq 2^{m-1}$.

where for $W_0 \ldots W_{2^m}, \approx \frac{N}{2^m} - 1$ additions will make up each W_n, additional $2^m - 1$ summations will be required to form the global sum G and $2^{m-1} - 1$ additions will be required to generate each DPA waveforms for 2^m key hypotheses.

4.3. Curve Combining

Pre-calculating certain curve combinations enables groups of curves that occur in the same set for one hypothesis, to be recycled in subsequent hypothesis testing. Since we are dealing with 2^m representative curves, precomputing all possible $2^m!$ curve combinations is obviously infeasible. Therefore we propose to partition the curves into groups of size x and precompute the different possible combinations for each group.

For example, for $x = 2$, adjacent curves are summed. We define each pair as the value $W_{2n,2n+1}$ where $n = 0...2^{m-1}$ and n is incremented by two.

$$W_{2n,2n+1} = W_{2n} + W_{2n+1}$$

The use of the combined curves $W_{2n,2n+1}$ in the evaluation of the set S_0, results in three possible scenarios for each pair:

1. The pair occurs *i.e.* $W_{2n} + W_{2n+1}$ appears in S_0. The probability of this occurring is $\frac{1}{4}$. In this case, one additional summation must be performed.
2. The pair does not appear in S_0, *i.e.* the pair is in G. The probability of this happening is also $\frac{1}{4}$. In this case no action is performed.
3. The two curves W_{2n} and W_{2n+1} appear in two separate sets. There is a higher probability of this happening, *i.e.* $\frac{1}{2}$. In this case a single addition is required.

The expected number of additions per Δ_n (assuming the global set already exists), is $\frac{3}{4} \times 2^{m-1}$. This is because there are 2^{m-1} groups of three elements (W_{2n}, W_{2n+1} and $W_{2n,2n+1}$), one of which will be used to add to S_0 with probability $\frac{3}{4}$.

If $x = 3$ then the following combinations of curves will be created from W_{3n}, W_{3n+1} and W_{3n+2}:

$$W_{3n,3n+1} = W_{3n} + W_{3n+1}$$

$$W_{3n+1,3n+2} = W_{3n+1} + W_{3n+2}$$

$$W_{3n,3n+2} = W_{3n} + W_{3n+2}$$

$$W_{3n,3n+1,3n+2} = W_{3n} + W_{3n+1} + W_{3n+2}$$

Following the same reasoning as above, the number of additions is $\frac{7}{8} \times \frac{2^m}{3}$. For all values of x this can be generalised to:

$$\text{Additions per Hypothesis} = \left(\frac{2^x - 1}{2^x} \right) \left(\left\lfloor \frac{2^m}{x} \right\rfloor - 1 \right) - \frac{2^{2^m \bmod x} - 1}{2^{2^m \bmod x}}$$

This comprises of two expressions as x will not always divide evenly into 2^m, which will leave $2^m \bmod x$ elements to be grouped together separately. Note that this is only an approximation of the amount of additions required for each set. In practice the number of additions involved in generating Δ_n will depend on the contents of the set, and whether the precomputed combinations appear or not.

The amount of pre-calculation involved (incorporating G, W_n and the precomputed combinations) is:

$$\text{Pre-Additions} = N - 1 + \left((2^x - x - 1) \left\lfloor \frac{2^m}{x} \right\rfloor \right) + \left(2^{2^m \bmod x} - (2^m \bmod x) - 1 \right)$$

Therefore, total pre- and post-calculations, which will result in the production of 2^m DPA waveforms is given by:

$$\text{Total Calculations} = 2^m \times \text{Additions per Hypothesis} + \text{Pre-Additions}$$

Memory requirements are obviously a vital factor, as the more pre-computed values, the more storage they will take up and the more time it will take to load these values into memory, which will effect the overall attack performance. In order to balance the time-memory tradeoff and achieve the optimal attack, we give the following formula to derive for a given value of x, the memory that is required. The formula allows an attacker to relate the number of precomputed values to their resources.

$$\text{Memory Required} = (2^x - 1) \left\lfloor \frac{2^m}{x} \right\rfloor + \left(2^{2^m \bmod x} - 1 \right) \tag{3}$$

This value gives the number of representative curves W_n which need to be stored in memory. Each point in this curve will be stored in a 32-bit word so that no information is lost. The value generated in (3) will be multiplied by $4\times$ the size of one acquisition (assuming that the values acquired are byte sized).

4.4. Chosen Plaintext Differential Power Attacks

The pre-calculations previously made for S-box ℓ_j, unfortunately will be redundant for ℓ_{j+1}. This is due to the fact that we will be focusing on a later section of the current consumption waveforms, which when classified according to the partial input $P_{i,j}$ will fall into different equivalence classes W_n than before. Therefore for S-box ℓ_{j+1}, the regeneration of the representative curves will be required.

In classical DPA the message given to the algorithm under attack is random. However if we can perform a chosen plaintext attack we can utilise the precalculated W_i for use in subsequent S-boxes. The simplest case is where input to S-box ℓ_1 is the same for $\ell_1 \ldots \ell_{N_S}$. For example, construct the plaintext so that all plaintext bytes are equal, *i.e.* byte[1] = byte[2] = ... = byte[16] in AES. This means that there are 256 possible values for the plaintext. Calculating the DPA waveform for the first S-box will calculate the DPA waveform for all others at the same time, giving sixteen peaks at the points in time in which the sixteen key bytes are being manipulated. Using this method may not always be advantageous as some confusion can arise as to which peak corresponds to which key byte.

Obviously the use of this technique is dependant on the algorithm and the eligibility checks that the plaintext undergoes before it is encrypted. A similar and valid attack is an attack on an implementation of DES, where the plaintext is generated such that the

$P_{i,j}$ entered into $\ell_{j \bmod 2=0}$ is equal for all even S-boxes, and $P_{i,j}$ entered into all odd S-boxes $\ell_{j \bmod 2=1}$ is equal for all odd S-boxes. All the even numbered S-boxes can use the same set of data generated during the pre-calculation for the first S-box. The odd numbered S-boxes also use this data but with a permutation on the value associated with each representative curve. This does not affect the quality of the results produced as each S-box uses a different permutation. The DPA peak will be at the same level as if a random plaintext was used.

Note that these optimisations are applicable when the attack is concentrating on the first round of a secret key algorithm. If the attack focuses on the last round where the DPA waveforms are related to the ciphertext, these optimisations will be useless as the data can not be controlled.

5. Results

We will describe our optimisations in terms of performing DPA on DES, where 1000 acquisitions current consumption acquisitions have been taken. This has been seen experimentally to often be sufficient to determine some relationship between the current consumption and the data manipulated. It may be necessary to use more acquisitions, or possible to use less, but 1000 has usually proven to be a good starting point.

Given $N = 1000$ current consumption waveforms w_i, the following table details the number of operations that must be performed in the act of generating the differential traces for the key hypotheses.

	Precalculation	Additions per hypothesis	Additions per S-box	Curves Required	Memory Required
Theoretical DPA	–	998	63872	–	–
Optimisation 1: Global Sum	999	487	32167	1	4
Optimisation 2: Equivalence Classes	999	31	2983	65	260
Optimisation 3:					
2 bits	1031	23.3	2519	96	384
3 bits	1083	18	2235	148	592
4 bits	1175	14.1	2075	240	960
5 bits	1322	11.6	2064	387	1548
6 bits	1580	9.8	2207	645	2580
7 bits	2079	8.4	2619	1144	4576
8 bits	2975	7.0	3421	2040	8160
9 bits	4513	6.5	4928	3578	14312
10 bits	7088	5.9	7468	6153	24612

The more bits are grouped together, the more memory is required to conduct the attack. It has been assumed the the current consumption acquisitions consist of a million points where each point is one byte, therefore we will allow for the representative curve to take up four times as much memory as that of a raw data curve.

As shown in the table the best results are obtained when five bits are grouped together at a time. However, the memory requirement for this is 1.5 Gigabytes. The amount of additions when three bits are combined is slightly higher but requires a much more reasonable amount of memory.

The optimal location for the storage of the representative curves is obviously in the computers RAM. This is because the access times are significantly faster than those of a hard drive, especially as the amount of data being processed is too large for the hard drive to store in it's cache.

6. Conclusion

In this paper we presented a number of optimisations that can be used with Kocher's original algorithm to significantly reduce the computation time. These optimisations allow an attacker to search for data dependence in a short period of time. This can be used as a preparatory phase to other forms of SCA, such as CPA [13]. These types of treatment can help to reduce false positives by reducing the occurrence of "ghost peaks" as described in [13].

In the example given, the time taken for the processing of all the hypotheses for one six-bit section of the key is reduced by a factor of thirty. In actuality, this time will be further decreased as the acquisitions on the computer's hard drive are only accessed during the construction of the representative curves W_n. The rest of the processing takes place in RAM.

The ideas expressed in Section 4.4 have not been discussed in the example, as the gain for the overall attack depends on how the message can be manipulated. The gain for an attack where the plaintext can be freely manipulated should reduce execution time by a factor of approximately sixty.

In our analysis we assume the resolution of the current consumption acquisitions is one million points. In practice this can vary depending on a number of factors, such as the storage capacity of the oscilloscope, the amount of time spent localising the S-boxes, and the algorithm being attacked. In the case of AES, larger S-boxes are used, and so there will be a greater number of key hypotheses, which will result in an increase in the number of precomputed values to be stored. The worst possible scenario is where the memory requirement becomes unmanageable and pre-computation actually inhibits the attack. There are two approaches that an attacker can employ to combat this situation. In the case where the acquisitions captured are large, one can split the acquisition into smaller sections and perform the respective operations on these sections, and subsequently concatenate the files to construct the full DPA waveform. Alternatively, (3) can be used to determine how much pre-computation is possible with the memory available, allowing an attacker to achieve a maximum benefit from the optimisations described.

References

[1] P. Kocher, J. Jaffe, and B. Jun. Differential power analysis. In M. Wiener, editor, *Advances in Cryptology – CRYPTO 99*, volume 1666 of *Lecture Notes in Computer Science*, pages 388–379. Springer Verlag, 1999.

[2] T. Messerges. Securing the aes finalists against power analysis attacks. In B. Schneier, editor, *Fast Software Encryption – FSE 00*, volume 1978 of *Lecture Notes in Computer Science*, pages 150–164. Springer Verlag, 2000.

[3] J.S. Coron. Resistance against differential power analysis for elliptic curve cryptosystems. In C.K. Koc and C. Paar, editors, *Cryptographic Hardware and Embedded Systems – CHES 99*, volume 1717 of *Lecture Notes in Computer Science*, pages 292–302. Springer Verlag, 1999.

[4] T. Messerges, E. Dabbish, and R. Sloan. Investigations of power analysis attacks on smartcards. In *USENIX Workshop on Smartcard Technology*, 1999.

[5] S.B. Ors, E. Oswald, and B. Preneel. Power analysis attacks on an fpga – first experimental results. In C.D. Walter, C.K. Koc, and C. Paar, editors, *Cryptographic Hardware and Embedded Systems – CHES 03*, volume 2779 of *Lecture Notes in Computer Science*. Springer Verlag, 2003.

[6] L. Goubin and J. Patarin. Des and differential power analysis, the duplication method. In C.K. Koc and C. Paar, editors, *Cryptographic Hardware and Embedded Systems – CHES 99*, volume 1717 of *Lecture Notes in Computer Science*, pages 158–172. Springer Verlag, 1999.

[7] M.L. Akkar and C. Giraud. An implementation of des and aes, secure against some attacks. In D. Naccache, C.K. Koc and C. Paar, editors, *Cryptographic Hardware and Embedded Systems – CHES 01*, volume 2162 of *Lecture Notes in Computer Science*, pages 309–318. Springer Verlag, 2001.

[8] S. Chari, C.S. Jutla, J.R. Rao, and P. Rohatgi. Towards sound approaches to counteract power-analysis attacks. In M. Wiener, editor, *Advances in Cryptology – CRYPTO 99*, volume 1666 of *Lecture Notes in Computer Science*, pages 398–412. Springer Verlag, 1999.

[9] L. Goubin. A sound method for switching between boolean and arithmetic masking. In C.K. Koc, D. Naccache and C. Paar, editors, *Cryptographic Hardware and Embedded Systems – CHES 01*, volume 2162 of *Lecture Notes in Computer Science*, pages 3–15. Springer Verlag, 2001.

[10] J.S. Coron and A. Tchoulkine. A new algorithm for switching from arithmetic and boolean masking. In C.K. Koc, C.D. Walter and C. Paar, editors, *Cryptographic Hardware and Embedded Systems – CHES 03*, volume 2779 of *Lecture Notes in Computer Science*, pages 89–97. Springer Verlag, 2003.

[11] J.J. Quisquater and D. Samyde. A new tool for non-intrusive analysis of smartcards based on electromegnetic emissions, the sema and dema methods. 2001.

[12] K. Gandolfi, C. Mourtel, and F. Olivier. Electromagnetic analysis: Concrete results. In C.K. Koc, D. Naccache, and C. Paar, editors, *Cryptographic Hardware and Embedded Systems – CHES 01*, volume 2162 of *Lecture Notes in Computer Science*, pages 251–261. Springer Verlag, 2001.

[13] E. Brier, C. Clavier, and F. Olivier. Correlation power analysis with a leakage model. In M. Joye and J.J. Quisquater, editors, *Cryptographic Hardware and Embedded Systems – CHES 04*, volume 3156 of *Lecture Notes in Computer Science*, pages 16–29. Springer Verlag, 2004.

Security and Embedded Systems
D.N. Serpanos and R. Giladi (Eds.)
IOS Press, 2006

A Process Algebra Approach to Authentication and Secrecy

Lăcrămioara AŞTEFĂNOAEI and Gabriel CIOBANU [1]

Romanian Academy, Institute of Computer Science, Iaşi

Abstract. In this paper we investigate security properties like authentication and secrecy. We express a security protocol in a process algebra called Spi calculus. We describe Needham-Schroeder public key protocol in Spi, and give some results regarding its authentication and secrecy. Finally we present some verification procedures for the authentication protocols described in Spi calculus.

Keywords. Authentication, secrecy, Needham-Schroeder protocol, process algebra, bisimulation

1. Introduction

Formal methods can be useful in detecting and solving security problems. They have been used in the analysis of communicating protocols since 70's, but their application in security properties became useful only since 90's, when researchers found out flaws with the help of a formal approach [6].

According to [4], we can distinguish four general approaches of security protocols:

1. modelling and verifying security protocols using methods and tools which are not specially designed for security;
2. developing expert systems to study and investigate different scenarios;
3. modelling and verifying security protocols using logics based on knowledge and belief;
4. developing formal model on the algebraic term-rewriting properties of security and cryptographic systems.

Following the first approach, we use a process algebra called Spi calculus, which is an extension of the π-calculus [8] with primitives for encryption and decryption; see [1] for more details on Spi calculus. A process algebra approach has several advantages:

1. it is easy to express communication through channels;
2. it is easy to model private communication by using some specific "scoping rules";
3. it is not required to model explicitly possible intruders, and only refer to their interactions and behaviour.

---

[1] Corresponding Author: Gabriel Ciobanu, Romanian Academy, Institute of Computer Science, 700506 Iaşi, Romania. E-mail: gabriel@iit.tuiasi.ro.

The last advantage can facilitate an easy-to-understand model of some security proto-cols. An intruder can be treated as a testing process I. Considering testing processes, we prove that a certain authentication protocol is secure, and its implementation respects the formal specification. In this way, by using process algebra, we decrease the difficulty of expressing an intruder in the authentication protocols.

2. Basic Model

We work with processes representing senders, receivers and servers. A server is the only process which can be trusted. Any other process in the system could represent a potential intruder. Our processes communicate through public channels, on which they transmit encrypted messages. Depending on the communication protocol, a key is public or pri-vate. The system is represented by one or more instances of the protocol (a sender, a re-ceiver and a server) running concurrently. We make some assumptions in our approach. A well suited environment for security protocols is represented by **Dolev-Yao** model [3]. This model assumes **perfect cryptography** and **all-mighty intruder**. Perfect cryptogra-phy means that one cannot know an encrypted message without the corresponding key, and one cannot guess a secret key. All-mighty intruder expresses a complete control over the medium, namely one can obtain any message sent or received, can intercept, modify, delete, replay, and invent messages.

Considering a Dolev-Yao model, we are mainly concerned about the security prop-erties. Some important security properties are

1. **authentication**: capability of identifying the other partner engaged in a commu-nication,
2. **secrecy**: confidential information should be available only to the partners of the communication,
3. **integrity**: assurance of no alteration of message content,
4. **non repudiation**: assurance that a signed document cannot be repudiated by the signer,
5. **fairness**: in a contract, no party can obtain advantage by ending the protocol first.

We concentrate on the first two of them, namely authentication and secrecy. We use the notation $A \to B : \{K_S, A\}_K$, where $\{K_S, A\}_K$ is a message sent by A to B. The key K of $\{K_S, A\}_K$ is used to denote the encryption of the message $\{K_S, A\}$. This notation in-tuitively provides both authentication and secrecy of the key K_S. Authentication is given by the fact that B is sure that K_S really comes from A, and secrecy is given by the fact that nobody else knows K_S. Using this notation, we describe **Needham-Schroeder** pub-lic key protocol [9]. This is an authentication protocol used for several years in practice until Lowe discovered it was not secure [6]. We present both the original version of the protocol, and Lowe's improvement.

First we mention a few things about public keys. A process X has a public key K and a private key K^{-1}. Everybody knows K, but only X knows K^{-1}. X uses its private key K^{-1} to encrypt messages, and the others should decrypt its messages using its public key K. Messages encrypted with K can be successfully decrypted only by X, using K^{-1}.

We present here the original Needham-Schroeder public key protocol. We use the notion of nonce, meaning a random variable.

1. $A \rightarrow S : B$

    A requests B's public key from a server S

2. $S \rightarrow A : \{K_B, B\}_{K_S^{-1}}$

    S sends B's public key and B's name to A, encrypted with its private key K_S^{-1}; A decrypts the message using S's public key K_S, and finds out B's nonce.

3. $A \rightarrow B : \{N_A, A\}_{K_B}$

    A sends a nonce N_A together with its name to B, encrypted with B's public key; B decrypts it with its private key, and gets the name of the sender.

4. $B \rightarrow S : A$

    B requests A's public key from S.

5. $S \rightarrow B : \{K_A, A\}_{K_S^{-1}}$

    S sends A's public key to B; B decrypts the message using S's public key K_S, and finds out A's nonce.

6. $B \rightarrow A : \{N_A, N_B\}_{K_A}$

    B generates a nonce N_B, and sends it together with N_A to A, both encrypted with the public key K_A. A decrypts the message using its private key K_A^{-1}; if A finds N_A, A assumes it is from B in response to the original message.

7. $A \rightarrow B : \{N_B\}_{K_B}$

    A encrypts N_B with B's public key, and sends it to B. B decrypts the message; if B finds N_B, B assumes it is a response from A.

Lowe proved in [6] that this protocol has a flaw. An intruder could initiate a communication with B, pretending to be A. We describe how this happens, by emphasizing only the relevant new steps with respect to Needham-Schroeder original protocol. In these new steps, I is someone on the net with a false identity. I can trick an honest participant A by pretending to be someone else (e.g., B). 3. $A \rightarrow I : \{N_A, A\}_{K_I}$

    A initiates communication with I.

3'. $I_A \rightarrow B : \{N_A, A\}_{K_B}$

    I_A is I impersonating A. I initiates a communication with B pretending to be A.

6'. $B \rightarrow A : \{N_A, N_B\}_{K_A}$

    B thinks it is talking to A. B generates a nonce N_B and sends it together with N_A to A, encrypted with K_A. A decrypts the message.

7. $A \rightarrow I : \{N_B\}_{K_I}$

    A thinks it has a message from I, and replies. A encrypts N_B with I's public key, and sends it to I.

7'. $I_A \rightarrow B : \{N_B\}_{K_B}$

    I completes the protocol with B.

Our approach is based on a process algebra called Spi calculus [1]. We assume the reader is also familiar with the π calculus (more details can be found in [8]). We mention here only the difference between Spi and π-calculus. Spi has some primitives that make it easy to describe cryptographic protocols; it extends π-calculus with:

- a new term $\{M\}_K$ called **shared-key encryption**, representing the cipher-text obtained by encrypting the term M under the key K using a shared-key crypto system such as DES.

- a new process *case L of* $\{x\}_K$ *in P* required by decryption, representing a process which attempts to decrypt the term L with the key K; if L is a cipher-text of the form $\{M\}_K$, then the process behaves like $P[M/x]$, otherwise, it is deadlocked.

Regarding Needham-Schroeder public key protocol, we define in Spi the following processes: a sender A, a server S, a receiver B, and an intruder I. Process A has one parameter, representing its partner of communication; we denote by $A(Y)$ the fact that A wants to start a communication with Y. We describe $A(Y)$, S, and B in Spi:

$$A(Y) \quad \overset{\Delta}{=} \quad \overline{c}_S \langle Y \rangle. \tag{1}$$
$$c_S(x).case\ x\ of\ \{K, Z\}_{K_S^{-1}}\ in\ [Z\ is\ Y]\ \overline{c}_Y \langle\ \{N_A, A\}_K \rangle. \tag{2}$$
$$c_Y(x).case\ x\ of\ \{N_1, N_2\}_{K_A}\ in\ [N_1\ is\ N_A]\overline{c}_Y \langle\ \{N_2\}_K \rangle. \tag{3}$$
$$talk(A, Y) \tag{4}$$

In (1), by channel $\overline{c}_S$, A tells the server that it wants to communicate with Y. Then A waits for an answer compound from two names, namely Y and Y's public key K_Y. If A is able to decrypt the response, then A sends to Y a nonce N_A and its name, both encrypted with K_Y (2). A waits for Y's reply which must be composed by two nonces (A's nonce and Y's nonce), encrypted with A's public key. If A decrypts this reply, then it sends Y's nonce back to Y, by channel $\overline{c}_S$ (3). After this, A and Y are able to communicate by $talk(A, Y)$.

$$S \quad \overset{\Delta}{=} \quad c_S(x).\overline{c}_S \langle \{K_x, x\}_{K_S^{-1}} \rangle.S$$

S listens channel c_S. It responds to messages constituted only from one name, let it be Y. The server substitutes x by Y in its response $\{K_x, x\}_{K_S^{-1}}$ on channel $\overline{c}_S$.

$$B \quad \overset{\Delta}{=} \quad c_B(x).case\ x\ of\ \{N, Z\}_{K_B}\ in\ \overline{c}_S \langle Z \rangle. \tag{1}$$
$$c_S(x).case\ x\ of\ \{K, T\}_{K_S^{-1}}\ in\ [T\ is\ Z]\ \overline{c}_B \langle\ \{N, N_1\}_K \rangle \tag{2}$$

B listens channel c_B. If B receives a message from Z, then B asks the server for Z's public key (1). If B receives Z's public key K_Z, B responds to Z with Z's nonce N and a new nonce N_1, both encrypted with K_Z (2).

The general Needham-Schroeder protocol is given by $Syst(Y) = A(Y) \mid S \mid B$. Our specification of the system is defined as $Syst_{spec} = A(B) \mid S \mid B$. The specification is what would be ideal to happen, namely A speaking directly and exclusively to B, by the help of S.

Definition 2.1 *Two processes P and Q are **testing equivalent** if and only if for any testing process T we have $P \mid T$ is observational equivalent with $Q \mid T$. The observational equivalence is defined in [1]. Roughly speaking, two processes are observational equivalent if both of them reach the same configuration after a number of steps. We use the notation $P \simeq Q$ for P is testing equivalent with Q and $P \approx Q$ for P is observational equivalent with Q.*

We intend to prove that $Syst(Y)$ and $Syst_{spec}$ are not testing equivalent. If $Syst(Y) \not\simeq Syst_{spec}$ then the authentication property does not hold. If the authenticity holds for $Syst(Y)$, then $talk(A, Y)$ should be the only communication in the system. To the contrary, we prove that there exists another communication $talk(Y, B)$.

Proposition 2.2 *Considering the Spi processes* $A(Y)$, S *and* B, *we have that*

$$Syst(Y) \not\simeq Syst_{spec}.$$

Proof $Syst(Y) \not\simeq Syst_{spec}$ means that $Syst(Y)$ and $Syst_{spec}$ do not pass all the tests in the same way. Particularly, we construct a test I as an informal description of the intruder. Let I be the process defined as it follows:

$$I \; \triangleq \; c_I(x).case \; x \; of \; \{N_Z, Z\}_{K_I} \; in \; \overline{c}_B\langle\{N_Z, Z\}_{K_B}\rangle. \tag{1}$$
$$c_I(x).case \; x \; of \; \{N_Z\}_{K_I} \; in \; \overline{c}_B \; \langle\{N_Z\}_{K_B}\rangle.talk(I, B) \tag{2}$$

It means that I waits to see if someone, say Z, is willing to communicate with it. If so, I decrypts the message and encrypts it using B's public key, and then forwards the new message to B (1). Looking at the content of the message, B thinks that Z is trying to communicate, and replies to Z with a new nonce. Z receives B's response and thinks it is from I. So Z sends B's secret nonce to I, and I is now able to communicate independently with B (2).

Clearly, we do not want to have I communicating with B. However, in $Syst(I) \mid I$ it is possible to have $talk(I, B)$. On the other hand, $Syst_{spec} \mid I$ does not allow such a communication. Namely, we have no interaction between I and the specification $Syst_{spec}$. The only possibility is that A communicates with B, as it is desirable. Following the reaction rules of [1], $A(B) \mid B \mid S$ evolves into $talk(A, B)$. A sends to B its name and a nonce N_A encrypted with B's public key (which A has taken from S). B replies with A's nonce and its own nonce N_B encrypted with A's public key. A sends back B's nonce, so now B is sure that it communicates with A. I is listening on channel c_I, but nobody sends data on this channel, and therefore I cannot interact.

Lowe's contribution consists in changing message 6. B's reply should include also its name in the message. Each time the process A is receiving a message of form $\{X, N_A, N_X\}_{K_A}$, it continues only if X is the recognized communication partner. According to Spi syntax, this means that $A(Y)$ is deadlocked if X is different of Y. Therefore, A does not send B's information to unreliable parties, and I is not able to masquerade with B pretending to be A.

We present the changes in the previous protocol. Now B includes its name in the first reply to A:

$$B_{fixed} \quad \triangleq \quad c_B(x).case \; x \; of \; \{N, Z\}_{K_B} \; in \; \overline{c}_S\langle Z\rangle.$$
$$c_S(x).case \; x \; of \; \{K, T\}_{K_S^{-1}} \; in \; [T \; is \; Z] \, \overline{c}_B\langle \, \{\textbf{B}, N, N_1\}_K\rangle$$

Process A changes accordingly, namely A checks the origin of the message:

$$A_{fixed} \quad \triangleq \quad \overline{c}_S\langle Y\rangle.$$
$$c_S(x).case \; x \; of \; \{K, Z\}_{K_S^{-1}} \; in \; [Z \; is \; Y] \, \overline{c}_Y\langle \, \{N_A, A\}_K\rangle.$$
$$c_Y(x).case \; x \; of \; \{T, N_1, N_2\}_{K_A} \; in \; [\textbf{T is Y}] \; [N_1 \; is \; N_A]$$
$$\overline{c}_Y\langle \, \{N_2\}_K\rangle.talk(A, Y)$$

Proposition 2.3

(i) *For any honest process* B, $Syst_{fixed} \mid B$ *evolves to* $talk(A, B)$.
(ii) *For any intruder* I, $Syst_{fixed} \mid I$ *evolves to a deadlock.*

Proof

(i) B is an honest process. A initiates a communication with B sending a nonce N_A. B responds with a message composed of B's name, B's nonce, and A's nonce. A checks if the reply really comes from B, and if the first nonce is N_A. If this checking is successful, then A is able to communicate with B. Thus $Syst_{fixed} \mid B$ evolves to $talk(A,B)$.

(ii) I is an intruder, meaning I is not an honest participant. A sends a message to I, and waits for a reply. If the message does not come from I, A does not continue. Thus A does not divulge B's nonce. I knows how to decrypt only messages encrypted with K_I. I cannot change the information from a message that does not belong to it (meaning a message encrypted with another key). Therefore I is not able to make A think its message comes from B. A does not reply to a message that does not come from A's recognized communication partner, so I does not have any information required to start a communication with B.

3. Software Verification

A possible advantage of expressing a security protocol in a process algebra is to verify properties of communicating protocols by using automatic tools. Spi calculus is an appropriate proces algebra allowing us to express easily security properties without modelling the intruder, and without some other assumptions. However we have not yet a model checker for Spi calculus. A possible approach is to translate Spi calculus into other formal specifications. We describe our attempts in the following picture:

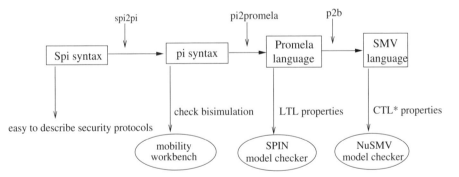

As a first step, we translate the Spi calculus description into a π-calculus description by using an existing tool called *spi2pi*. As it is proved in [2], such a translation of a protocol is relevant to the original description. More precisely, if we have in Spi a protocol P and a test E, as well as their encodings $[\![P]\!]$ and $[\![E]\!]$ in the π-calculus, then

P satisfies E iff $[\![P]\!]$ satisfies $[\![E]\!]$.

We can use a model checker for the π-calculus; we use Mobility Workbench (MWB), a software tool able to check various (temporal) properties, deadlocks and bisimulations [10]. We mention that the code obtained from this translation from Spi to π is relatively long, and MWB is quite slow.

In a second step we use a software tool to translate the π code into Promela, a specification which can be passed to SPIN [5], a model-checker for properties expressed in Linear Temporal Logic (LTL). In our experiments, we have used a tool called *pi2promela*. We have found some difficulties in the fact that the π code cannot have any free variables or names, as well as in obtaining only local variables in the resulting Promela code. This is an impediment to express LTL properties automatically; we had to adjust the code making some variables global.

We run the Promela code of the protocol without the intruder and we obtain the following message state chart:

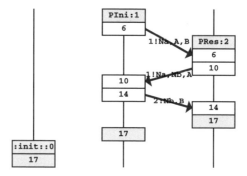

The protocol with the intruder is described by an atomic statement in which we have three processes Sender, Receiver and Intruder running together, as this is visible in the following message state chart:

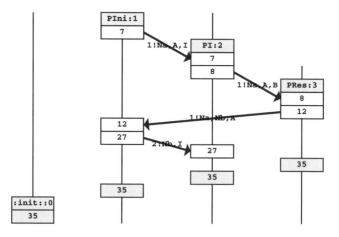

As it could be remarked, the protocol accomplish its purpose when an intruder is not present: Sender authenticates to Receiver and vice-versa, and after that Sender and Receiver can communicate securely. In the presence of an intruder with a typical behaviour, Sender divulges Receiver's nonce to Intruder. This means that Intruder is able to be considered by Receiver as being Sender, breaking the secret and the authentication property. We verify this aspect by using some LTL formulas and obtaining negative responses and an counter-examples.

As a final step we translate Promela code to SMV[7], a formal description for NuSMV model-checker. NuSMV is an "on-the-fly" model-checker able to verify properties expressed in CTL* (this feature is an advantage). We use a tool *p2b*, but it imposes several restrictions, and the results are not very promising.

As a conclusion of these software experiments, we found that it is not easy to integrate the existing tools, and it will be useful to have a verification tool for Spi calculus. For each description of a system in Spi calculus, the model checker should build a labelled transitional system. In order to verify the authenticity property for Needham-Schroeder protocol, we can consider two transition systems corresponding to $Syst(I)$ and $Syst_{spec}$. We check if these two systems are testing equivalent, meaning that in composition with a testing process I they behave in the same way. We can reduce the space of processes by taking into consideration only those that can interact with the system at a given step. Depending on the channel they communicate on, we can group them in equivalence classes. In case of a failure, we can trace back the evolution, and finally obtain a counterexample. This would be particularly useful in fixing the protocols.

4. Conclusion

We present the way process algebras can be a general framework for describing security protocols. We are mainly interested in Spi calculus, because of its simplicity and its expressiveness. Taking advantage of the testing equivalence, there is no need to model an intruder. In this paper we express Needham-Schroeder public key protocol in Spi and give some results regarding its authentication and secrecy. We take in consideration other formal methods and software tools, and see how they relate with the security problem.

References

[1] M. Abadi, A.D. Gordon. A Calculus for Cryptographic Protocols: The Spi Calculus. *Information and Computation* 148(1), pp. 1–70, Elsevier, 1999.

[2] M. Baldamus, J. Parrow, B. Victor. Spi calculus translated to π–calculus preserving may-tests. In *Proceedings LICS*, pp. 22–31, 2004.

[3] D. Dolev, A. Yao. On the security of public-key protocols. *IEEE Transaction on Information Theory* 29(2), pp. 198–208, 1983.

[4] S. Gritzalis, D. Spinellis, P. Georgiadis. Security protocols over open networks and distributed systems: formal methods for their analysis, design, and verification. *Computer Communications* 22(8), pp. 695–707, 1999.

[5] G.J. Holzmann. *SPIN Model Checker*, Addison Wesley, 2004.

[6] G. Lowe. An attack on the Needham-Schroeder public-key authentication protocol, *Information Processing Letters* 56(3), pp. 131–136, 1995.

[7] K.L. McMillan. *Symbolic Model Checking*. Kluwer Academic, 1993.

[8] R. Milner. *Communicating and Mobile Systems: the π-calculus*, Cambridge University Press, 1999.

[9] R.M. Needham, M.D. Schroeder. Using encryption for authentication in large networks of computers. *Communications ACM* 21(12), pp. 993–999, 1978.

[10] B. Victor, F. Moller. The Mobility Workbench: A tool for the π-calculus. In D. Dill (Ed.): *Proceedings CAV*, Lecture Notes in Computer Science vol. 818, pp. 428–440, Springer, 1994.

44

Security and Embedded Systems
D.N. Serpanos and R. Giladi (Eds.)
IOS Press, 2006

Intellectual Property Protection Using Embedded Systems

A.G. FRAGOPOULOS and D.N. SERPANOS

Department of Electrical & Computing Engineering, University of Patras, Greece

{afragop,serpanos}@ee.upatras.gr

Abstract. Development of innovative mechanisms for protection of Intellectual Property (IP) is a necessary and important activity in modern computing systems. Many parties participate in creation and distribution of protected property, such as creators, distributors, manufacturers, vendors, providers and the end-users. There have been various mechanisms for IP protection deployed already, but we need to reconsider some of them or deploy new ones, taking in advantage new trends and technologies. Embedded systems can be used as means to protect IP and implement DRM mechanisms into larger general purpose systems or into mobile consumer devices, like PDAs, mobile phones and mobile players, which are quite constrained environments. In this paper, we investigate and summarize existing methods to protect IP with the use of embedded systems.

Keywords. Embedded systems, security, intellectual property, digital rights management, trusted platforms, DRM, mobile DRM

Introduction

Development of innovative mechanisms for protection of Intellectual Property (IP) is of major importance in modern computing systems. Many parties participate in the creation and distribution of protected property, such as creators, distributors, manufacturers, vendors, providers and the end-users. Several mechanisms for IP protection have been already deployed, but we need to reconsider some of them or deploy new ones, taking advantage of new trends and technologies. Basically, provision of digital entertainment, like real time applications, video-on-demand, music downloading, games, ring tones and others, using mobile devices provides a revenue stream for various providers, while unauthorized copying, cloning and re-distribution can lead to correspondingly great revenue loss, e.g. $40 million loss in US, since 2004 [1]. Moreover, the deployment of new technologies like UMTS, GPRS, MMS, and 3G services provide high bandwidths to the users, allowing them to easily download and distribute protected content over the Internet. Finally, the potential to use of mobile devices as means for ubiquitous and pervasive computing leads to a new class of mechanisms for IP protection, namely mobile Digital Rights Management, m-DRM.

Embedded systems can be used as means to protect IP and implement DRM mechanisms into larger general purpose systems or into mobile consumer devices, like PDAs, mobile phones and mobile players, which are quite constrained environments.

In this paper, we investigate and summarize existing methods to protect IP with the use of embedded systems; these methods have been proposed either by academia or by the industry of mobile appliances.

1. What Should We Protect?

Under the umbrella of IP protection, we can embody the prevention, control and tracing of unauthorized cloning, upgrade and modification of any hardware, software or other type of protected content, like, for example, downloaded music or video, which resides into the device. Various types of software are installed into the mobile devices. Furthermore, in the context of digital entertainment, different types of digital objects, such as music data, video clips, e-books, etc., are held into such appliances as well.

In the implementation of IP protection mechanisms, we need to take into consideration the role of various parties. For example, the end-user of a mobile appliance can be considered as an un-trusted entity by the contents provider, while the end-user has to be re-assured about his privacy concerns.

2. Design Challenges

Several challenges arise in the design and implementation of IP protection mechanisms for use in embedded systems. We summarize them as follows.

We are facing dynamically changing environments, where the security requirements keep changing day by day. There is a wide deployment of network technologies that provide high data rates, which in conjunction with the fact that mobile devices are connected to the Internet raises various concerns regarding IP protection. Moreover, the nature of embedded systems, which have limited storage space and processing power and which are power constrained, makes application of IP protection mechanisms a challenging task.

An effective IP protection mechanism should be easily adaptable under changing conditions and new requirements, without loss of its original purpose of existence. We may distinguish between two different design approaches: *a static programmable design and a non-static one*. In a static programmable approach, once the IP protection mechanism is deployed to the system, it is not easy to modify and update the mechanism, due to possible appearance of new security requirements. A static IP protection mechanism can be vulnerable and finally compromised by malicious users, for example DVD-CSS[1] technology, hacked quite easy. Furthermore, a static mechanism lacks flexibility and adaptability in new security environments. A non-static programmable mechanism is more flexible and adaptable under changing requirements and also has more benefits compared with the previous approach. For example, in a non-static IP protection mechanism, some part of the mechanism can be implemented and distributed to legitimate users, through embedded devices, e.g. smart cards, allowing further improvements and enhancements of the mechanism, while retaining more personalized the distribution of protected contents.

---

[1] http://www.windowsitpro.com/Article/ArticleID/20234/20234.html.

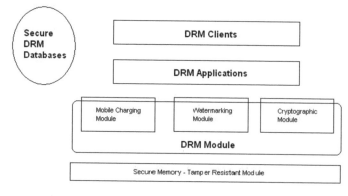

Figure 1. A tamper-resistant memory is needed to store the device's operating system, protected content, cryptographic keys and other sensitive data. The DRM module comprises of a charging module for applying charging mechanisms, a watermarking module for detection and removal of possible embedded watermarks and fingerprints, and a cryptographic module for implementing necessary cryptographic primitives. The DRM clients send requests to content providers, while DRM applications are used to render protected contents.

3. Protecting Intellectual Property

Digital Rights Management (DRM) is a means to protect Intellectual Property. According to Hartung et al. [2], a DRM scheme should provide: (a) conditional access to protected content, (b) interface to charging mechanisms, (c) encryption/decryption mechanisms for protected content, (d) an interface for key management, since legitimate users are verified and authenticated with the use of well established protocols, (e) identification and tracing of protected data, and (f) prevention and control of copying and redistribution of protected content. In case of m-DRM especially, which applies to mobile appliances, we have to implement DRM mechanisms under hard constraints.

Yan [3] proposes an abstract architecture for m-DRM, shown Fig. 1, taking into consideration three different use cases that apply in such environments: *(a) digital contents downloading, (b) broadcasting of contents and (c) personal contents management.*

Trusted platforms constitute an alternative method to provide a secure space for deployment of DRM mechanisms. According to TCPA [4], trust can be defined as "*... the expectation that a system shall exhibit a specific behavior under well defined circumstances*". So, such a system can ensure data integrity and user privacy, while retaining content's rights intact against tampering. One of the primary purposes of a trusted system is to implement digital rights management mechanisms. A commercial trusted architecture for application in embedded systems has been proposed by Intel Corporation is the **Intel ® Wireless Trusted Platform** [5] utilizing the **Certicom Security Architecture** [6].

In the following sections, we provide an overview of proposed methods for deployment of DRM mechanisms utilizing (a) cryptographic primitives, (b) watermarking and fingerprinting techniques, (c) smart cards, and (d) trusted systems.

4. Cryptographic Based DRM Mechanisms

Cryptography can be used by itself as a means for protection of intellectual property. Use of cryptography can ensure confidentiality and integrity of protected data. Basically, a content provider encrypts the data that he/she wants to keep protected using symmetric key algorithms and data are delivered to the legitimate users encrypted in such form. The legitimate users are authenticated to the content provider, while it might be necessary for data integrity mechanisms to be applied.

It becomes clear that, a system for IP protection should be capable to implement various cryptographic primitives efficiently, securely, at the right time and with low cost. These primitives include: *symmetric-key algorithms*, such as AES [7], for encryption and decryption of protected content, *public-key algorithms*, such as RSA [8], Elliptic-Curve Cryptography[2] (ECC) [9], for authentication purposes, digital signatures,[3] and key exchange – transfer of keys for decryption of contents between contents provider and legitimate users — and *hashing algorithms*, like SHA-1 [10] and MD-5 [11], for checking the integrity of data.

4.1. Minimal Cost Encryption Scheme

Kim et al. [12] propose a method to protect MPEG-4 video files, for use in MPEG-4 video streaming services. Such services constitute standard services in modern mobile phones. In their scheme, they use only cryptography, encrypting some a portion of each object of the MPEG-4 file, using DES algorithm [13]. Their idea is to encrypt minimum segments of every Video Object Plane (VOP) of the MPEG-4 file, exploiting the structure of MPEG-4 files. The encrypted files are stored in a media streaming server, which is accessible for files downloading by legitimate subscribers/holders of handheld devices. The decryption of media takes place on the mobile terminal. They claim that, the encryption of the first 8 bytes of each VOP can provide adequate IP protection of such video streams in mobile environments.

5. Watermarking – Fingerprinting

Cryptography alone is not sufficient to protect rights of digital assets, because nothing can prevent possible re-distribution or un-authorized copying or storing of plain content, after it has been passed from the device's cryptosystem and is held in plain form at the user's side. In general, users are considered as un-trusted sources by the content providers.

Digital watermarking/fingerprinting can provide adequate security of intellectual property, because it allows the association of some cryptographic information – embedded marks – with the contents to be protected. Also, it allows possible tracing of pirate copies by the content provider. A combination of cryptographic and watermarking/fingerprinting technologies should be used for the deployment of DRM systems.

---

[2] ECC is an efficient candidate as a public-key algorithm for use in embedded systems. It reduces the key size, while retaining the same level of security with RSA, saving storage space, hardware area and power consumption [36,37]. The major drawback is its complexity, because its development requires very strong mathematical background.

[3] Use of digital signatures can provide non-repudiation between contents provider and legitimate users. Also, content is typically signed digitally by the manufacturer. Mechanisms that are often implemented include Diffie – Hellman (D-H) key exchange [38] and El Gamal's digital signature scheme [39].

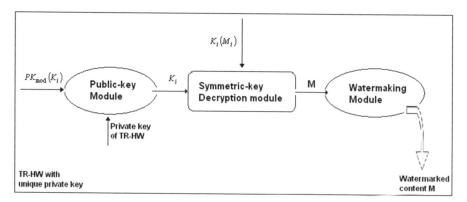

Figure 2. Architectural view of the tamper resistant hardware module used for (i) decryption of content key K_i, using the private key of the TR-HW, (ii) decryption of content with key K_i and (iii) watermarking of the original content M, before it is sent to the player.

5.1. Watermarking

In 1998, Motorola [14] marked its own original mobile phone batteries with a holographic image and also put on them a non-volatile re-programmable EEPROM, in order to protect its intellectual property concerning the use of original mobile phones batteries. When the battery was plugged on the mobile device, the mobile phone's charging system was authenticating the battery; in case of an erroneous response, i.e. identification of a non-original battery, the battery was not charged and warning alerts were displayed.

5.2. Fingerprinting

Asymmetric fingerprinting [15] is a method where each digital asset has a unique embedded mark, which inter-relates the user with the specific content, allowing the content provider to trace back the specific content and check for possible violation of IP rights.

Bao [16] propose a scheme for content protection of multimedia data using a tamper-resistant hardware (TR-HW), which utilizes asymmetric fingerprinting technique. The key generation ("*key-gen*") and fingerprinting ("*fing*") protocol parts of the method are performed on the TR-HW, which is held by the buyer. In case of audio files fingerprinting, the TR-HW can be implemented with 8-bit CPU smart cards. Figure 2 presents an architectural view of the TR-HW and a negotiation scheme between the holder of the TR-HW and the content provider for downloading an encrypted file from the content provider's database; the figure uses the following notation: PK_{mod} is the public-key of the TR-HW, K_i is the symmetric-key of encrypted content M_i, and M is the decrypted plain content.

Potlapally [17] propose Thor, an IP protection system that uses fingerprinting and cryptographic techniques for data that are stored on discs, like CDs and DVDs. In the heart of Thor's security system lays a smart card, which implements a security protocol, handles various cryptographic operations and provides secure storage. The smart card resides into the player's disc reader; its architecture is shown in Fig. 4.

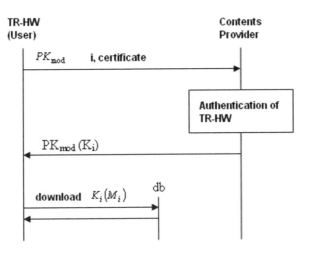

Figure 3. The content provider holds a database, where he/she stores various digital objects encrypted using symmetric algorithms, each content M_i encrypted with key K_i. The TR-HW (user) sends to the content provider its public-key, the module's serial number, its digital certificate and the id for the requested content. The module is authenticated by the content provider side and, in case of successful authentication, the content provider returns key K_i to the module, encrypted with the module's public key. Then, the user can download the requested encrypted content from the database and send it as input to the TR-HW for further handling, according to the procedure, which is described in Fig. 2.

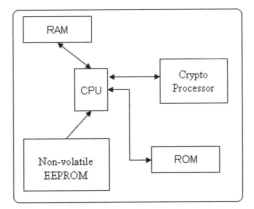

Figure 4. Thor's smart-card architecture.

In this scheme, some part of DRM mechanism is held by the protected media, as the disc manufacturer places the following data at the beginning of the disc:

a)   his unique ID,
b)   a digital signature – HEADER, which includes the fingerprint locations, and
c)   the encrypted data.

The smart card holds into its EEPROM a key-table with the public keys of all manufacturers and Thor's protocol. When a disc is inserted into the player, an authentication process takes place, where the smart card determines the existence of the fingerprint and decides about the disc's validity. In case of positive recognition, bulk encrypted data that are stored in the disc are decrypted using symmetric algorithms.

Domingo-Ferrer and Herrera-Joancomarti [18] propose an IP protection system based on anonymous fingerprinting.[4] They propose a protocol suite to implement various primitives of anonymous fingerprinting, utilizing smart cards to perform the necessary security functions. In short, a scenario is as follows: the user generates a sequence of keys $k_1, k_2, \ldots, k_n$ and sends them to the registration authority (RA). The RA certifies[5] the keys and sends back to the user n digital certificates, one for each key. When the user wants to make a purchase, the user sends to the content provider the item request, a key and its certificate. A proposed fingerprinting protocol is executed between the user and the content provider; finally, the content provider sends the requested item to the user.

6. Smart Card Based DRM Systems

Numerous methods have been proposed and implemented by the academic community using smart cards as the key components of their system. Use of smart cards has many advantages, such as low cost and efficient implementation of security functions in constrained environments. Moreover, smart cards can be used as trusted systems for storing, manipulation and execution of sensitive data.

Song et al. [19] propose and show the implementation of a system for IP protection for use in cable TV (CATV) networks. Within the OpenCable system, they implemented a security module using the ARM7TDMI[6] 32-bit RISC secure embedded microprocessor to handle various conditional access functions, to communicate with other system modules and to perform necessary cryptographic primitives for content protection, i.e. authentication, generation of copy protection keys, hash functions, and Diffie-Hellman key-exchange algorithms. They also implemented conditional access mechanisms using smart cards, which contain subscribers' records and also allow possible security updates, always in close cooperation with the security module.

Frikken et al. [20] propose a DRM smart card based scheme using commutative one-way functions, which—among other functions—allows revocation of expired smart cards, while preserving privacy of legitimate card holders. The environment can be described as follows. Content provider server S holds copyrighted media and each legitimate subscriber holds a smart card (SC), which allows him to access the server. The proposed protocol suite satisfies the following requirements:

1. access protection,
2. user privacy (the system cannot distinguish among requesting users),
3. revocation of SCs,
4. non-interactivity between client SC and server S,
5. efficiency, in terms of communication and computation, and
6. forward and backward security.

---

[4] Anonymous Fingerprinting [40] is a method for fingerprinting digital objects, into which the content provider neither has knowledge of the fingerprinted copy nor of the buyer's identity. This method alleviates the drawback of asymmetric fingerprinting, which relates to privacy issues of legitimate users. In this method, if the content provider finds a fingerprinted copy, he/she has to request the help of an external partner – registration authority – to identify the owner of the copy.

[5] The public key algorithm that is used is ElGamal's signature scheme [41].

[6] For further information, see http://www.arm.com/products/CPUs/ARM7TDMI.html.

Ueno et al. [21] propose a content protection system using smart cards that hold user profile information. Furthermore, various attributes like device ownership, family and friend relationships with the user can be stored into the smart card. The device that holds the contents has also its own profile information stored in an IC chip, allowing mutual authentication between the content provider server and the user's smart card.

Aura and Gollmann [22] propose a scheme for management and distribution of software licenses, which uses smart cards as tokens carrying license data. Each smart card has a unique public-private key pair for authentication purposes and contains a card certificate and a license certificate, which are signed by the software manufacturer with a master key. The smart card also contains the public part of the manufacturer's master key. Each smart card can be used as a single token containing license for various software programs. The proposers prove the security of protocols for binding the licenses with the smart cards, transferring licenses between smart cards and buying licenses over the Internet.

Lin et al. [23] propose a content protection scheme for Video-On-Demand (VOD) applications using hierarchical key management and utilizing smart cards to perform the necessary security protocols. Videos are classified into various classes, depending on its content. A user may request some videos from different classes. The content provider does some hard computation,[7] generates some encrypted information and embeds it into the smart card. The smart card contains the following: (a) smart card key – a shared key between user and content provider, (b) some pre-computed cryptographic information of each class of content, and (c) a user private key. The user takes the smart card and a unique pin code. The last requirement is that the end-user's set-top box must have an embedded smart card reader. The user inserts his pin code as a first step for authentication and the device communicates with the content provider, in order to authenticate the user. As soon as the user is identified, the content provider sends to the user's smart card – through the device interface – some encrypted parameters related with the requested content. Then the smart card calculates the decryption key of the requested video.

7. Trusted Architectures

Messerges and Dabbish [24] propose a DRM system for use in mobile phones, posing the demand that the part that implements DRM policy has to be implemented as a trusted system. Their system can be seen schematically in Fig. 5. The DRM manager is responsible for authentication of licenses and contents, for enforcing digital rights and for content decryption. A protected digital content has a license of use and its license has to be authenticated before it can be used by an application. Before the decryption of the content, there may be additional information required, e.g. checking device credentials and querying a secure database for further instructions. After that, the content is decrypted and sent to a trusted agent, which is an application that is trusted to access and manipulate decrypted content data. The security agents are in close co-operation with the security hardware and provide: (a) *Memory management*, (b) *Cryptographic*

---

[7] The model which has been proposed by Lin and Lee for hierarchical key management requires the implementation of cryptographic computations over finite fields generated by well chosen elliptic curves. The necessary computations are taking place on the content provider side, which is assumed to have the resources to perform them.

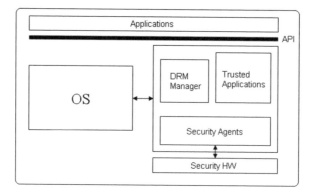

Figure 5. A trusted architecture for DRM implementation in a mobile device.

Figure 6. Spy component as a trusted system for protection of Intellectual Property.

operations, and (c) *Key management.* Secure memory is required in order to store sensitive data like phone private keys, while retaining the ability to be linked with erase mechanisms in case of attacks. Security agents are used to implement cryptographic algorithms like RSA [8] and ECC [9] for digital signatures, authentication and verification, SHA-1 [10] to process licenses and AES [7] to decrypt DRM protected contents. Key management can be implemented through a software module, having as primary job the safe storing and management of various keys, i.e. phone private keys, public keys, certifications, identification numbers, etc.

Lipton and Serpanos [25,26] propose the use of a special hardware agent, named spy, as a means for IP protection in several environments. Clearly, even if the content provider side is secure, one cannot trust the client, which, in general, is considered as an un-trusted source. They proved that the existence of a special, tamper-proof hardware component that resides on the client system, as shown in Fig. 6, is necessary to ensure protection of content provider Intellectual Property.

The spy is a hardware module which (a) acts as a passive I/O system, (b) can detect I/O activity and (c) has limited memory and computational power. It works in master mode in the client system and is monitoring the CPU. In a Video-on-Demand environment, for example, the user downloads the video from the content provider and stores it temporarily in the RAM of client system. There is an application that reproduces the content and it is assumed that it is the only application that runs on the system. If the user tries to copy or transmit the reproduced (decrypted) data, then some kind of I/O activity must take place at the client system, such as a disc access or a network transmission; such activity will be noticed by the spy, which, in turn, will notify the content provider in order to stop video transmission. Figure 7 shows the operation of this simple protocol.

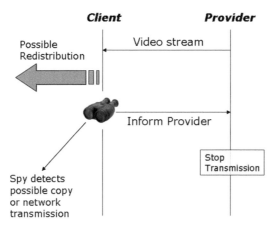

Figure 7. A simple protocol demonstrating *spy* operation.

Sibert et al. [27] propose DigiBox, a self-protecting container with a Secure Processing Unit (SPU), for use in information commerce, which provides protection of information's digital rights as well as easy control of protected content. On the proposed scheme, IP protection is based on well implemented cryptographic primitives, such as Triple DES [28] and RSA [8]. The security processing has to be performed into a "*secure processing unit*" —SPU—, in order to be cryptographically strong. SPU contains a CPU, memory, storage for applications and keys and it should be implemented in tamper-resistant hardware cryptographic modules.

Yan [3] proposes a high level model of a DRM system, which can be implemented in embedded systems, like a mobile device or a PDA. Yan claims that the system can provide DRM protection for downloadable digital content, broadcast contents and personal content management. The proposed scheme is based on trusted systems notion and can be seen in Fig. 1.

Smith et al. [29] stress the use of secure co-processors as trusted modules that offer secure storage space—to store sensitive data—and secure execution of critical software, despite any tampering attacks against the module. Such a co-processor comprises of (a) a CPU, (b) a bootstrap ROM, (c) a crypto processor—not necessarily—, and (d) secure memory, volatile and non-volatile. The module is encapsulated in a tamper-proof shell and there is an external I/O interface for communication with the rest of the system, as shown in Fig. 8. In case of a tampering attack, the protected content is erased from the secure memory.

Yee [30,31] proposes and demonstrated an implementation of Dyad, a secure co-processor, which can be used for copy protection of software packages. From its nature, such a module can reside into potentially un-trusted environments. The software, or at least some critical parts of it, is stored into the secure memory of the co-processor and only authenticated users can install or execute it in their systems. The software provider encrypts the copy-protected software using a randomly chosen key, which is encrypted with the secure co-processor's public-key and then stored into its non-volatile memory. As soon as the user is authenticated as a legitimate one, the secure co-processor can decrypt the key, using its own private key, decrypt the software and execute it.

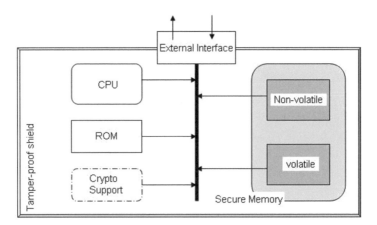

Figure 8. Generic structure of a secure co-processor.

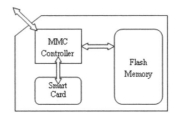

Figure 9. Functional view of a secure MMC.

Commercial DRM Applications

Various commercial applications have been implemented to protect Intellectual Property in commercial appliances. We briefly describe some of them, since there are no technical details for most of them.

Sony released the MagicGate™ [8] (MG) Memory Stick [32] as recording/playback media for various Sony commercial appliances, such as walkmans, MP3 players, etc. Sony stresses the necessity for copyright protection of music content, especially in such devices, and claims that the MG memory stick can be used as a copy-protection system which provides (a) authentication between the memory stick and the appliance and (b) content encryption and decryption. The drawback is that, both the memory stick and the appliance should incorporate MG technology.

Secure MultiMediaCards (MMCs) [33] provide a means for mobile DRM, integrating the mobile device to a secure multimedia device. As can be seen in Fig. 9, MMC is enhanced with an integrated chip that has full smart card functionality and which may provide an environment for secure storage and execution of protected content, as required by a DRM system.

ARM[9] has implemented ARM TrustZone™ [10] [34,35], an integrated hardware and software system, which provides a trusted and safe environment for various security

---

[8] MagicGate is a trademark of Sony Corporation.
[9] See http://www.arm.com.
[10] TrustZone is a trademark of ARM Limited.

functions. Protection of digital rights management in embedded devices is required urgently and the proposed platform can be quite helpful in this direction. The architecture is based on the notion of Trusted Platform and it distinguishes two "parallel" execution environments, one non-secure and one trusted. Critical parts, such as crypto hardware, a random number generator module, a boot ROM and key storage, are found into the "secure world". The TrustZone secure kernel can be implemented as a System-on-Chip module, consisting of the following:

- an embedded CPU, which executes code for trusted applications like DRM,
- an on-chip secure ROM,
- an on-chip non-volatile memory, which stores sensitive data like encryption keys, and
- secure volatile memory for temporary storage of data.

8. Conclusions

We presented various approaches for protection of Intellectual Property. Implementing them in embedded systems is a challenging task, due to the nature of embedded systems, with limited storage and processing power, power constraints, low cost requirements, etc. Mobile DRM comes to the fore, due to the explosive spread of use of mobile devices in various aspects of human transactions. Cryptography in conjunction with fingerprinting techniques can used as means to build efficient Intellectual Property protection systems. Tamper-resistant hardware modules like smart cards may be used to build trusted architectures, leading to environments that offer secure storage for protected content.

References

[1]   MOBILEDIA, "Online Shoplifters Grab Ringtones Worth $301 Million by 2006", online at http://www.mobiledia.com/news/33336.html, 2005.
[2]   F. Hartung and F. Ramme, "Digital rights management and watermarking of multimedia content for m-commerce applications", *Communications Magazine, IEEE,* vol. 38, pp. 78–94, Nov. 2000.
[3]   Z. Yan, "Mobile Digital Rights Management", Nokia Research Center, *Tech. Rep.* TML-C7 ISSN 1455–9749, 2001.
[4]   TCG, "What is Trusted Computing Group?" online at https://www.trustedcomputinggroup.org/home, 2005.
[5]   Intel Corp., "Intel Wireless Trusted Platform: Security for Mobile Devices", *White Paper,* online at http://whitepapers.silicon.com/0,39024759,60091578p-39000381q,00.htm, pp. 1–8, 2004.
[6]   Certicom Corp., "Giving Your Mobile Device a Competitive Edge", Presentation Slides from Webinar, online at http://www.certicom.com, 2005.
[7]   Inst. of Standards and Tech. (NIST), "Advanced Encryption Standard (AES), Federal Information Processing Standards Publication 1997", November 26, 2001.
[8]   R.L. Rivest, A. Shamir and L. Adleman, "A method for obtaining digital signatures and public-key cryptosystems", *Commun ACM,* vol. 21, pp. 120–126, 1978.
[9]   N. Koblitz, "Elliptic Curve Cryptosytems", *Math. of Comp.,* vol. 48, pp. 203–209, Jan. 1987.
[10] NIST, "Secure Hash Standard, FIPS PUB 180-2", pp. 1–75, Aug. 2002.
[11] L. Rivest, "The MD5 Message-Digest Algorithm", Recommendation RFC 1321, online at http://www.faqs.org/rfcs/rfc1321.html, Apr. 1992.
[12] Gunhce Kim, Dongkyoo Shin and Dongil Shin, "Intellectual property management on MPEG-4 video for hand-held device and mobile video streaming service", *IEEE Transactions on Consumer Electronics,* vol. 51, pp. 139–143, 2005.
[13] B. Schneier, *Applied Cryptography: Protocols, Algorithms, and Source Code in C,* Wiley, 1995.

[14]   Motorola, "Motorola announces availability of new wireless phone batteries for increased performance and safety, featuring new hologram", online at http://www.ftp.cl.cam.ac.uk/ftp/users/rja14/mototola_battery_auth.html, 1998.
[15]   B. Pfitzmann, M.E. Schunter, *Asymmetric Fingerprinting,* online at *http://citeseer.ifi.unizh.ch/pfitzmann96asymmetric.html*, 1996.
[16]   F. Bao, "Multimedia content protection by cryptography and watermarking in tamper-resistant hardware", in *MULTIMEDIA '00: Proceedings of the 2000 ACM workshops on Multimedia*, pp. 139–142, 2000.
[17]   N.R. Potlapally, "Optical Fingerprinting to Protect Data: A Proposal." *IEEE Computer,* vol. 35, pp. 23–28 online at http://computer.org/omputer/o2002/r4023abs.htm, 2002.
[18]   J. Domingo-Ferrer, Herrera-Joancomarti, "Efficient Smart-Card Based Anonymous Fingerprinting", in *CARDIS '98: Proceedings of the the International Conference on Smart Card Research and Applications*, 2000, pp. 221–228.
[19]   Won Jay Song, Won Hee Kim, Bo Gwan Kim, Minho Kang and Munkee Choi, "Contents protection system using smart card interface for digital CATV network based on the OpenCable specification," *IEEE Transactions on Consumer Electronics,* vol. 49, pp. 693–702, 2003.
[20]   K.B. Frikken, M.J. Atallah and M. Bykova, "Remote Revocation of Smart Cards in a Private DRM System", in *ACSW Frontiers*, online at http://www.crpit.com/confpapers/CRPITV44Frikken.pdf, 2005, pp. 169–178.
[21]   M. Ueno, M. Kanbe, T. Kobayashi and Y. Kondo, "Digital Rights Management Technology Using Profile Information and Use Authorization", *NTT Tech. Rev. Online*, 2 *(12),* online at http://www.ntt.co.jp/tr/0412/letters.html.
[22]   T. Aura and D. Gollmann, "Software license management with smart cards", in *Proceedings of USENIX Workshop on Smartcard Technology*, 1999, pp. 1–19.
[23]   C. Lin, J.S. Chou and T.Y. Lee, "A Secure Scheme for Users Classification and Contents Protection in Video-on-demand Systems", in *Proceedings of International Conference on Informatics, Cybernetics, and Systems 2003,* 2003, pp. 1325–1330.
[24]   T.S. Messerges and E.A. Dabbish, "Digital rights management in a 3G mobile phone and beyond", in *Proceedings of the 2003 ACM workshop on Digital rights management*, 2003, pp. 27–38.
[25]   R.J. Lipton, S. Rajagopalan and D.N. Serpanos, "Spy: A Method to Secure Clients for Network Services", in *ICDCS Workshops*, 2002, pp. 23–28, http://sd.omputer.org/omp/proeedngs/dsw/2002/1588/00/15880023abs.htm.
[26]   D.N. Serpanos and R.J. Lipton, "Defense Against Man-in-the-Middle Attack in Client-Server Systems", in *ISCC*, 2001, pp. 9–14, http://sd.omputer.org/omp/proeedngs/s/2001/1177/00/11770009abs.htm.
[27]   O. Sibert, D. Bernstein and V.D. Wie, "DigiBox: A Self-Protecting Container for Information Commerce", in *Proceedings of the First USENIX Workshop on Electronic Commerce*, 1995, pp. 171–183.
[28]   Inst. of Standards and Tech. (NIST), *FIPS Publication 46–1: Data Encryption Standard*, 1988.
[29]   S. Smith and S. Weingart, "Building a High-Performance, Programmable Secure Co-processor", *IBM Research Report*, vol. RC 21102, February 1998.
[30]   B. Yee, "Using Secure Co-processors", *PhD Thesis*, Carnegie Mellon University, pp. 1–104, May 1994.
[31]   B.S. Yee and J.D. Tygar, "Secure Coprocessors in Electronic Commerce Applications", in *Proceedings of the First USENIX Electronic Commerce Workshop*, 1995.
[32]   Sony Corp., "Memory Stick Copyright Protection Technology – MagicGate", *Sony Global CX-news*, 2005, online at http://www.sony.net/Products/SC-HP/cx_news/vol20/.
[33]   Giesecke & Devrient GmbH, "Secure MultiMediaCards", pp. 2, 2005.
[34]   ARM, "TrustZone Technology Overview", White Paper, 2005, http://www.arm.com/products/CPUs/arch-trustzone.html.
[35]   T. Alves and D. Felton, "TrustZone: Integrated Hardware andSoftware Security", *ARM Corp. (White Paper)*, pp. 1–12, July 2004, http://www.arm.com/products/CPUs/arch-trustzone.html.
[36]   J. Krasner, "Using Elliptic Curve Cryptography (ECC) for Enhanced Embedded Security", *'Catch the Curve' White Paper Series by Certicom Corporation,* vol. 3, pp. 1–30, November 2004.
[37]   Certicom, "An Elliptic Curve Cryptography (ECC) Primer," *'Catch the Curve' White Paper Series,* vol. 1, pp. 1–24, June 2004.
[38]   W. Diffie, M.E. Hellman, "New Directions in Cryptography", *IEEE Trans. on Information Theory,* vol. 22, pp. 644–654, 1976.
[39]   T.E. Gamal, "A Public Key Cryptosystem and a Signature Scheme Based on Discrete Logarithms", *IEEE Transactions on Information Theory,* vol. IT-31, pp. 469–472, July 1985.
[40]   B. Pfitzmann and M. Waidner, "Anonymous Fingerprinting", in *EUROCRYPT*, 1997, pp. 88–102.
[41]   T.E. Gamal, "A Public Key Cryptosystem and a Signature Scheme Based on Discrete Logarithms", in *Advances in Cryptology: Proceedings of CRYPTO 1984*, LNCS 0196, pp. 18, 1985.

Security and Embedded Systems
D.N. Serpanos and R. Giladi (Eds.)
IOS Press, 2006

57

Challenges in Deeply Networked System Survivability

Philip KOOPMAN, Jennifer MORRIS and Priya NARASIMHAN
Carnegie Mellon University, Pittsburgh, PA, USA

Abstract. Deeply networked systems are formed when embedded computing systems gain connectivity to each other and to larger enterprise systems. New functionality also brings new survivability challenges, including security across the embedded/enterprise interface. Addressing the needs of deeply networked system survivability is an open challenge that will require new approaches beyond those used for enterprise systems.

Introduction

A deeply networked system is formed when embedded computing subsystems are connected to each other and to enterprise systems, often via the Internet [20]. By increasing access to information and computing resources, these systems promise to provide new capabilities and opportunities. Unfortunately, deep networking also introduces survivability issues that have, thus far, received little attention.

Consider an automotive control application (such as a road-condition sensor or intake air quality sensor, Fig. 1) which is connected via the vehicle's embedded networks to an automotive telematics infrastructure [2]. In this system, external servers could optimize performance for a given emissions requirement by reconfiguring the ratio of internal combustion to battery power in the car's engine, based on data from the internal vehicle sensors and other external sources (such as traffic conditions). However, what happens if someone penetrates the servers and commands all hybrid vehicles to perform 100% internal combustion on a smoggy day? What happens when a fault in a

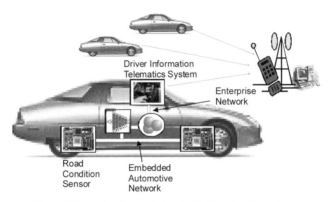

Figure 1. Example of a coupled embedded + enterprise system.

vehicle's telematics connection disrupts enterprise server operations? Worse, what happens when someone uses the enterprise-to-embedded communication channel to break into a vehicle and cause it to behave in an unsafe manner?

Given the proliferation of embedded applications that are increasingly connected to the Internet [19,16,15], including automobiles [9] and train control [6], it becomes imperative to find strategies that can safely and securely connect the two types of systems. In particular, deeply networked systems must ensure the survivability of embedded applications [12,10,18] with critical functionality.

1. Embedded Survivability

Embedded systems are often used in critical applications, and there is much previous work in creating dependable systems for transportation applications, among others. In addition to newer security-based approaches, classical approaches have included hardware fault tolerance, software fault tolerance, and techniques to assure high software quality for critical systems ([4] are proceedings from a primary conference on these topics).

Classical work in this area assumes closed systems in which external attackers cannot gain access to the system. For this reason, most embedded systems have little or no native security capabilities. For example, the real-time embedded networks currently used in mainstream automobiles have no security mechanisms available for network messages.

1.1. Embedded System Differences

It seems likely that traditional approaches won't solve many security problems in typical embedded systems, because the constraints and application domains differ tremendously from enterprise systems. A description of many of the differences can be found in [11]. The following points discuss the differences most relevant to survivability.

Many embedded systems interact with the external world by reading sensor values and changing actuators. Several properties of this real-world interaction that increase the difficulty of maintaining essential functions in the face of a failure or attack are:

- Reactive and real time. Embedded systems often perform periodic computations to close control loops. Even small timing variations (less than one second in many cases) that destabilize a single control loop can cause complete system failure.
- Critical. Embedded systems are often used in life- or mission-critical applications. This means that even minor disruptions to service can have unacceptably high cost.
- Non-recoverable. Because embedded systems have actuators that change the physical world, it may be difficult or impossible to "roll back" a state change caused by a faulty system as can be done with errant financial transactions.
- Exceptional. Embedded systems often operate in harsh environments with analog inputs, potentially subjecting them to many hardware faults.

Embedded systems have to remain survivable even though they usually are far more constrained than enterprise systems. Common embedded system constraints include:

- Small size & weight; battery power. Severe constraints on size, weight, and power often limit the amount of memory and computational power available.
- Low cost. Cost pressure usually results in the least capable CPU possible being used. Indeed, 8-bit CPUs dominate the market by volume [21].
- 24x7 operation of single nodes. Continuous operation, often with a single CPU dedicated to a particular function, makes it impracticable to have periodic downtime for applying patches, updates, or other preventive maintenance functions.
- Use of embedded networks. Most embedded systems are too low-cost to permit the use of Ethernet, TCP/IP, or other enterprise communication techniques. Instead, they use specialized embedded real-time networks such as CAN and TTP/C that don't support TCP/IP efficiently.
- Lack of system administrator. While it might be realistic to have a system administrator for every personal computer, most embedded systems are not designed to be continually patched or require software management. (Who should be the sysadmin for an air conditioner?)

Because of these various issues, it is clear that techniques used in enterprise systems cannot be expected to work as-is in an embedded environment.

1.2. Issues at the Embedded/Enterprise Interface

Most embedded systems aren't designed to connect to the Internet. Rather, most designs assume that the manufacturer has complete control over the software and network interface to every node. Moreover, they are typically built under the assumption that the system designer has taken into account all likely failure modes, that there are no misbehaving nodes (with misbehavior due possibly to software defects, unforeseen hardware defects, or malicious attackers), and that all system inputs conform to system requirements. Once a system is connected to the Internet, even indirectly, these assumptions are no longer valid.

2. Embedded System Design Approach Differences

Because embedded systems have so many differences in constraints and domain characteristics from typical enterprise systems, it should come as no surprise that their design approaches are often fundamentally different. These differences affect which approaches are viable for creating survivable systems.

2.1. Event-Based vs. Time-Based Operation

Enterprise systems are typically transactional and event-triggered in nature, which means that they usually focus on preserving data and tend to center around end-to-end request-response semantics. Usually the emphasis is on statistically good performance under various loading conditions, and it is often acceptable to refuse admission to tasks during overloads. "Best effort" servicing of aperiodic tasks is often acceptable.

Embedded systems often focus on interacting with continuous, physical systems with hard deadlines. Even minor disruptions to service can have unacceptably high cost. Periodic operation of all aspects of the system to makes it easier to ensure that worst case timing properties are acceptable. Such operation is often called "time triggered" system design (e.g., as discussed in [13]).

Time triggered design makes possible optimizations such as leaving time stamps (or even message identifiers) off messages and instead relying on the fact that the system assures timely message arrival to identify messages. A focus on worst case performance leads, in many cases, to static periodic execution schedules to ensure that every task has the computational resources it needs to run at its worst-case highest frequency. (Dynamic scheduling techniques can also be used, but in the end resources must still be reserved for worst-case loading conditions.)

Embedded systems designed for worst-case situations are at first glance more survivable to overload situations than typical enterprise systems. This is because no matter how many events an attacker or fault from the enterprise system throws at it, excessive loads applied to one task will not compromise resources used for other tasks.

2.2. Discrete vs. Continuous Applications

The interface between event- and time-based portions of deeply embedded systems creates additional types of vulnerabilities to faults and attacks. Beyond the usual issues of authentication and integrity, there are also timing vulnerabilities in continuous-time applications. Assuming that the embedded system has a typical time-triggered design approach, only one incoming message of a particular type can be processed per processing cycle (for example, one message of a particular type every 250 msec). If the data is being used for a control application, the system is likely designed to expect a fresh value for each and every control cycle. Even small disruptions in timing on the enterprise side, whether from congestion, faults, or malicious attacks, force exception handling mechanisms to be developed for the interface to the enterprise side. Exceptions that almost certainly must be handled include: missed messages (there may not be time for a successful retry on the enterprise side), erratically spaced messages (if two messages arrive during a single cycle, does the system queue one to let it get stale, combine the messages, or just throw one away?), severely clumped messages (if ten messages arrive all at once after a long delay, how does the system catch up given only enough capacity to process one incoming message per cycle?), duplicated messages, and messages that arrive too often over an extended period of time. Dealing with many of these scenarios will force tradeoffs between spending money on extra resources to deal with some fraction of overloads vs. discarding data.

Message transfer from embedded to enterprise systems requires a low pass filter between the periodically generated time-triggered messages and the event-triggered processing paradigm of the enterprise system. For example, it may be important to transmit the status of an embedded airbag sensor to an enterprise system. In a time-triggered embedded system, the state of the airbag (deployed or not) might be reported ten times per second via a network message to achieve 100 msec latency. But reporting ten times per second from millions of vehicles is an unacceptable enterprise server load. One job of the embedded/enterprise gateway on each vehicle must be to apply a low-pass filter to values, and only generate an event-driven enterprise message when an airbag is deployed. The gateway must also deal with spurious messages due to sensor failures or coordinated attacks.

2.3. Fault Handling Approaches

Enterprise systems typically use a checkpoint-rollback recovery strategy to make their significant amounts of state more survivable. Rollback reverts to a consistent, previously saved state snapshot to facilitate recovery or restart in the event that a failure occurs.

Embedded systems often use roll-forward recovery, because they cannot roll back in dealing with the irreversible physical world. Typically, embedded systems contain far less state than their enterprise counterparts. Thus, while enterprise systems focus primarily on data-integrity, ordering and state-consistency protocols, embedded systems tend to focus more on time-sensitive, scheduling protocols where data is extracted and processed from the system in real time, often grows stale quickly, and can be discarded. This makes fault recovery for embedded systems very different from enterprise recovery approaches.

2.4. Physical Security & Repair Incentive

In general, enterprise survivability relies on the assumption that equipment owners have a vested interest in keeping their entire system secure and fault-free, so as to obtain full value from their capital equipment investment. Another underlying assumption is that it is possible to limit access or turn off machines in a crisis. For example, centralized service providers often deny individual users access to their equipment (for example, cut off network access or shut down the machine) if that equipment has been compromised, in order to avoid disruption to other users.

Embedded system owners may not have incentive to perform repairs and maintain physical security. Indeed, there is financial incentive to break into some smart cards used to store cash value or keep satellite TV access logs. In other instances, physical tampering can remove externally imposed constraints such as increasing vehicle performance at the expense of flouting anti-pollution laws or risking unsafe operating conditions.

Even if such faults or tampering could be detected, simply shutting down an embedded application and/or blocking its communication are likely to be unacceptable. A shut-down function would be complicated by the fact that it would have to be owned by someone other than the owner of the physical equipment. (Would you want the manufacturer of your vehicle or your local police department, for example, to have a "kill switch" for your car?) If the embedded system send safety critical information, (fire alarms from a dwelling; airbag deployment alarms from a vehicle; medical alert alarms from a home security system), termination of communication might be prohibited without a lengthy process of warnings and opportunities for repair. And of course an external kill function would likely prove a tempting target for attackers to trip maliciously.

3. Embedded Enterprise Gateway Requirements

The usual approach for attempting to resolve problems at the embedded/enterprise interface is to use a gateway or "firewall" node to isolate the embedded system from faults and attackers originating on the enterprise side (e.g., [1,17,22]). However, there is little or no guidance available on the types of services that have to be in such a gateway node to ensure the resulting system is survivable. Typical proposed approaches for this interface currently focus on the use of encryption (e.g., [7]) and in industrial applications often use VPN. But, based on our observations, the following types of additional services are likely to be needed in at least some systems to ensure survivability for a wide variety of deeply networked system applications.

3.1. Trusted Time Base

A trusted time base that is shared among all embedded gateways and enterprise servers within a deeply networked system could provide a foundation for resolving timing disruptions and ambiguities. This could improve survivability by:

- Distinguishing whether a tightly spaced group of messages arriving at a gateway were generated at almost the same time, were bunched up due to congestion, or were subject to a man-in-the-middle timing attack.
- Detecting timing jitter in messages sent between embedded subsystems via an enterprise network due to load variation or a control-loop destabilization attack.
- Enabling compensation for message aging in closing inter-subsystem control loops.

In some applications the embedded network will have to make available "freshness" data for various values transmitted periodically, because the assumption of end-to-end periodic operation doesn't hold for data that has been exposed to the enterprise side of the system.

3.2. "Firewall" Protection in Both Directions

It is just as important to protect the enterprise system against an embedded subsystem as the other way around. Thus, we expect enterprise/embedded gateway nodes to be composed of a matched pair of gateway functions in opposing directions. Each side of the gateway will have opposite notions of whom to trust, complicating gateway management.

As the embedded-to-enterprise side of the gateway converts periodic time-triggered data to event-triggered messages, it will have to manage issues such as ensuring delivery via acknowledgements, self-throttling of message loads, filtering of inappropriate messages, time stamping messages, and in general ensuring that faults or attacks on the embedded side of the interface don't propagate to the enterprise side.

In addition to traditional firewall functions, the enterprise-to-embedded side of the gateway will have to manage the conversion of incoming event-based messages to time-triggered messages. This will include deciding what values to provide to periodic tasks when event-based messages are missed, delayed, clumped, repeated, or sent too fast.

3.3. Limiting Damage from Compromised Servers

A significant potential vulnerability in deeply networked systems comes from enterprise servers that are given direct or indirect control authority over embedded system actuators. We believe that such control authority will inevitably creep in to most deeply networked systems. As an example, Koopman [12] describes a real-time energy pricing scenario in which a malicious failure of an enterprise server can cause an arbitrary number of houses to change their power usage, resulting in a potential physical attack on the electric power grid.

Avoiding vulnerabilities due to compromises of enterprise servers might be difficult. A starting point might be to limit, by design, the number of embedded systems that are permitted to take information from any particular enterprise server (even via indirect paths), thus limiting the consequences of a fault or compromise of that server.

4. Related Work

Firewall designs for enterprise systems are well known, and secure the connection between internal and external systems by blocking unauthorized traffic [3]. This might be achieved by applying filters to the packet level, the application level, or the physical port level. Although these enterprise-centric security designs can be effective at blocking unauthorized communication, they are inadequate for the attack scenarios that we have identified for deeply networked systems. The SCADA community has been active in embedded security (e.g., [7,8]). To this point published results have focused on patch management and encryption of data sent over physically insecure links.

The TTP safety-critical embedded network protocol incorporates the concept of a "temporal firewall" [14] to isolate time-critical activities, but does not deal with embedded systems connected to the Internet. That refers more to the isolation of time-sensitive and non-time-sensitive tasks from each other within an embedded system.

Duri et al., have proposed a framework for automotive telematics applications to ensure the privacy and integrity of user-supplied data in the enterprise system [5]. That technique uses trusted processors to collect and aggregate user data to be sent to authenticated application. However, it focuses on authorization rather than message timing attacks.

5. Conclusions

Deeply embedded systems combine embedded and enterprise computing, offering tremendous potential but also new survivability challenges. Embedded systems have significantly different assumptions and approaches to computing, necessitating different approaches to survivability than those used in enterprise systems. Moreover, the interface between time-triggered, real-time embedded computing and event-triggered, transaction-oriented enterprise computing presents unique survivability challenges.

This work is supported in part by the General Motors Collaborative Research Laboratory at Carnegie Mellon University, NSF CAREER Award CCR-0238381, an NSF Graduate Research Fellowship, and Army Research Office grant number DAAD19-02-1-0389. Any opinions, findings, conclusions or recommendations expressed in this publication are those of the authors and do not necessarily reflect the views of the National Science Foundation or other sponsoring organizations.

References

[1]   AEEC Letter 01-112/SAI/742. *Draft 1 of Project Paper 664, 'Aircraft Data networks' Part 5 'Network Interconnection Devices'*, May 2001.

[2]   Robert Bosch GmbH. Audio, *Navigation & Telematics in the Vehicle: Bosch Technical Instruction.* Bentley Publishers, July 2002.

[3]   Cheswick & Bellovin. *Firewalls and Internet Security: Repelling the Wily Hacker.* Addison Wesley, June 1994.

[4]   *Dependable Systems and Networks Conference Proceedings*, IEEE Computer Society Press, June 2005.

[5]   S. Duri, J. Elliott, M. Gruteser, X. Liu, P. Moskowitz, and R. Perez. Data protection and data sharing in telematics. *Mobile Networks and Applications*, 9(6): 693–701, December 2004.

[6]   A. Fabri, T. Nieva, and P. Umiliacchi. Use of the internet for remote train monitoring and control: the rosin project. *In Proceedings of Rail Technology '99*, 1999 September 16.

[7]   AGA/GTI SCADA Encryption Web Site, *http://www.gtiservices.org/security/index.shtml*, August 1, 2005.

[8]   W. Iversen. Hackers step up SCADA attacks. *Automation World*, October 2004.

[9]   L. Kahney. Your car: The next net appliance. *Wired News*, 2001 March.

[10] P. Kocher, R. Lee, G. McGraw, A. Raghunathan, and S. Ravi. Security as a new dimension in embedded system design. In *Proceedings 41st Design Automation Conference*, pages 753–760. IEEE Press, June 2004.

[11] P. Koopman, "Embedded System Design Issues – the Rest of the Story", In *Proceedings of the 1996 International Conference on Computer Design*, Austin, October 7–9 1996.

[12] P. Koopman. Embedded system security. *IEEE Computer*, 37(7): 95–97, July 2004.

[13] H. Kopetz. *Real-Time Systems: Design Principles for Distributed Embedded Applications.* Kluwer, 1997.

[14] H. Koptez and R. Nossal. Temporal firewalls in large distributed real-time systems. *In Proc. 6th IEEE Comp. Soc. Wkshp. on Future Trends of Distributed Comp. Sys.*, pp. 310–315. IEEE Computer Soc., October 1997.

[15] P. Krishnamurthy, J. Kabara, and T. Anusas-Amornkul. Security in wireless residential networks. In *IEEE Transactions on Consumer Electronics*, volume 48, pages 157–166. IEEE Press, February 2002.

[16] S. Kuo, Z. Salcic, and U. Madawala. A real-time hybrid web-client access architecture for home automation. In *Proceedings of the 2003 Joint Conference on Information, Communications and Signal Processing and the Pacific Rim Conference on Multimedia*, volume 3, pages 1752–1756. IEEE Press, December 2003.

[17] P. Polishuk. Automotive industry in europe takes the lead in the introduction of optical data buses. *Wiring Harness News*, November 2001.

[18] S. Ravi, A. Raghunathan, P. Kocher, and S. Hattangady. Security in embedded systems: Design challenges. *ADM Transactions on Embedded Computing Systems (TECS)*, 2(3): 461–491, August 2004.

[19] J.W. Szymanski. Embedded internet technology in process control devices. In *Proceedings 2000 IEEE International Workshop on Factory Communication Systems*, pages 301–308. IEEE Press, September 2000.

[20] D. Tennenhouse. Proactive computing. *Communications of the ACM*, 43(5): 43–50, May 2000.

[21] J. Turley, "The Two Percent Solution," *Embedded Systems Programming*, January 2003.

[22] C.A. Wargo and C. Chas. Security considerations for the e-enabled aircraft. In *Proceedings of the IEEE Aerospace Conference*, volume 4, Big Sky, MT, March 2003.

Security and Embedded Systems
D.N. Serpanos and R. Giladi (Eds.)
IOS Press, 2006

Multimedia Watermarking

Bede LIU[1]

Department of Electrical Engineering, Princeton University, USA

Abstract. Watermarking is the insertion of information into a host data, for a variety of applications, including ownership identification, authentication, and to provide additional functionalities. We review here some of the recent works on multimedia watermarking, focusing on (1) watermarking binary images, (2) watermarking curves, and (3) image communication.

Keywords. Multimedia watermarking, data hiding, image communication

1. Introduction

Watermarking is the insertion of information into a host multimedia data, usually imperceptibly with the help of human perceptual models. The inserted watermark can be used for a variety of purposes, including ownership identification, authentication, and to provide additional functionalities in the use of the host data [1,2]. Because the watermark is often inserted imperceptibly, watermarking and data hiding are sometimes used synonymously. Watermarking for authentication is designed to reveal any alteration of the host multimedia data and also to provide additional information such as where alterations have been made.

A number of approaches have been shown to be effective for watermarking multimedia data. The detection of the presence of the watermark can be carried out with or without using the original host data. Signal processing, either intentional or unintentional, can affect the inserted watermark. Intentional processing includes deliberate attempt at removing or obliterate the watermark. Unintentional processing may include compression, scanning and printing, etc.

We review in this paper some of the recent works on multimedia watermarking, focusing on watermarking binary images for authentication and annotation. We will also discuss briefly two related problems: watermarking curves and watermarking for image communication.

1.1. Two Examples

A well known watermarking method for images is the spread spectrum approach [3], shown in Fig. 1. The largest M of the DCT coefficients, denoted by X, are selected for the insertion of watermark. A pseudo random signal (PRS) W is generated as the watermark and added to X with a weighting factor α to form the marked coefficients according to $(1 + \alpha W) X$. The inverse DCT is taken of these marked and those not se-

---

[1] Corresponding Author: Bede Liu, Department of Electrical Engineering, Princeton University, Princeton, NJ 08544, USA. E-mail: liu@princeton.edu.

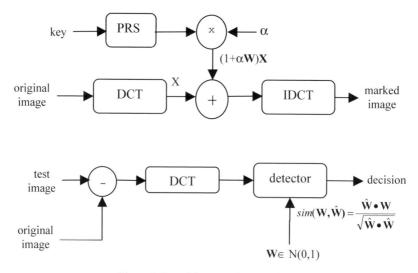

Figure 1. Spread Spectrum Watermarking.

lected for watermarking. The result is the watermarked image. That the strength of the inserted watermark is related to the size of the DCT coefficients helps to reduce the visual distortion introduced by the watermark insertion.

To detect whether or not a given watermark is present in a test image, DCT is taken of the difference of the test image and the watermarked image. The result is correlated with W, and then compared with a threshold. The presence of W can be used for certain claims, such as ownership. The embedded watermark can also be detected without the original, but less reliably. This approach has been shown to be robust when the marked image is subject to moderate compression and some other processing.

Shown in Fig. 2 is an example of watermarking for image authentication, where a known pattern (b) is inserted in the host image (a) to produce the marked image, from which the inserted watermark (b) can be extracted. The marked image is visually indistinguishable from the original unmarked image. Suppose the marked image is modified to produce image (c). Then the watermark extracted from the altered image becomes that of (d), which is different from the original watermark, revealing not only that the marked image has been modified but also where the modification took place.

The alterations were made on the image of Fig. 2 where it is relatively easy to insert watermarks without causing visual distortion because of the moderately rich texture there. There are other regions in the image which are 'smooth'. The insertion of watermark in those regions would be difficult or even impossible, since a slight modifications in those regions can produce noticeable visual distortion. The need for inserting watermark in these regions is to be able to reveal possible alterations there. Figure 3(a) shows the smooth blocks of Fig. 2(a), and Fig. 3(b) is a histogram showing how many coefficients in each block can be modified without producing artifacts. It is seen that modifications cannot be made in about 20% of the blocks.

(a)
(c)

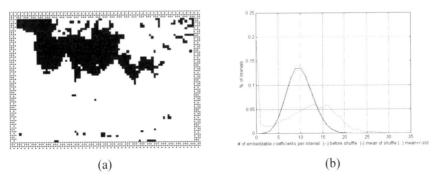

(b)
(d)

Figure 2. An example of watermarking to detect alteration.

(a)
(b)

Figure 3. (a) smooth region of Fig. 2(a), (b) histogram of embeddable coefficients in each block.

1.2. Insertion in Smooth Regions

It is, however, possible to embed information in the smooth regions [2] by using shuffling, whereby the information to be inserted in a smooth region is actually embedded in different parts of the image. The coefficients of all the blocks are concatenated to form a single string, as shown in the first line of Fig. 4. Because of smooth regions, some of the blocks will have no embeddable coefficients. A random shuffle is then performed on the string to form a different string shown on the second line of Fig. 4.

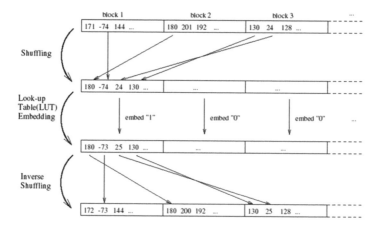

Figure 4. Shuffling to embed information in smooth regions.

This string is then partitioned into blocks. It can be shown [4] that because of the shuffle, all blocks will have embeddable coefficients with probability close to 1. Embedding is then done on this shuffled string, and a reverse shuffle follows the embedding. Shuffling also enhances security since the shuffling table or a key for generating the table is needed to correctly extract the hidden data.

2. Watermarking Binary Images

Most of the previous works on image watermarking have been concerned with color or grayscale images, where the pixels may take a wide range of values. In these images, the changing of most pixel values by a small amount may not cause visible artifacts under normal viewing conditions. This property of human visual system plays a key role in watermarking of media data.

However, an increasing number of images we encounter today are binary, or with a very limited number of values the pixels may take. These images include maps, archived records, signatures, *substitute checks* [5]. Because of the ease with which images can be copied and modified, the annotation and authentication of binary images as well as the detection of tampering are important problems to be addressed. It is difficult to watermark these images because modification of pixel values in these images will likely to produce noticeable artifacts. For binary images in particular, the only modification on the pixels that can be performed is to "flip" a white pixel to black or vice versa. And these changes can only be made on pixels at the boundary.

To insert a watermark into binary images, one may also modify some features such as curvature or thickness of strokes. We shall briefly review one approach to hide data in general binary images, including scanned text, figures, and signatures. The hidden data can be extracted without using the original unmarked image. The approach can be used for detecting whether a binary document has been altered or not, and for hiding annotation labels or other side information in binary images.

2.1. Insertion of Watermark

An image is partitioned into blocks and one bit is embedded in each block by changing one or more pixels in that block. For example, a "0" can be embedded by making the number of black pixels in that block an even number. Similarly, making the number of black pixels to be odd can embed a "1".[2] This method can be extended straightforwardly to embedding more than one bit in each block.

The question remains as to which pixel or pixels in each block are to be changed. While human visual model plays a key role to minimize visual artifacts in watermarking grey scale or color images, visual model for binary images have not received much attention. A simple way is introduced in [6] to quantify how noticeable a change will be caused by the flipping of a pixel. This is done by examining the pixel and its immediate neighbors to produce a numerical *flip score*. Changing a pixel with higher scores generally introduces less artifacts and a 0 score means no flipping.

It is not practical to examine exhaustively each pixel and its neighborhood to decide how noticeable a change will be caused by flipping that pixel. However, one can determine the flip score by examining a small window centered around that pixel and using a smooth measure and a connectivity measure. The smooth measure is derived from horizontal, vertical, and diagonal transitions in the local window, and the connectivity measure is derived from the number of the black and white clusters. If the flip of a pixel changes the connectivity or significantly changes the smooth measure of the neighborhood centered at the pixel, then the pixel has a low flip score.

Using this approach, all 3x3 patterns can be ranked in terms of how noticeable the change of the center pixel will be. The results can be refined by examining a larger neighborhood, say 5x5. Special cases are also handled in such large neighborhood so as to avoid introducing noise on special patterns such as sharp corners.

2.2. Embedding in Smooth Regions – Shuffling

For binary images, no pixel can be flipped in the interior of an all white and all black regions. However, the shuffling approach discussed previously can be applied to binary images as well. Embedding is done after shuffling, and inverse shuffling is performed to get a marked image.

Figure 5 illustrates an example of using watermarking to detect alteration. A "hidden" data of 976 bits are inserted into the original binary image of Fig. 5(a). The hidden date contains an 800 bit "PUEE" pattern of Fig. 5(g). The watermarked image is shown in Fig. 5(b), which is visually indistinguishable from the original, even by examining the magnified portion, Figs 5(c) and 5(e). An alteration, Fig. 5(f), is made on the marked image of Fig. 5(b). The extracted watermark is then the random pattern, Fig. 5(g), rather than the original embedded pattern, thus indicating that alteration has taken place.

The overall system of this approach is shown in the block diagram of Fig. 6.

---

[2] A generalization is to pick a "quantization step size" Q and to make the total number of black pixels in a block to be an even multiples of Q in order to embed a "0", and an odd multiple of Q to embed a "1". In this case, a larger value of Q would make the embedding less sensitive to noise, at the expense of introducing more noticeable artifacts. This odd-even embedding can be viewed as a special case of using a lookup table for embedding.

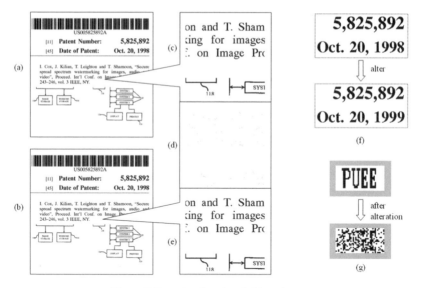

Figure 5. Detecting alterations in binary image.

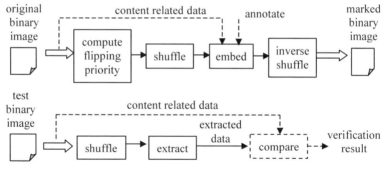

Figure 6. Embedding in binary images and extraction.

3. Watermarking Curves

Curves, including signatures, contour maps, and sketches, form a special class of binary images. They can be watermarked by inserting a spread spectrum signal in the control points of the B-spline for the curve [7].

Consider a curve of m+1 points $P = (p_x, p_y)$, where p_x and p_y are the coordinates. Denote its B-spline approximation by $p^B(t) = \sum_{i=0}^{n} c_i B_{ik}(t)$, where $c_i = (c_{xi}, c_{yi})$ is the i-th control point, and $B_{ik}(t)$ is a kth order blending function. The control points may also be written as $C = (c_x, c_y)$. A watermark (w_x, w_y) is scaled by α and added to the control points, so the marked control points becomes $(c_x + \alpha w_x, c_y + \alpha w_y)$. The watermarked curve is constructed from the B-spline, by using the marked control points. To detect whether or not the watermark has been inserted into a test curve $P^* =$

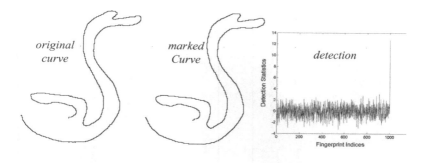

Figure 7. Watermarking curve via B-spline.

$(\mathbf{p}^*_x, \mathbf{p}^*_y)$, the control points $\mathbf{C}^* = (\mathbf{c}^*_x, \mathbf{c}^*_y)$ is extracted, from which the original control points are subtracted and the result normalized by α to give the estimated watermark $(\mathbf{w}^*_x, \mathbf{w}^*_y)$. The estimated watermark can be correlated with the inserted watermark and the result compared with a threshold. Figure 7 shows an example of watermarking a curve using this approach, where the number of control points is 100.

4. Image Communication – Error Concealment and Error Resilience

In image communication, error concealment refers generally to the recovery of lost information. Error resilience refers to reducing the vulnerability to error. There is considerable redundancy present in multimedia data, which can be used to recover lost information. If the lost information is isolated, natural looking interpolation can be made using information derived from neighboring blocks. The computation typically begins with an estimation of some features of the lost information, such as edges, motion information, etc. These features are then used for interpolation to recover the lost information. However, feature estimation may require considerable processing resources at the receiver. Such processing can be performed at the encoder and sent to the decoder for concealment. Sending side information can be done using data hiding at the expense of slight degradation of image quality, but without increasing the bit rate [8]. Using this approach, the receiver saves about 30% computation for concealment, as the feature information needed for concealment are pre-computed at the encoder and inserted into the data bit stream to be used by the receiver when needed.

Error resilient approach can be employed in MPEG coded video to improve the performance of error concealment at the decoder with minimal increase in bit rate. Most of error concealment methods in MPEG are either spatial which is usually applied to I frames, or temporal which is usually applied to P and B frames. To isolate the damaged blocks, the order with which the blocks are sent can be shuffled [9]. To help the recovery of motion information, interframe-wise parity bits of motion vectors in successive intraframe are embedded in the video using data hiding. This approach can give a reasonable image quality for packet loss up to 25%.

5. Conclusion

Watermarking is the insertion of information into a host data, often using understanding of human perception so that the inserted watermark does not cause visual artifacts. Watermarking or data hiding are used for a variety of applications, including ownership identification, authentication, and to provide additional functionalities. We review here some of the recent works on multimedia watermarking, focusing on watermarking binary images, watermarking curves, and image communication.

Acknowledgement

The author acknowledges the support of New Jersey State Commission of Science and Technology and the help of Min Wu and Peng Yin in preparing this paper. There is a large body of literature on watermarking. The author apologizes to those authors whose papers are not included in the Reference because of page limitation.

References

[1] I. Cox, J. Bloom, and M. Miller, *Digital Watermarking*, Morgan Kaufmann, 2001.
[2] M. Wu and B. Liu, *Multimedia Data Hiding*, Springer-Verlag, 2002.
[3] I. Cox, J. Killian, F. Leighton, and T. Shamoon, "Secure spread spectrum watermarking for multimedia," *IEEE Trans. Image Processing*, Dec 1997, 1673–1687.
[4] M. Wu and B. Liu, "Data hiding in image and video: Part-I – fundamental issues and solutions", *IEEE Trans. on Image Proc.*, June 2003, 685–695.
[5] Check 21 (http://www.federalreserve.gov/paymentsystems/truncation/faqs2.htm#ques1).
[6] M. Wu and B. Liu, "Data hiding in binary image for authentication and annotation", *IEEE Trans. on Multimedia*, August 2004, 528–538.
[7] H. Gou and M. Wu, "Robust digital fingerprinting for curves," *IEEE ICASSP'05*, March 2005, 529–532.
[8] P. Yin, H. Yu, and B. Liu, "Error concealment using data hiding," *IEEE ICASSP*, 2001, 1453–1456.
[9] P. Yin, M. Wu, and B. Liu, "A robust error resilient approach for mpeg video transmission over internet," *Visual Communication of Image Processing* (SPIE), 2002, 103–111.

Security and Embedded Systems
D.N. Serpanos and R. Giladi (Eds.)
IOS Press, 2006

A Platform for Designing Secure Embedded Systems

Haris LEKATSAS [a], Jörg HENKEL [b], Venkata JAKKULA [a] and
Srimat CHAKRADHAR [a]

[a] *NEC Labs, Princeton, USA*
[b] *University of Karlsruhe, Germany*

Abstract. Multimedia systems become increasingly ambient and as such require compact, lightweight, low power etc. designs that were not major constraints in earlier desktop-based systems. At the same time, DRM (Digital Rights Management) is playing an important role in the multimedia industry and hence requires copyright protection.

In this paper we introduce our Cypress platform that is tailored to provide solutions to these issues. Specifically, the platform addresses as the first approach of its kind the combined data/code compression and their encryption in a unified architecture.

Keywords. media encryption, media compression, embedded systems, microarchitecture

1. Introduction

Multimedia systems pose stringent constraints on compactness, lightweight, low power consumption etc. The unique memory demands (large memory size, concurrent memory accesses, high memory throughput) of a multimedia system make its memory subsystem a prime target for optimization. The situation is worsened by the fact that systems featuring embedded multimedia grow increasingly complex as the demand for functionality is enhancing from one device generation to the next. An example is a cellular phone that beyond its core function of a communication device provides multiple embedded multimedia functions like video (embedded digital camera, sending and receiving video clips), music player, gaming etc. The demand for increased chip size that comes with the embedded multimedia features is virtually growing faster than what can be alleviated through higher integration densities of new silicon technologies. This aspect has to be seen in the context of a cell phone that is in fact expected to feature smaller size, lighter weight, lesser power consumption etc., from generation to generation. These contradictory demands and constraints need to be addressed through a portfolio of optimization strategies.

The proliferation of embedded systems in recent years has boosted interest especially in code compression [6,7] and there are numerous solutions proposed or implemented in academia and in industry [4]. Apart from compression an important issue in embedded multimedia systems is the protection of sensitive (e.g. copyrighted) multimedia data (music, video) during transmission or even during the runtime of a multimedia system. Encryption can solve this problem by allowing unencrypted multimedia data or code to reside only at levels of memory hierarchy that are very close to the processor (possibly on-chip only) where it is difficult for a potential adversary to gain access and reverse-engineer the code or data. An important emerging area of commercial significance is streaming media that involves rapid, secure transmission of audio and video packets over the Internet. These packets employ compression and encryption. A client receiving these packets is expected to decompress and decrypt the stream in real-time to provide the required QoS (Quality of Service) for video and audio playback. Web pages also routinely include code (Java applets, Servlets, ActiveX Controls etc.) that is transported securely over public networks. Browsers decrypt, decompress and execute the code snippets to provide feature-rich animations and interactivity. However, mobile device that use these services do not yet provide widespread download and execution support for these dynamic technologies. Due to projections (e.g. by NEC and others) future mobile multimedia devices will embed dedicated hardware that handles combined compression and encryption of data and code.

We present an encryption methodology using existing encryption standards, which works as a complement to our compression technology but is integrated in our approach. The whole work is embedded in our framework that addresses as the first approach of its kind the combined compression of data and code and their encryption. The framework allows to prototype diverse compression and encryption schemes and it comprises a parameterizable platform for hardware architecture plus a design flow.

2. Related Work

As far as combined compression/encryption systems are concerned, Shaw et al. [9] proposed a pipelined architecture that combines compression and encryption. Our focus is to provide a encryption framework that allows to offer random access without compromising security, which works well with our compression/decompression architecture. As for comp[ression technologies, the state-of-the-art is as follows:

The MXT technology by IBM (Tremaine et al. [2]) was one of the first systems that incorporates compression and decompression during runtime of a software application. This work targets servers and has been covered by various patents [8].

Benini et al. [3] proposed a compressed memory system where the focus is on energy reduction. Kjelso et al. [5] presented a technology called X-match that improves performance when using memory compression.

Compression has also been used to improve virtual memory management. Douglis [11] modified the Sprite operating system to compress pages of memory with the LZRW1 algorithm [13]. Cate and Gross [12] proposed using the filesystem to automatically compress the least recently used files and decompress them when a user accesses them. Both these techniques aim to improve virtual memory size, improve bandwidth, and improve performance.

Taunton describes the use of dictionary compression for a low-cost computer (RISC iX) using the ARM processor [14]. Compression is used to fit the system software on a small hard drive. Each page of text and data of the executable image on disk is compressed.

3. Motivation and Problem

3.1. Problem

Previous work on code compression focused on compressing the instruction segment (but not the data segment) of the executable file only. Limiting to instruction code eases the design: Since instructions do not change during execution (with the exception of the rare case of self-modifying code) as data, it is possible to compress the instruction code offline (before execution) once and then decompress small portions at runtime as needed. Secondly, indexing compressed instructions, i.e. locating the same in the compressed stream is substantially easier than in the case where runtime compression is required (see below).

However we found that very often and especially in the case of multimedia applications executables contain large areas of data such as the *.bss* areas that correspond to data that are written to and read from during runtime. Leaving out compression for the data areas of an executable file will under certain circumstances diminish any good results achieved from the compressed instruction part. As an example, Table 1 shows some executables of various multimedia applications that we came across that require large *.bss* (data) areas. It therefore shows the need for combined data and instruction code compression.

For the above experiments we used our benchmark set which we describe in more detail in Section 5. Figure 1 shows the corresponding compression results when compressing the instruction segment (code part) of the executable only.

The first bar corresponds to size reduction of the instruction segment. The second bar shows the overall executable file reduction. Clearly, while the first bar shows that code compression does indeed compress instructions well, the second bar shows that due to large data areas there is no real benefit in many cases.

Data compression introduces the following new challenges:

- **Online compression.** Data will be read from and written back to memory during runtime.
- **Indexing.** It is necessary to provide a means for locating data in the memory.
- **Memory management.** Online compression introduces gaps (unused memory space) in the memory layout, as original memory addresses cannot be used to store data.

Table 1. Break-down of executable files in an instruction code portion and data portion showcasing the need for combined data/code compression techniques.

Appl.	Code [Kb]	Data [Kb]	Total [Kb]
AES	153	103	256
CRC	91	59	150
DMC	42	1238	1280
KEY	8	504	512
MPEG	97	87	184
SSL	2921	151	3072

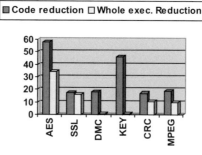

Figure 1. Compression of executable files when instruction code is compressed solely: it diminishes the compression ratio of the whole executable file when not considering the data sections.

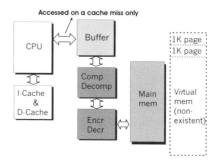

Figure 2. Levels of memory hierarchy.

- **Unknown memory requirement.** Unlike instruction compression, it is not known before execution how much memory will be required.

These issues indicate a significant performance overhead in data compression/decompression such that it is beneficial to carry out compression/decompression at higher memory hierarchy levels as IBM did between the L3 cache and the main memory [2].

3.2. Our Contribution

Existing system architectures with multiple levels of memory hierarchy have always been designed with a focus on performance; We, however, need to focus on memory size reduction for embedded multimedia applications. The main contributions of our platform:

1) An architecture that provides combined compression/decompression and encryption/decryption.
2) A parameterizable hardware platform and a design flow that allow us to explore the design space for this architecture and adapt it to the requirements of a certain multimedia application. Among others, our design platform comprises a simulator that works with a commercial processor.

4. Our Platform

4.1. Com/Decompression Enc/Decryption Algorithms

The focus of Cypress is to adapt and architecturally combine compression and encryption algorithms for implementation in embedded multimedia systems. As a platform, Cypress can accommodate many standard algorithms as long as the following constraints are fulfilled:

- Compression/decompression needs to be able to be implemented efficiently in hardware.
- Prospective algorithms need to provide *random access* The page size is therfore crucial for an efficient implementation On the other hand, if the buffer page is too big, the added hardware is too large to justify the additional gain in compressibility and/or security.

We experimented in our platform with many *com/decompression algorithms* including *Gzip*, *Bzip2* or *DMC* [10]. Throughout, efficient implementations were achieved with page sizes ranging between 1KB to 16KB.

Enc/Decryption needs to be combined with com/decompression. A dilemma with with many popular encryption standards is the lack of random access to encrypted data. Most block cipher algorithms, which are typically used in security applications, work in block chaining mode that inherently prevents random access. The simplest mode that a block cipher can operate in, and that does not incorporate any chaining, is the Electronic Codebook mode (ECB mode). In this mode, the data to be encrypted are separated into blocks and are encoded completely independently. While this method ensures random access at the block level, it is very insecure: blocks that contain the same code will be encrypted to the same ciphertext, giving valuable information to a potential adversary. Other chaining modes that are considered adequately secure, e.g. where the output of block i is fed to block $i + 1$, do not allow for random access. One method that is secure and does allow for random access is *counter mode*. The main idea is to encrypt a counter and to exclusive-or the encrypted counter value with the plaintext. Since the counter value can be made accessible by both the encryption and the decryption hardware, we found that random access is indeed possible. Figure 3 illustrates counter mode where P represents the plaintext and C the ciphertext. The counter value for block i can be given by $i + IV(mod264)$ where IV an initial counter value.

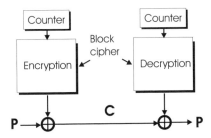

Figure 3. Random access in encryption.

For that reason, we use the above-described mode throughout the presented results and applied it exemplary to the *Advanced Encryption Standard* (*AES*).

4.2. Cypress Common Com/Decompression, Enc/Decryption Architecture

There are two major problems as far as the architecture in concerned: a) to locate compressed data during read operations, and b) to find a free location to store newly compressed/encrypted data[1] during write operations. The dividing of data areas in pages is important for efficiency. Pages at the size of bytes or words, for example, would result in large memory requirements in order to be able to allocate these small (since many) pages afterwards. The Cypress platform allows to vary page size from 1kB to 16kB. Pages smaller than 1kB would results in too unfavorable compression ratios.

In the rare event where compression cannot yield any size reduction, pages are stored in their original form.

In the general case, a *n* KB page will compress to *any* size less or equal to *n* KB. This variable size can complicate indexing compressed pages significantly; therefore, we chose compressed pages sizes as a multiple of what we call the *CFrame* size. In the following for explanatory reasons we will set the CFrame size to 64 bytes, and the page size to 1kB.

Furthermore, we imposed a rule on block alignment: all CFrames have to be aligned on a 64-byte boundary. Using these rules we design a table for mapping compressed pages in memory. Each table entry corresponds to a compressed page and it stores the locations of 16 CFrames. By allocating space for 16 blocks per page (when page size is 1kB), we ensure that any page can be stored in the table regardless of its compression ratio. An additional advantage is that the mapping table has fixed size and therefore can be easily indexed by the first bits of the page pointer. The alternative would be to save space for pages that compress well and to not allocate the space for 16 CFrames pointers. However this would complicate the hardware design.

Note that the mapping table is stored in memory along with the compressed data. Each bit pointer points to a 64-bit boundary (according to the CFrame alignment).

The mapping table described above provides a means for finding a compressed page in memory. We also need another structure to help us locate free space during writes when attempting to write a page back to memory. This structure is a set of pointers pointing to free space. It works as a FIFO and it is blocked in chunks of 64 bytes.

Eventually, all hardware blocks that together comprise the compression/decompression and encryption/decryption operations are shown in Fig. 4.

Figure 4. Hardware blocks of compression/decompression and encryption/decryption.

---

[1]Note, that unlike data, code needs only to be decompressed and decrypted since only reads are necessary.

4.3. Platform Parameters

Cypress allows to customize the following parameters: a) **Compression IP:** A wide variety of De/compression, algorithms can be implemented and simulated. b) **Encryption IP:** same holds for de/encryption IP. c) **Separate compression software for code & data** d) **CDC Buffer size:** The designer can easily modify the buffer size to exploit the best area/performance trade-off. e) **Page size:** f) **CFrame size:** The CFrame parameter affects mainly memory fragmentation. This parameter, too, can be tuned easily using our platform. g) **Buffer miss policy:** Cypress currently supports two different buffer miss policies: LRU and Round Robin. h) **Unified and separate buffers:** Code and data exhibit different locality; this can be best exploited by providing two separate buffers. Our platform permits using a unified buffer as well as two separate buffers. i) **CPU independency**.

4.4. Cypress Design Flow

To evaluate the area overheads and performance of our system we keep track of the following metrics during the simulation phase: a) the total *cycle count*, b) the amount of *memory fragmentation*, c) the CDC buffer size miss ratio as an indirect measure of performance, d) the number of page write-backs which refers to the amount of times compression and encryption of data is performed and e) the number of page reads which is equal to the number of times decompression and decryption is conducted.

The main steps of our design space exploration algorithm can then be summarized as follows:

After compilation, the multimedia application (code and data) is initially compressed and encrypted. An allocation of free memory spaces follows:

Besides the initially compressed code and data areas we need to allocate free space for data that will be written during the runtime of the application. Our experimental results show that more than 50% compression is an attainable goal. However, since an application will show varying compression ratios dependent on the input, the compression ratio needs to be estimated. Our estimation is based on a conservative measure on average compression ratio for a large set of differing inputs for a certain application.

After setting initial platform parameters, the tuning part works as shown in Fig. 5. It is important to understand that the selection of the parameters is application specific, an acceptable practice in the embedded market arena. As shown in Fig. 5 if our contraints are not met, a different compression algorithm may be selected. Our platform is largely compression algorithm independent. The main characteristics a compression algorithm should have to be feasible are a) fast hardware implementation b) good compressibility. For this reason, table-driven techniques where replacing compressed codes is done by table-lookup are typically the most efficient techniques. The topic of this paper is not the compression algorithm itself; the reader can get more insight into compression algorithms for embedded systems by reading our previous paper [4].

The order in which parameters are selected and fixed is crucial for the final result: in the given form it is made sure that parameters with the largest impact on performance and area are selected first. The parameters with lesser impact are then subsequently used for fine-tuning. When using this scheme and comparing it with a complete search for some smaller applications, we were always able to find the pareto-optimum points of the design space.

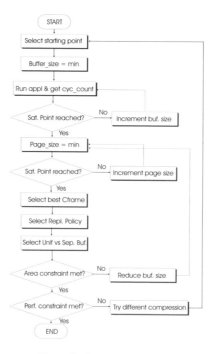

Figure 5. Cypress design flow.

5. Experimental Results using the Cypress platform

We used a set of multimedia-related applications to showcase the usefulness of our Cypress technology. The applications are: **AES**, an implementation of the Advanced Encryption Standard, **CRC**, a telecommunications software package, **DMC**, a compression/decompression algorithm, **KEY**, an image processing application, and **MPEG**, an MPEG4 encoder, and **SSL**, a suite of security algorithms.

According to the design space exploration described earlier, we have determined and fixed parameters individually for each application. The final parameters are shown in Table 2 as they represent the best compromise for compression ratio, performance and hardware overhead. It can be seen that large applications like SSL tend to require a larger CDC, larger page size, larger buffer line size and a larger CFrame size. However, there is no linear dependency between the size of these parameters and the size of the respective

Table 2. Best platform parameters for each application according to design space exploration.

Parameter	AES	CRC	DMC	KEY	MPEG	SSL
CDC size	32 Kb	16 Kb	64 Kb	64 Kb	32 Kb	64 Kb
Page size	1 Kb	512 b	2 Kb	2 Kb	1 Kb	32 Kb
CDC line size	1 Kb	512 b	2 Kb	2 Kb	1 Kb	16 Kb
Cframe size	64 b	64 b	128 b	128 b	64 b	256 b
Replacem. policy	LRU	LRU	LRU	RR	LRU	RR
Unified/Split Buffer	Unified	25/75	Unified	Unified	Unified	Unified

application. These parameters are clearly dominated by the application's size but also depend on the data/code access characteristics. The replacement policy and split/unified buffer option, however, are not notably dependent on the size of the application but do highly depend on the access pattern to memory and on control flow characteristics of an application. Finding the right combination of these parameters is a search through a multidimensional search space and it requires, beyond a heuristic search algorithm (as presented earlier), a platform that allows to rapidly prototype and measure diverse options.

We achieve effective compression ratios of 50% or more for large applications. For smaller applications compression ratios are smaller as expected since the compression/decompression hardware overhead is relatively quite high. The relative contribution of this part becomes insignificant the larger the application is.

The significant chip area reductions do not come entirely for free, though. In fact, we observe a performance penalty in the proximity of 10% in average.

Furthermore, our platform offers the incorporation of seamless encryption in case the application requires that. Due to our technique as described earlier, compression and encryption are architecturally combined. The most notable benefit is that no further performance degradation incurs compared to the case of compression only. For that reason we compare the quality of our combined code/data compression and encryption technology to one where compression and encryption are decoupled (i.e. serialized) or in other words where the code/data is first compressed and then encrypted.[2] As depicted in Fig. 6 we encounter in most cases performance improvements or only slight degradations over a system featuring serialized de-/compression decryption. This needs to be seen under the fact that a serialized system is by far more area consuming since a separate hardware for both de-/compression and decryption is needed with additional buffer between the two stages. Again, our technology is optimized for embedded multimedia as pointed out before.

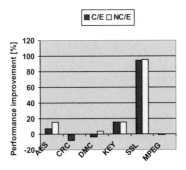

Figure 6. Performance improvement over serial decryption system.

---

[2] Note that compression would always be followed by encryption and not vice versa since otherwise compression would not be possible according to information theory.

6. Conclusion

We have presented an overview of the Cypress platform for combined data/code compression and encryption. It decompresses and decrypts code on-the-fly and it both decompresses/compresses and decrypts/encrypts data on-the-fly. Processing both compressed data and code guarantees that the executable file will benefit from compression no matter whether the code or data section in an executable of an application dominates. In addition, the seamless integration of encryption provides an efficient, hardware-sharing with compression solution, for the increasing demand of security. The Cypress platform features besides the parameterizable hardware architecture a suite of software tools that allow to evaluate and to optimize a specific multimedia applications.

References

[1] L. Benini, A. Macii, E. Macii, and M. Poncino. Selective Instruction Compression for Memory Energy Reduction in Embedded Systems. *IEEE/ACM Proc. of International Symposium on Low Power Electronics and Design (ISLPED'99)*, pages 206–211, 1999.

[2] B. Tremaine, P.A. Franaszek, J.T. Robinson, C.O. Schulz, T.B. Smith, M.E. Wazlowski, and P.M. Bland. IBM Memory Expansion Technology. IBM Journal of Research and Development, Vol 45 (2), March 2001.

[3] L. Benini, D. Bruni, A. Macii, E. Macii. Hardware-Assisted Data Compression for Energy Minimization in Systems with Embedded Processors. Design, Automation and Test in Europe, 2002.

[4] H. Lekatsas, J. Henkel, and V. Jakkula. Design of an One-cycle Decompression Hardware for Performance Increase in Embedded Systems. 39th Design Automation Conference, June 2002.

[5] M. Kjelso, M. Gooch, and S. Jones. Main memory hardware data compression. 22nd Euromicro Conference, pages 423–430. IEEE Computer Society Press, September 1996.

[6] Gideon Frieder and Harry J. Saal. A process for the determination of addresses in variable length addressing. Communications of the ACM, 19(6):335–338, June 1976.

[7] J.E.L. Peck, V.S. Manis, and W.E. Webb. Code compaction for minicomputers with INTCODE and MINICODE. Technical Report TR-75-02, Department of Computer Science, University of Britisch Columbia, 1975.

[8] IBM MXT Technology related patents: US Patent No. 5,761,536 and 6,240,419.

[9] Chandrama Shaw, Debashis Chatterji, Pradipta Maji Subhayan Sen, B.N. Roy, P. Pal Chaudhuri. A Pipeline Architecture For Encompression (Encryption + Compression) Technology. 16th International Conference on VLSI Design. January 2003.

[10] T.C. Bell and J.G. Cleary and I.H. Witten. Text Compression. Prentice Hall, New Jersey, 1990.

[11] F. Douglis. The Compression Cache: Using On-line Compression to Extend Physical Memory. Proceedings of the 1993 Winter USENIX Conference, 1993.

[12] V. Cate and T. Gross. Combining the Concepts of Compression and Caching for a Two-Level Filesystem. Proceedings of the Fourth International Conference On Architectural Support for Programming Languages and Operating Systems (ASPLOS IV), pp. 200–211, Palo Alto, April 1991.

[13] R.N. Williams. An Extremely Fast Ziv-Lempel Data Compression Algorithm. Proceedings of the IEEE Data Compression Conference 1991 (DCC'91), pp. 362–371, 8–11 April, 1991.

[14] M. Taunton, "Compressed executables: an exercise in thinking small", In Proceedings of the Summer 1991 USENIX Conference, pp. 385–403, 1991.

Security and Embedded Systems
D.N. Serpanos and R. Giladi (Eds.)
IOS Press, 2006

Cryptographic Insecurity of the Test & Repeat Paradigm

Tomáš ROSA

eBanka, a.s., Václavské náměstí 43, 109 00 Prague 1, Czech Republic, EU

trosa@ebanka.cz

Abstract. Let $f(x)$ be a certain cryptographic function and let g, g: $Im(f) \rightarrow$ {true, false}, be an integrity test saying whether a particular value of $f(x)$ fits into predefined integrity boundaries or not. The "Test and Repeat" paradigm is then characterized by the following pseudocode: *repeat let $y = f(x)$ until $g(y) = true$*. On a first look, it may seem like a kind of best programming practice that can only improve overall security of the module. Especially, an architect can see it as a rather strong countermeasure against attacks based on computational faults – so called fault attacks. In this article, however, we will show that such a practice can induce particular cryptographic weaknesses. Therefore, it cannot be regarded as a general security improvement. Especially, it can even increase a vulnerability to the fault attacks. Its usage in cryptographic modules shall, therefore, undergo a proper cryptanalysis before being actually deployed.

Keywords. Fault attack, Side channel, Covert channel, DSA, Vernam cipher, RNG, Lattice, Cryptanalysis

Introduction

In practice, we can meet the "Test and Repeat" (TAR) paradigm in many software and hardware applications, including cryptographic modules. Roughly speaking, it is a technical construction that encapsulates the following two very basic demands of computing systems architects:

1. To prevent a propagation of faulty results.
2. To ensure certain level of robustness of the application being designed.

The first aim is achieved by using the test part of TAR, while the second one is achieved by repeating the computation together with the test part several times before giving up the whole operation. Arranged in this way, TAR might also be regarded as a rather strong countermeasure against fault attacks [1,2], especially against those ones based on an analysis of faulty results of a corrupted computation.

This paper was written as a tutorial note of a cryptologist to security engineers who design the hardware and-or software architecture of cryptographic modules. We will see two illustrative examples serving as a proof that TAR shall not be regarded as a general countermeasure, since there are realistic attacks that can be even right allowed or, at least, accelerated and hidden by it. The first example in §1 concerns a subliminal covert channel [2] occurring in Vernam's one-time pad [3] equipped with a random number generator [3] which uses TAR. The second example in §2 discusses a fault attack presented in [4]. This attack is focused on DSA and we will see that it can pass totally undetected when a "reasonable" TAR is applied. Moreover, TAR actually helps an attacker to keep her attack hidden and unrecognized here.

1. Case 1: TARed RNG

Let us imagine the following scenario that is based on real situations arising in the military area: Alice works with highly secured classified information which Bob wants to see. However, despite working for the same company, Bob does not possess the required clearance level. So, he seduces Alice and convinces her to cooperate with him on the classified data theft. To prevent such attacks, there are often strict technical countermeasures applied, so Alice cannot simply copy the clear data on a CD ROM and pass them to Bob. She can only do some operations with the clear data within her terminal. Any data written to any removable media or sent through a network are encrypted. An undesirable way allowing Alice to inconspicuously send the clear data to Bob is then referred to as a covert channel or even as a subliminal covert channel [2,5,6], depending on a technique used to create the channel. Obviously, a considerable effort is made to eliminate all these channels [6].

Now, let us assume that for encrypting the networked data from Alice, the system uses the Vernam's one-time pad cipher [3]. Denoting the plaintext data from Alice as an N-bit binary vector $M = (m_1, m_2, \ldots, m_N)$, the corresponding ciphertext $C = (c_1, c_2, \ldots, c_N)$ is computed as:

$$C = M \oplus K, \text{ i.e. } c_i = m_i \oplus k_i, \text{ for } 1 \leq i \leq N, \tag{1}$$

where $K = (k_1, k_2, \ldots, k_N)$ is a keystream of the same length as the message being encrypted. The keystream is a-priori unknown for both Alice and Bob. Arranged this way, the scheme is close to being unconditionally secure, i.e., for instance, unbreakable regardless an attacker computing power. A necessary condition is, however, that the keystream bits are independent and uniformly distributed random binary variables. Therefore, the scheme needs what is usually called a cryptographically strong random number generator (RNG). Note that in practice, such a generator would probably be based on a physical source of randomness (diode noise, etc.) which needs to be checked periodically for a malfunction (manifesting itself as a statistical irregularity in output data). Such a testing shall, however, not be arranged as TAR: If a statistical singularity occurs, the device must be put out of working order. Note that such a singularity does not imply that the device is really corrupted. Actually, a lot of alarms will be false. Therefore, in practice, it may be tempting to design a "cost saving" RNG which will automatically restart after the alarm giving the hardware next chance to pass the test. Unfortunately, devices with this behavior were already met in practice.

Provided that a TARed RNG is used for the keystream computation and Bob has an access to the ciphertext C, the construction of a subliminal covert channel from Alice to Bob is easy: Let us denote the statistical test applied on each L-bit binary block $B = (b_1, b_2, \ldots, b_L)$ produced by this RNG as $g: \{0, 1\}^L \rightarrow \{\text{true, false}\}$. If $g(B) = \text{true}$, then the block passed the test. Otherwise, the RNG generates a new block and repeats the test. For the sake of simplicity, let $L \mid N$ and assume the keystream is constructed from N/L blocks as $K = B_1 \| B_2 \| \ldots \| B_{N/L}$. Then there is no i, $1 \leq i \leq N/L$, such that

$g((k_{L(i-1)+1}, k_{L(i-1)+2}, ..., k_{Li}))$ = false, since all the blocks producing an alarm were filtered out by TAR. If Alice sends a plaintext message M consisting of N zero bits, we get C satisfying:

$$g((c_{L(i-1)+1}, c_{L(i-1)+2}, ..., c_{Li})) = \text{true, for all } 1 \le i \le N/L, \tag{2}$$

since $M = 0$ implies $C = K$ according to Eq. (1). On the other hand, if Alice encrypts a block of N uniformly distributed independent random bits, then for all $1 \le i \le N/L$, there is a nonzero probability p that $g((c_{L(i-1)+1}, c_{L(i-1)+2}, ..., c_{Li}))$ = false. The value of p corresponds with the probability of the false alarm for the particular test being used. Therefore, observing C long enough, Bob can distinguish if Alice encrypted a zero message or a message of random bits. From here, Bob can gain 1 bit of information. He gets another bit from another transmission, and so on. The expected length T of a ciphertext needed for 1 bit transmission can be estimated as $T = Lp^{-1}$. For example, let the testing function g implement the continuous RNG test defined in §4.9.2 of FIPS 140-2 [7] with the block size $L = 16$ b. This test returns false if and only if the two consecutive blocks of 16 bits produced by the tested RNG are the same. Therefore, the probability of a false alarm is $p = 2^{-16}$ and $T = 16*2^{16} = 2^{20}$. So, Bob needs to observe approx. 1 Mb of ciphertext for gain of 1 bit of secret information from Alice. We see, that the channel can be hardly used for a transmission of common data files, nevertheless, it may suffice for revealing a secret password, safe lock combination, etc. Moreover, Alice and Bob can use error control codes to increase a reliability of their covert channel. We can also observe that for a certain types of messages, the covert channel discussed above can spontaneously convert to a side channel allowing an attacker to gain some secret information even without cooperation with the sender.

1.1. A Cautionary Note

Although we may reasonably assume that a professional cryptographer should avoid designing the aforesaid illustrative scheme, it is worth noting that the problem can be more complicated. Let us assume that an RNG is put of working order immediately as the test says false. However, the service of a keystream generation must remain available. To maintain required availability, several backup RNGs may be installed. Each of them starts when its ancestor stops. The problem with covert channel might seem to be solved, but it is not. If all of these RNGs use the same statistical tests, then we still know that $M = 0$ implies Eq. (2), while for a random M, there can be false alarms detected over the ciphertext C. Therefore, a communication from Alice to Bob is still allowed. We see that the problem of reasonable fault detection versus covert channels minimization deserves closer attention, which is, however, beyond the scope of this paper.

2. Case 2: TARed DSA

It is well known cryptanalytical result that the security of a DSA [8] private key strongly depends on statistical properties of temporary nonces (i.e. Numbers-used-ONCE; usually denoted as k) used for a particular signature generation. Such a nonce must have a uniform distribution on a certain interval and must be kept secret. Otherwise, an undesirable subliminal side channel is created that enables a consecutive leakage of the private key information in every signature made. Having collected enough such signatures, an attacker can recover the whole private key with a trivial complexity on a general personal computer or a notebook. In 2002, Nguyen and Shparlinski presented a theoretically stable and practically very fruitful approach [9] to private key recovering which employs a lattice-based solution of Nguyen's variant of the hidden number problem (HNP) introduced in 1996 by Boneh and Venkatesan [10]. They results show, for instance, that we can recover the whole private key knowing only as few as the lowest three bits of each nonce for only 100 signatures made.

In 2004, the paper of Naccache, Nguyen, Tunstall, and Whelan was made public on IACR's ePrint (eprint.iacr.org) [11]. It connects the results obtained by Nguyen and Shparlinski together with a vulnerability to a fault injection observed for a certain kind of smartcard. Naccache et al. demonstrated that it was possible to use the fault injection to substitute known values for the lowest bytes of each nonce k. Besides the others, it is interesting to observe that this is such a kind of fault attack that cannot be prevented simply by checking each signature for faults by verifying its validity using a public key. Obviously, every signature made in this way is valid. So, despite seeming robust on a first look, it turns out that a countermeasure based on TAR is totally useless against this attack. The article [4] went further this way. It presented such a lattice-based fault attack on the DSA scheme that becomes even more dangerous when the device under attack behaves according to a "reasonable" TAR scenario: Using the public key, the device checks every signature made whether it is valid or not. Only valid signatures can be read from the device – this constitutes the test part of TAR. Furthermore, the module restarts the signing procedure automatically, until a valid signature is computed or the number of attempts is out of a predefined boundary – this is the repeat part of TAR. Since designers of such a module would probably require certain level of robustness and independence, we may reasonably assume that the device would allow even hundreds of repetitions before it blocks.

2.1. Implicit Verification of DSA Signatures

Let (p, q, g) denote DSA public parameters according to [8]: p, q are primes, such that $2^{1023} < p < 2^{1024}$, $2^{159} < q < 2^{160}$, $q \mid p - 1$, and g is a generator of a cyclic multiplicative subgroup G of Z_p^* of order $|G| = q$. Furthermore, let x be a private key, $x \in Z$, $0 < x < q$, and let y be a public key, $y = g^x \bmod p$. We assume that a cryptographic module employing TAR paradigm (possibly as a countermeasure against fault attacks) would behave according to the following algorithm. The notation of input parameters respects the fact that, in practice, the public parameters are usually stored independently with both records of the public and the private key.

Algorithm 1. Signing a message using DSA with implicit verification.
Input: Message to be signed m, private key record (p, q, g, x), public key record (p, q, g, y), repeat boundary B.
Output: Signature (r, s) or FAILURE.
Computation:

1.   Let $i = 1$.
2.   Choose an integer nonce k at random, such that $0 < k < q$.
3.   Compute $r = (g^k \bmod p) \bmod q$.

4. Compute $s = (h(m) + rx)k^{-1} \bmod q$, where $kk^{-1} \equiv 1 \pmod q$ and h denotes the hash function SHA-1[12].
5. If $r = 0$ or $s = 0$ then go to 2.
6. Compute $u = h(m)s^{-1} \bmod q$, where $ss^{-1} \equiv 1 \pmod q$.
7. Compute $v = rs^{-1} \bmod q$.
8. Compute $w = (g^u y^v \bmod p) \bmod q$.
9. If $w = r$ then return (r, s).
10. $i \leftarrow i + 1$
11. If $i > B$ then return FAILURE.
12. Go to 2.

□

As we can see, the algorithm describes formally what a programmer would do naturally if she was asked to implicitly verify every signature made whether it is valid or not before letting it go out from a cryptographic module. Steps 2 to 4 cover the signature generation, while steps 5 to 9 do the signature verification. Both parts are written according to [8]. Another thing that would the programmer do naturally in such a situation is to employ an automatic repeat function which would retry the signing operation several times before the algorithm echoes a failure to a calling process. This constitutes the repeat part of TAR which is driven by the boundary denoted as B. Note that for a small value of the boundary (circa $B \leq 20$), such an algorithm can also originate due to a user activity: The user, for instance, wants to send a signed e-mail, while the device says that there is something wrong about a signing module. We can reasonably expect that she would try to sign her message several times before she gives it up. The more eager the user is the higher B we get.

2.2. Embedding the Fault Side Channel

On a first glimpse, Algorithm 1 described above can be regarded as being resistant against fault attacks, since no faulty signature can leave perhaps the innermost place of the cryptographic module. Such a reasoning which could be inspired by typical symptoms of fault attacks on RSA (c.f. [1,2,13,14]), can, however, be terribly misleading here. An example of fault attack that passes undetected in such a situation can be found in [11]. A fault attack that can be even right allowed thanks to relying on such a "fault tolerant" algorithm was then presented in [4]. A brief description of the attack follows.

Let d be an integer, such that $d \mid p - 1$ and $\gcd(d, q) = 1$. Furthermore, let β be an integer, $1 < \beta < p$, of order $\mathrm{ord}(\beta) = d$ in Z_p^*. Now, let us suppose that an attacker substitutes the value of $g' = g\beta \bmod p$ in place of g in the private key record in Algorithm 1. Such a change can be theoretically possible, since g is a part of non-secret public parameters whose protection architects often tend to underestimate. For instance, in the CryptoAPI subsystem of the MS Windows platform, there is a function CryptSetKeyParam with the parameter KP_G reserved for such a purpose [15]. It is left up to designers of cryptographic modules how to implement this function and whether to allow such modifications at all. There is, however, no warning about how dangerous this functionality can be. Therefore, we may reasonably assume that at least some architects will allow the attacker to freely change the value of g. Several problems with integrity of a key material were also identified by Clulow for the PKCS#11 security standard platform [13]. There was also a successful attack based on DSA public parameters modification described by Klíma and Rosa in [14]. We shall, therefore, fully anticipate the possibility of such a modification when we discuss security aspects of a particular signing procedure.

Now, let us denote r' and s' the variables from Algorithm 1 computed for a substituted value of $g' = g\beta \bmod p$. We can write:

$$r' = (g^k\beta^k \bmod p) \bmod q, \tag{3}$$

$$s' = (h(m) + r'x)k^{-1} \bmod q, \; kk^{-1} \equiv 1 \pmod{q}. \tag{4}$$

Let us assume that in step 8, the module uses the value of the correct generator g. That means that the attacker will not affect the public key record which is usually loaded from an independent storage – possibly from a user's public key certificate [3]. Note that the attack is possible even if the attacker changes the generator in both of the public and private key records [4]. Let us denote u' and v' the values computed in steps 6 and 7, respectively. Using their definitions together with Eq. (4) over GF(q), it follows that:

$$u' + v'x \equiv h(m)(s')^{-1} + r'(s')^{-1}x \equiv (h(m) + r'x)(s')^{-1} \equiv k \pmod{q}. \tag{5}$$

Now, let us denote w' the value computed in step 8. Since the algorithm uses the unaffected value of g of order q, we can use Eq. (5) and write:

$$w' = (g^{u'}y^{v'} \bmod p) \bmod q = (g^{u'+v'x} \bmod p) \bmod q = (g^k \bmod p) \bmod q. \tag{6}$$

Basing on Eqs. (3) and (6), we can rewrite the condition the signature (r', s') must pass in step 9 as:

$$w' = r' \Leftrightarrow (g^k \bmod p) \bmod q = (g^k\beta^k \bmod p) \bmod q. \tag{7}$$

Since we can neglect an influence of "inner" collisions in the mapping $\varphi(k) = (g^k\beta^k \bmod p) \bmod q$ (c.f. [16]), we can claim that with a probability close to 1 the following condition is necessary and sufficient to release the signature (r', s') in step 9:

$$\beta^k \bmod p = 1, \text{ i.e. } k \equiv 0 \pmod{d}. \tag{8}$$

We see that the attacker gets nontrivial direct information about the nonce k whenever Algorithm 1 releases a signature pair (r', s'), since she knows that whatever the nonce is, it must be an integer divisible by a known value d. This creates a vital side channel that she can use to recover the whole value of the private key using a slightly modified approach from [9]. A detailed description of the computation is given in [4]. Here, we present the following table showing certain experimental results.

Each numbered row of Table 1 corresponds to an experimental fault attack on a particular randomly generated DSA instance. The divisor d was chosen automatically by the attacking program to be small enough while producing a usable side channel for the attack. Small values are desirable, since the probability that step 9 releases a particular signature can be estimated as d^{-1}. The number of TAR iterations follows a geometric distribution, so the expected value and the variance of the number of signatures computed before releasing a valid signature is then $EX = d$ and $\text{Var}(X) = d(d-1)$, respectively. Sometimes, there was no suitable divisor found with respect to a realistically tight boundary of repetitions (several hundreds). The number of signatures in Table 1 denotes the number of valid signatures used for a successful private key reconstruction. The total number of signatures illustrates the number of invalid signatures

Table 1. Experimental fault attacks on several randomly chosen DSA instances.

Exp. No.	Divisor *d*	#Signatures	#Signatures Total	Exp. Duration
1	12	70	880	182 s
2	12	55	688	66 s
3	15	61	923	120 s
4	12	55	649	63 s
5	2	weak channel	N/A	N/A
6	14	48	550	44 s
7	22	46	912	67 s
8	12	55	832	76 s
9	2	weak channel	N/A	N/A
10	12	65	621	118 s

produced and discarded within TAR. The duration of each experiment shows how effective the whole attack is, since this time covers the DSA instance generation, the attack preparation, the signatures generation, and the private key reconstruction. The platform used for the experiments was a general office notebook with Pentium M/1.5 GHz and Windows 2000. The code was written in C++ and supported by the Shoup's NTL library [17].

3. Conclusion

We saw that the "Test and Repeat" paradigm cannot be regarded as a robust countermeasure against fault attacks, since there are realistic strategies that pass undetected by it. We also saw that there are attacks which can be even right allowed thanks to relying on the "power" of this approach. Therefore, despite being a bit paradoxical on a first glimpse, we shall use it very carefully in a cryptographic modules design. Of course, this is not to say that we shall not use it at all. We just shall bear on our minds that we must not rely solely on this approach and that we have to design and implement it properly. The caution mainly addresses the phase of a design verification in which we shall check every possible attack scenario to see whether our implementation can resist it or not. Otherwise, the situation about overall cryptanalytical attacks can become even worse, since some of them may become hidden and accelerated, some of them even right allowed.

Acknowledgements

I am grateful to Vlastimil Klíma for many helpful comments and inspiring suggestions on the previous versions of the paper.

References

[1]   Boneh, D., DeMillo, R.-A., and Lipton, R.-J.: *On the Importance of Checking Cryptographic Protocols for Faults*, in Proc. of EUROCRYPT '97, pp. 37–51, Springer-Verlag, 1997.
[2]   Rosa, T.: *Modern Cryptology – Standards Are Not Enough*, Ph.D. Thesis, 2004.
[3]   Menezes, A.-J., van Oorschot, P.-C., and Vanstone, S.-A.: *Handbook of Applied Cryptography*, CRC Press, 1996.
[4]   Rosa, T.: *Lattice-based Fault Attacks on DSA – Another Possible Strategy*, in Proc. of Security and Protection of Information 2005, pp. 91–96, Brno, 2005.
[5]   Simons, G.-J.: *The History of Subliminal Channels*, IEEE Journal of Selected Areas in Communications, Vol. 16, No. 4, pp. 452–462, April 1998.
[6]   Bishop, M.: *Computer Security – Art and Science*, Addison-Wesley, 2003.
[7]   FIPS PUB 140-2: *Security Requirements for Cryptographic Modules*, National Institute of Standards and Technology, May 25 2001.
[8]   FIPS PUB 186-2: *Digital Signature Standard (DSS)*, National Institute of Standards and Technology, January 27 2000, updated: October 5 2001.
[9]   Nguyen, P.-Q., and Shparlinski, I.-E.: *The Insecurity of the Digital Signature Algorithm with Partially Known Nonces*, Journal of Cryptology, Vol. 15, No. 3, pp. 151–176, Springer-Verlag, 2002.
[10] Boneh, D., and Venkatesan, R.: *Hardness of Computing the Most Significant Bits of Secret Keys in Diffie-Hellman and Related Schemes*, in Proc. of CRYPTO '96, pp. 129–142, Springer-Verlag, 1996.
[11] Naccache, D., Nguyen, P.-Q., Tunstall, M., and Whelan, C.: *Experimenting with Faults, Lattices and the DSA*, in Proc. of Public Key Cryptography – PKC'05, pp. 16–28, Springer-Verlag, 2005.
[12] FIPS PUB 180-1: *Secure Hash Standard (SHA-1)*, National Institute of Standards and Technology, January 2001.
[13] Clulow, J.: *On the Security of PKCS #11*, in Proc. of CHES 2003, pp. 411–425, Springer-Verlag, 2003.
[14] Klíma, V., and Rosa, T.: *Attack on Private Signature Keys of the OpenPGP format, PGP$^{(TM)}$ Programs and Other Applications Compatible with OpenPGP*, IACR ePrint archive, 2002/076, http://eprint.iacr.org, 2001.
[15] Microsoft CryptoAPI, *MSDN Library*, October 2001.
[16] Brown, D.-R.-L.: *Generic Groups, Collision Resistance, and ECDSA*, IEEE 1363 report, February 2002.
[17] Shoup, V.: *Number Theory C++ Library (NTL)*, http://www.shoup.net/ntl/.

Security and Embedded Systems
D.N. Serpanos and R. Giladi (Eds.)
IOS Press, 2006

A Privacy Classification Model Based on Linkability Valuation

Dan CVRČEK [a,b], Vashek MATYAS [a] and Marek KUMPOŠT [a]

[a] *Masaryk University in Brno*
[b] *Brno University of Technology*

Abstract. Many papers and articles attempt to define or even quantify privacy, typically with a major focus on anonymity. We propose new means of describing (obviously only observable) characteristics of a system to reflect the role of contexts for profiling – and linking – users with actions in a system. We believe this approach should allow for evaluating privacy in large data sets.

1. Introduction

Evidence-based systems work basically with two sets of evidence (data describing interaction outcomes). The primary set contains evidence that is delivered (or selected from locally stored data) according to a given request content. That data is used for reputation evaluation to grant/reject access requests. Data in this first set may contain information from third parties representing evidence about behaviour collected by other nodes – recommenders.

The secondary set comprises data relevant to a local system. That data is used for self-assessment of the local system security in various contexts (it may be a non-deterministic process in a certain sense). This set may be also referenced as derived or secondary data. Note that there may be an intersection between the two evidence sets with implications to privacy issues that we are investigating in related projects [2,3].

The approach of reputation systems is rather probabilistic and this feature directly implies properties of security mechanisms that may be defined on top of such systems. The essential problem arises with recommendations that may be artificially created by distributed types of attacks (Sybil attack [5]) based on large number of nodes created just to gather enough evidence and achieve maximum reputation that would allow them to launch their attack(s).

1.1. A Note on the Common Criteria and Freiburg Privacy Diamond Models

Our work on the privacy model started with a proposal for formal definitions of existing Common Criteria concepts/areas of privacy and their comparison with the Freiburg Privacy Diamond model (FPD) [14]. Recent research in anonymity systems [4,8,11] demonstrates that it is usually unfeasible to provide perfect anonymity and that implementations of privacy enhancing systems may provide only a certain level of privacy (anonymity, pseudonymity). This lead to definitions of several metrics that can quantify level of privacy achievable in a system, most often a (remailing) mix.

The Common Criteria class Privacy deals with aspects of privacy as outlined in their four families. Three of these families have a similar grounding with respect to entities (i.e., users or processes) whose privacy might be in danger. They are vulnerable to varying threats, which make them distinct from each other. These families are Unobservability, Anonymity, Unlinkability, and Pseudonymity.

1.2. Motivation

While working on related issues [3], we became aware of the need to define the Common Criteria concepts (called families) dealing with privacy in a bit more precise fashion. As we were examining definitions of privacy concepts/families as stated in Common Criteria, two negative facts emerged. First, the definitions are given in an existential manner, and secondly, not all aspects of user interactions relevant to privacy are covered. Both issues come from research carried out in the areas of side-channel analysis and security of system implementations, showing that it is not sufficient to take into account only the idealised principals and messages. It is also very important to consider the context, in/with which the interactions are undertaken. Information like physical and virtual (IP, MAC addresses) positions of users and computers, time, type of service invoked, size of messages, etc. allow to profile typical user behaviour and successfully deteriorate privacy of users in information systems.

We propose to introduce context information (side/covert channels, like physical and virtual location of users and computers, time, type of service invoked, size of messages, etc.) into the CC model and compare it with the FPD model that reflects only one very specific context information – location.

Our objectives for starting this work are as follows. Firstly, we want to provide a model that allows one to cover as many aspects of user interactions as is beneficial for improving quantification/measurement for different aspects of privacy; this model shall definitely provide for better reasoning/evaluation of privacy than Common Criteria and Freiburg Privacy Diamond models do. Secondly, and in a close relation to the first objective, we want to illustrate the deficiency of the Common Criteria treatment of privacy, and to provide a foundation that would assist in improving this treatment. Thirdly, with a long-term perspective, we aim to provide basis for partly or fully automated evaluation/measurement of privacy.

This paper does not address all aspects of data collection for privacy models, and neither does it suggest any means for improving the level of privacy protection.

2. Privacy in the Common Criteria

Since some of the discussions and proposals in this paper are based on the Common Criteria (CC) concepts, we refer the reader to [13] for a description of the acronyms and concepts used. In the CC view, the user does not access objects directly but through subjects – internal representation of herself inside TOE/TSC. This indirection is exploited for definition of pseudonymity as we will see later. Objects represent not only information but also services mediating access to TOE's resources. This abstract model does not directly cover communication like in (remailer) mixes as it explicitly describes only relations between users/subjects and resources of target information system. However, it is not difficult to extend the proposed formal definitions of major privacy concepts based on this model for communication models.

2.1. Privacy in the Common Criteria

Unobservability: *This family ensures that a user may use a resource or service without others, especially third parties, being able to observe that the resource or service is being used.* The protected asset in this case can be information about other users' communications, about access to and use of a certain resource or service, etc.

Anonymity: *This family ensures that a user may use a resource or service without disclosing the user identity. The requirements for Anonymity provide protection of the user identity. Anonymity is not intended to protect the subject identity.* The protected asset is usually the identity of the requesting entity, but can also include information on the kind of requested operation (and/or information) and aspects such as time and mode of use. The relevant threats are: disclosure of identity or leakage of information leading to disclosure of identity – often described as "usage profiling".

Unlinkability: *This family ensures that a user may make multiple uses of resources or services without others being able to link these uses together.* The protected assets are the same as in Anonymity. Relevant threats can also be classed as "usage profiling".

Pseudonymity: *This family ensures that a user may use a resource or service without disclosing its user identity, but can still be accountable for that use.* Possible applications are usage and charging for phone services without disclosing identity, "anonymous" use of an electronic payment, etc. In addition to the Anonymity services, Pseudonymity provides methods for authorisation without identification (at all or directly to the resource or service provider).

2.2. Privacy Families Revisited

Common Criteria privacy families are defined in an existential manner and any formal definition of them has to tackle a number of ambiguities. It is unrealistic to assume perfect/absolute privacy as demonstrated by several anonymity metrics, based on anonymity sets (number of users able to use a given resource/service in a given context) [9] or entropy assigned to a projection between service and user/subject identities (uncertainty about using a service) [11].

Our proposal for the CC model privacy formalisation is based on the following representation. The set S represents observations of uses of services or resources, P_{ID} is equivalent of subjects and *ID* stands for users as defined in the CC. Sets U_S and U_{ID} are sets of all possible service use observations and identities, respectively – not only those relevant for a given system. By stating *with probability not significantly greater than* in the following definitions, we mean negligible difference (lower than ε) from a specified value [1]. Let $\mathcal{A}$ be any attacker with unbounded computing power.

Our formal transcription of existential definitions of CC privacy families is as follows.

Unobservability – there is a space of encodings (U_S) from which some elements are defined to encode use of service/resource (S). However, $\mathcal{A}$ is not able to determine $\forall s \in S$ with a probability significantly greater than $1/2$ whether a particular $s \in S$ or $s \in (U_S - S)$.

Anonymity – there is a probability mapping $m_u : S \rightarrow U_{ID}$. When

1. $\mathcal{A}$ knows the set ID – then $\forall s \in S, u_{ID} \in ID$, she can only find $m_u(s) = u_{ID}$ with a probability not significantly greater than $1/|ID|$.

2. $\mathcal{A}$ does not know anything about ID (particular elements or size) – then for $\forall u_{ID} \in U_{ID}$, she cannot even guess whether $u_{ID} \in ID$ with a probability significantly greater than $1/2$. (The probability of finding $m_u(s) = u_{ID}$ would not be significantly greater than 0.)

Unlinkability – let us assume there is a function $\delta : m \times S \times S \rightarrow [no, yes]$. This function determines whether two service uses were invoked by the same $u_{ID} \in U_{ID}$ or not. Parameter m stands for a function that maps service uses (S) into a set of identities U_{ID} (e.g., m_u).

It is infeasible for $\mathcal{A}$ with any δ and any $s_1, s_2 \in S$, $s_1 \neq s_2$ to determine whether $m(s_1) = m(s_2)$ with a probability significantly greater than $1/2$.

Pseudonymity – there exists and is known to $\mathcal{A}$ an unambiguous mapping $m_u(s) = u$, $\forall s \in S$, $u \in P_{ID}$. There also exists a mapping $m_i(u) = u_{ID}, \forall u \in P_{ID}, u_{ID} \in ID$, but is subject to strict conditions and not known to $\mathcal{A}$. When $\mathcal{A}$

1. knows ID, she cannot determine correct u_{ID} with a probability significantly greater than $1/|ID|$;

2. does not know ID, she can only guess with a probability not significantly greater than $1/2$ whether $u_{ID} \in ID$.

These existential expressions can then be easily turned into probabilistic ones that allow for expressing different qualitative levels of all these privacy concepts/families. This can be done simply by changing the "not significantly greater than" expression to "not greater than Δ", where Δ is the given probability threshold.

3. Freiburg Privacy Diamond

FPD is a semiformal anonymity (and partly also unlinkability) model by A. Zugenmaier et al. [14,15]. The model originated from their research in the area of security in mobile environments. The model is graphically represented as a diamond with vertices User, Action, Device (alternatives for CC's user, service, and subject), and Location. The main reason for introducing *location* as a category here is probably due to the overall focus of this model on mobile computing.

Anonymity of a user u performing an action a is breached when there exists a connection between a and u. This may be achieved through any path in the diamond model. Let us recap basic definitions of the FPD model:

1. Any element x has got a type $type(x) \in \{User, Action, Device, Location\}$. Any two elements, such as $x, y \in \{e|type(e) = User \vee Action \vee Device \vee Location\}$, $type(x) \neq type(y)$ are in a relation R if the attacker has evidence connecting x and y.

2. An action is anonymous if $U_R = \{u \mid type(u) = User \wedge (u, a) \in R\}$ is either empty or $|U_R| > t > 1$, where t is an anonymity threshold defining minimum acceptable size of anonymity set.
3. There is the transitivity rule saying that if $(x, y) \in R$ and $(y, z) \in R$, and $type(x) \neq type(z)$, then $x, z \in R$.
4. The union of all initial relations known to an attacker $\mathcal{A}$ defines his initial view $View_{\mathcal{A}}$.
5. The transitive closure $\overline{View_{\mathcal{A}}}$ of $View_{\mathcal{A}}$ defines all the information an attacker $\mathcal{A}$ may infer from her initial view.

The book [14] also introduces three types of attacks with context information. Finally, the model assigns probabilities to edges in order to express attacker's certainty about existence of particular relations with some simple rules how to derive certainty for transitive relations.

4. Contexts in the Two Models

Contexts may be assigned to any element of the model. *ID* represents physical entities and we may know their mobile phone locations, addresses, patterns of network usage, etc. P_{ID} – virtual IDs – can be characterised by previous transactions and possibly virtual locations (a virtual location may be in some cases very effectively mapped on a physical location). Elements of S may be further characterised by type, provider, etc.

The edges between sets (their elements) represent sessions taking place in the system. The information we may gather about them are highly dependent on actual implementation of the system and may comprise contextual information such as time, length, routing path, content, etc.

The FPD model only briefly mentions context information but does not introduce any definition of it. The attacks based on context information do not say how to perform them but only defines changes in $\overline{View_{\mathcal{A}}}$ when an attack is completed.

Since the FPD model newly addressed the mobile computing environment, as opposed to the old-fashioned "static" environment, location had a very prominent role, as did the device to some extent. We have decided to treat these as "ordinary" context information, i.e. as any other additional information about the system that can link a user and an action (or more precisely, their identifiers).

5. Context Revisited – Basics of the PATS (Privacy Across-The-Street[1]) Model

We propose the following approach, inspired by the way location and device (descriptors) are represented in FPD. We suggest all context information available to an attacker to be represented as vertices in a graph, where edges are weighed with the probability of the two incident vertices (contextual information, user and service IDs) to be related/connected. Those connections may be between any two vertices, and a path connecting a user ID and a service ID with a certain probability value of the path suggests a link between the service use and the user ID exists.

---

[1] Main authors of this proposal worked for different institutions located across the street.

The graph reflects all knowledge of an attacker at a given time. Attackers with different knowledge will build different graphs for a system as will likely do the same attacker over some time.

What is not clear to us at the moment is the question whether pseudonyms should be treated differently from other contexts or not. Clearly they are more important in the model since their connection to users and actions defines level of pseudonymity achieved in the system. Yet at the moment we suggest all vertices to be treated equally, although we suspect that some of them might be more equal than others. :-)

5.1. Outline of the Graph Model

We denote the set of all vertices by V, the set of all identifiers of service instances by S, and the set of all user IDs by ID. There are no edges between any pair of elements of ID, only indirect paths through a linking context, and the same applies to elements of S. There is also a function W_{max} calculating overall probability weight for a path in the graph, and therefore also a way to determine the highest value $W_{max}(v_a, v_b)$ for a path between v_a and v_b. The value of any path is calculated as a multiplication of the weights (w) of all its individual edges, e.g. for the path $P = v_1, v_2, \ldots, v_i$ of i vertices of the graph, the value of the path P is $W(v_1, v_i) = w(v_1, v_2) \times w(v_2, v_3) \times \ldots w(v_{i-1}, v_i)$.

Unobservability (of service s_i) – a graph that $\mathcal{A}$ can build after observing a system at a given time does not include s_i at all.

Unlinkability (between two nodes v_1, v_2, at the level Δ) – a graph that $\mathcal{A}$ can build when observing the system at a given time has no path connecting v_1 with v_2 with the overall probability greater than Δ, i.e. provides $W(v_1, v_2) \leq 1/|V| + \Delta$, where $v_1, v_2 \in V$.

Anonymity (of a user $u_{ID} \in ID$, at the level Δ) – then $\forall\ v \in V$, when $\mathcal{A}$

1. knows the set ID, she can only find a path from v to u_{ID} with the weight not greater than $1/|ID| + \Delta$, such that $W_{max}(v, u_{ID}) \leq 1/|ID| + \Delta$;
2. does not know anything about ID (particular elements or size), she can only find a path from v to u_{ID} with the weight not greater than Δ, i.e. $W_{max}(v, u_{ID}) \leq \Delta$.

Pseudonymity (of a subject/pseudonym $u \in P_{ID}$, at the level Δ) – there exists a path known to $\mathcal{A}$ from any $s \in S$ to u with a satisfactory value of $W_{max}(s, u)$, but for $\mathcal{A}$ there is no knowledge of an edge from u to any $u_{ID} \in ID$ such that when $\mathcal{A}$

1. knows ID, the path from u to any u_{ID} has weight not greater than $1/|ID| + \Delta$, i.e. $W_{max}(u, u_{ID}) \leq 1/|ID| + \Delta$;
2. does not know anything about ID (particular elements or size), the path from u to u_{ID} has weight not greater than Δ, i.e. $W_{max}(u, u_{ID}) \leq \Delta$.

There are several proposals for formal frameworks for anonymity [6,7] and unlinkability [12]. Frameworks introduced in these papers define typed systems with several defined categories like agents, type of agents, messages [7] or an inductive system based on modal logic of knowledge [6]. We believe that our proposal would be more flexible and would cover context information as an inherent part of the model thus opening interesting questions.

6. Conclusions and Open Issues

This paper points out that contexts provide side-channels that are not covered neither by the Common Criteria Privacy Class, nor by the Freiburg Privacy Diamond model. We also believe that contexts in general are not well reflected in other current research attempts to quantify the levels (and deterioration) of privacy. A simplistic introduction of pseudonyms will not guarantee perfect privacy, and we need to have some means to quantify what levels of privacy is needed and/or achievable for specific scenarios.

One particularly interesting issue relates to the Common Criteria definition of unlinkability, as empirically reviewed by Rannenberg and Iachello [10] and more formally specified by us in a full version of this paper, is whether the unlinkable "items" in question should only be operations (service invocations) or whether other kinds of unlinkability should also be considered. We have provided a supporting evidence for a substantial revision of unlinkability specifications, while leaving the actual revision as an item for the future research.

We also provide our basic PATS model that is not so limited in the coverage of selected aspects of user interactions and therefore allows for better quantification/measurement of different aspects of privacy. This proposal, unlike the CC or FPD models, introduces a computational model (based on graph theory). One of the problems we are currently examining is atomicity for the vertices, i.e. contextual information. We currently review various approaches to this problem, being aware that the issue of atomicity has a critical impact on the possibility of graph normalisation and therefore also for the provision of the critical properties of completeness and soundness. This work in progress includes the issue of edge dependence, for it is clear that the edges are not completely independent. We can mark sets of nodes from distinct kinds of context (e.g., pseudonyms, IP addresses used in connections from the same provider) – let us call them *domains*. Then we can address additional graph properties, e.g., such that for all pairs of domains D_1, D_2, all sums of probabilities from any node in D_1 to all nodes in D_2 are not higher then a given value, typically 1.

The PATS approach allows for two definitions of anonymity, a weaker one considering a weight of the entire path from u_{ID} to s_i can be added to the stronger one above that considers the intermediate edges from u_{ID} only (to any other vertex – contextual information – that would then be identifiable).

Another interesting issue is the role of time that has a two-fold role – firstly, it can be a contextual information (time of an action invoked by a certain subject, i.e. three mutually connected vertices). Secondly, the probabilistic weights of edges in a graph change with time, as do the sets of vertices and edges as such. Obviously, the contextual role of time may be reflected by the latter view – time of an action invoked by a certain subject is denoted by existence of vertices describing action and subject identifiers, connected by an edge with weight 1, at the given time.

Acknowledgements

Thanks go to Andrei Serjantov and Alf Zugenmaier for their opinions and links to some interesting references in the area of privacy, and to Flaminia Luccio for valuable discussions of the PATS graph model details.

References

[1] M. Bellare. A note on negligible functions. Technical Report CS97-529, Department of Computer Science and Engineering, UCSD, 1997.

[2] V. Cahill et al. Using trust for secure collaboration in uncertain environments. *IEEE Pervasive Computing Magazine*, 2003 (July-September):52–61.

[3] D. Cvrček and V. Matyáš. Pseudonymity in the light of evidence-based trust. In *Proc. of the 12th Workshop on Security Protocols*, LNCS (forthcoming), Cambridge, UK, April 2004. Springer-Verlag.

[4] Claudia Diaz, Stefaan Seys, Joris Claessens, and Bart Preneel. Towards measuring anonymity. In Roger Dingledine and Paul Syverson, editors, *Proceedings of Privacy Enhancing Technologies Workshop (PET 2002)*, LNCS 2482. Springer-Verlag, April 2002.

[5] J. Douceur. The Sybil attack. In *1st International Workshop on Peer-to-Peer Systems (IPTPS'02)*, LNCS 2429, pages 251–260. Springer-Verlag, 2002.

[6] J.Y. Halpern and K. O'Neill. Anonymity and information hiding in multiagent systems. In *Proceedings of the 16th IEEE Computer Security Foundations Workshop*, pages 75–88, 2003.

[7] D. Hughes and V. Shmatikov. Information hiding, anonymity and privacy: A modular approach. *Journal of Computer Security, special issue on selected papers of WITS 2002*, 12(1):3–36, 2004.

[8] D. Kesdogan, D. Agrawal, and S. Penz. Limits of anonymity in open environments. In Fabien Petitcolas, editor, *Proceedings of Information Hiding Workshop (IH 2002)*, LNCS 2578. Springer-Verlag, October 2002.

[9] Andreas Pfitzmann and Marit Köhntopp. Anonymity, unobservability and pseudonymity – a proposal for terminology. In *Designing Privacy Enhancing Technologies: Proceedings of the International Workshop on the Design Issues in Anonymity and Observability*, LNCS 2009, pages 1–9. Springer-Verlag, 2000.

[10] K. Rannenberg and G. Iachello. Protection profiles for remailer mixes – do the new evaluation criteria help? In *16th Annual Computer Security Applications Conference (ACSAC'00)*, pages 107–118. IEEE, December 2000.

[11] A. Serjantov and G. Danezis. Towards an information theoretic metric for anonymity. In *Privacy Enhancing Technologies (PET)*, LNCS 2482, pages 41–53. Springer-Verlag, April 2002.

[12] S. Steinbrecher and S. Köpsell. Modelling unlinkability. In R. Dingledine, editor, *Privacy Enhancing Technologies (PET)*, LNCS 2760, pages 32–47. Springer-Verlag, 2003.

[13] The Common Criteria Project Sponsoring Organisations. *Common Criteria for Information Technology Security Evaluation – part 2, version 2.1*. August 1999.

[14] A. Zugenmaier. *Anonymity for Users of Mobile Devices through Location Addressing*. RHOMBOS-Verlag, ISBN 3-930894-96-3, Berlin, 2003.

[15] A. Zugenmaier, M. Kreutzer, and G. Müller. The Freiburg Privacy Diamond: An attacker model for a mobile computing environment. In *Kommunikation in Verteilten Systemen (KiVS) '03*, Leipzig, 2003.

Security and Embedded Systems
D.N. Serpanos and R. Giladi (Eds.)
IOS Press, 2006

A Run-Time Reconfigurable Architecture for Embedded Program Flow Verification

Joseph ZAMBRENO, Tanathil ANISH and Alok CHOUDHARY [1]
Department of Electrical and Computer Engineering, Northwestern University

Abstract. Poorly written software can pose a serious security risk. Applications designed for embedded processors are especially vulnerable, as they tend to be written in lower-level languages for which security features such as runtime array bounds checking are typically not included. The problem is exacerbated by the fact that these potentially insecure embedded applications are widely deployed in a variety of high-risk systems such as medical devices, military equipment, and aerospace systems. These observations motivate additional research into embedded software security. In this paper, we present a compiler module and reconfigurable architecture for verifying the integrity of embedded programs. Our architecture prevents several classes of program flow attacks, as opposed to many current approaches which tend to address very specific software vulnerabilities. We demonstrate the correctness and feasibility of our approach with an FPGA-based prototype implementation that is effective in protecting applications with minimal performance overhead.

Keywords. Security, software protection, buffer overflows, reconfigurable architectures

Introduction

Embedded applications are typically not the main focus of secure solutions providers, as the personal and business computing world has been the traditional target for wide-scale attacks. This is a cause for concern for two reasons. Firstly, embedded software tends to be written in low-level languages, especially when meeting real-time constraints is a concern. These languages tend to not have facilities for runtime maintenance which can often cover programming errors leading to security holes. Secondly, embedded systems are used in a variety of high-risk situations, for which a malicious attack could have devastating consequences.

Many current approaches merely apply stopgap measures – either by patching specific vulnerabilities or disallowing behavior that is representative of the attacks considered. While effective at preventing the most popular exploits, these approaches are not able to handle an unexpected weakness or an unknown class of attacks. Clearly, additional research is needed to find a more general solution.

[1]Corresponding Author: Alok Choudhary, Department of Electrical and Computer Engineering, Northwestern University, 2145 Sheridan Road, Evanston, IL 60208 USA; Tel.: +1 847 467 4129; Fax: +1 847 467 4144; E-mail: choudhar@ece.northwestern.edu.

In this paper, we present an architecture and compiler module that can prevent a more general class of attacks. The input program is first analyzed by our compiler to generate program flow metadata. When the application is loaded onto the processor, this data is then stored in the custom memories on our architecture. Since this approach requires only a passive monitoring of the instruction fetch path, we are able to continually verify the program's execution with a minimal performance penalty.

To demonstrate the correctness of our architecture, we implemented a prototype on a Xilinx ML310 FPGA development board. The results presented here detail the performance of the protected applications given various architectural configurations. The feasibility of the total approach is also considered, with experimental results on both the area consumption of our architecture and the increase in application size due to the inclusion of the program flow metadata.

The remainder of this paper is organized as follows. We start with an explanation of unchecked buffer vulnerabilities alongside their commonly-found exploits. In Section 2, we discuss several of the current approaches to addressing this problem. We then present our proposed solution in Section 3, followed by a description of the prototype we developed on the FPGA board. Finally, we conclude the paper in Section 5 with a brief overview of future efforts that are planned for this project.

1. Vulnerabilities and Attacks

Consider the simple application depicted in Fig. 1. In this C-style pseudo-code, function bar is called with an array of pointers to character arrays as its input. These input arrays are copied to a local array using the standard C library strcpy call before further processing is applied.

In this code example, since the strcpy call does not check to ensure that there is sufficient space in the destination array to fit the contents of the source string, it is

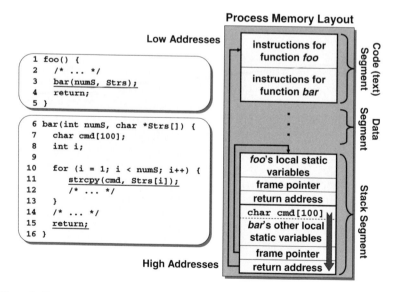

Figure 1. Process memory layout of an application with a potentially exploitable buffer overflow.

possible to write enough data to "overflow" the local array. In this example's process memory layout, the local variables for function `bar` are placed in the stack segment, just on top of run-time variables that are used to ensure proper program flow. The common convention is for the stack to grow backwards in memory, with the top of the stack being placed at lower physical addresses and local arrays growing upwards in memory.

When user input is placed into overflowable buffers, the application is vulnerable to the *stack smashing* attack [1]. Widespread exploits including the Code Red and SQL-Slammer worms have convincingly demonstrated that it is possible for an attacker to insert arbitrary executable code on the stack. The stack smashing attack works as follows:

- The attacker first fills the buffer with machine instructions, often called the *shellcode* since typical exploit demonstrations attempt to open a command-shell on the target machine.
- The remainder of the stack frame is filled until the return address is overwritten with a pointer back to the start of the shellcode region.
- When the vulnerable function attempts to return to its calling parent, it uses the return address that has been stored on the stack. Since this value has been overwritten to point to the start of the attacker-inserted code, this is where the program will continue.

The widespread notoriety of stack smashing exploits have led to a considerable amount of focus on their detection and prevention. In the future, it is likely that more complex attacks involving buffer overflows (see [2] for a description of *arc injection* and *pointer subterfuge*) will gain in popularity. Note that any arbitrary program flow modification can be potentially malicious, not just those involving unprotected buffers.

2. Current Approaches

Several compiler-based solutions currently exist for buffer overflow vulnerabilities. StackGuard [3] is a compiler modification that inserts a unique data value above the return address on the stack. The code is then instrumented such that this value is then checked before returning to the caller function. This check will fail if an overflowing buffer modifies this value. StackShield is a similar compiler extension that complicates the attack by copying the return addresses to a separate stack placed in a different and presumably safer location in memory. While they are effective, it should be noted that these protections can be bypassed in certain situations [4].

Other similar approaches include obfuscation-driven compiler transformations [5], where the goal is to limit code understanding through the deliberate mangling of program structure. In [6] a tamper-proofing approach is proposed where application integrity is asserted through the insertion instructions that perform code checksums during program execution. The modified applications are vulnerable to discovery using tools that can be built to automatically look for obfuscations or checksum instructions. Accordingly, these protections are only able to delay an eventual attack.

Designating memory locations as non-executable using special hardware tags is becoming a popular method for deterring buffer overflow attacks. Although available on a variety of older processors, most recently AMD has released hardware with their NX (No eXecute) technology and Intel has followed suit with a differently named yet functionally equivalent XD (eXecute Disable) bit. Software emulation of non-executable memory is a less secure option for processors that do not include functionality similar to the NX bit. These approaches are being widely adopted for general-purpose processors, however they do not address any type of program flow attack that doesn't involve instructions being written to and later fetched and executed from data memory.

There have been several hardware-based approaches to protecting software. The authors in [7] utilize their DISE architecture to implement a concept similar to StackShield in hardware. The SPEF framework proposed in [8] provides options for both obfuscating and introducing integrity checks to the input application, which are verified at run-time by custom hardware. The XOM architecture proposed in [9] attempts to ensure that instructions stored in memory cannot be modified, with specialized hardware being used to accelerate cryptographic functionality. The latency overhead introduced by encrypting the instruction fetch path can be considerable and may not be acceptable in real-time embedded systems; this problem is currently being examined by the computer architecture community [10,11]. Industry support for secure processors include the companies in the Trusted Computing Group (TCG) [12], which define the Trusted Platform Module, a hardware component that provides digital signature and key management functionality for software protection and Digital Rights Management (DRM).

3. Our Approach

When considering a static view of an application (Fig. 2), a *basic block* is defined as a subsequence of instructions for which there is only one entry point and one exit point. Basic block boundaries are typically found at jumps and branch targets, function entry and exit points, and conditionally executed instructions. The various types of program flow attacks can all be generalized as invalid edges in a flow graph at the basic block granularity:

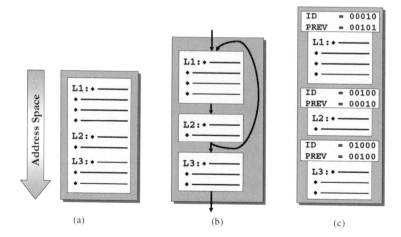

Figure 2. (a) Static view of an application's instructions. (b) Program-flow graph. (c) Runtime execution information added to the application via the PFencode compiler module.

- Flow passing between non-consecutive instructions in the same basic block.
- Flow passing between between two blocks with no originally intended relation.
- Flow passing between any two instructions that are not both at basic block boundaries.
- Flow passing from an instruction back to that same instruction, when that instruction is not both the entry and exit point of a single basic block.

Our approach operates at the basic block level. In the example of Fig. 2, flow passes unconditionally from block L1 into L2, where it may either loop back into L1 or pass conditionally into L3. This information is statically knowable by the compiler, which is typically able to break the input program into basic blocks for analysis. It is also possible to include a profiling pass to determine more complex program flows. Our compiler module, which we call PFencode, assigns identification labels to the basic blocks. These "IDs" are given a one-hot encoding, for reasons that will become apparent. For this example, block L1 is encoded as **00010**, L2 is encoded as **00100**, and L3 is encoded as **01000**.

Next, the compiler generates a table of predecessors for each basic block. Since the blocks are already encoded with a unique bit, we can create this "prevID" table by just ORing the IDs or all the blocks that are valid predecessors for each block. As an example, since since block L2 and the prefix code segment (with an ID of **00001**) are both valid predecessors of L1, the prevID value for L1 is defined as **00101**. The compiler also generates a value representing the length of each basic block.

Figure 3 shows a high level view of how our program flow checking architecture can be inserted into a standard CPU architecture. Our hardware component, which we call PFcheck, uses a snooping mechanism to analyze instructions being fetched directly between the processor core and the lowest level of instruction cache. Since the PFcheck architecture does not delay the instruction fetch path, it is not expected to incur the same negative performance impact as other approaches.

The architecture contains several customized memories which it uses to hold the program flow metadata values. The basic block base addresses are stored in a Content-Addressable Memory (CAM). Typically on a CAM lookup operation, the output is a unencoded value of the lines in the memory that match the target address. When an instruction is being fetched, the PFcheck component sends this address to the CAM. If

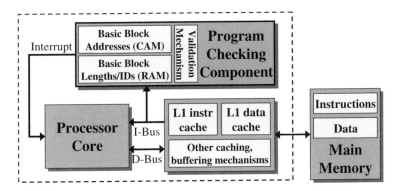

Figure 3. Insertion of the PFcheck component into a standard CPU architecture.

there is a match, this means that the instruction is an entry point for a basic block – the ID of that block is given as the output of the CAM.

The basic block lengths and prevID table are stored in a standard RAM. The only output required by the component is an interrupt signal, which is used to notify the system that an invalid flow has been detected. A more detailed description of a PFcheck implementation is given in the following section.

4. Implementation and Results

We implemented our prototype system on a Xilinx ML310 FPGA development board (Fig. 4), using version 7.1 of their Embedded Development Kit (EDK) for the design entry, simulation, and synthesis. The ML310 contains a XC2VP30 FPGA that has two PPC 405 processors, 13696 reconfigurable CLB slices, and 136 Block SelectRAM modules. The board and FPGA can act as a fully-fledged PC, with 256 MB on-board memory, some solid-state storage, and several standard peripherals.

We implemented our PFencode compiler as a post-pass of the GCC compiler targeting the Xilinx MicroBlaze soft processor [13]. We chose the MicroBlaze over the PPC for its simplicity and flexibility. Table 1 shows the results when we ran PFencode on a number of benchmarks customized to support MicroBlaze software libraries. For these relatively small applications, we found that the size of the metadata increased exponentially with the number of basic blocks. This is due to the fact that for an application with N basic blocks, our one-hot encoding approach requires an $N \times N$ memory to hold the entire prevID table. For the benchmarks that have relatively short basic blocks, this

Xilinx XC2PV30 FPGA

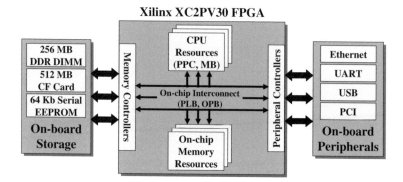

Figure 4. Architectural view of the Xilinx ML310 development platform.

Table 1. PFencode results for a variety of benchmarks.

Benchmark	App Size	Num Basic Block	Metadata Size	Percentage Increase
adpcm	15.8 kB	75	1.30 kB	8.2%
dijkstra	23.3 kB	257	10.3 kB	44.2%
laplace	15.6 kB	32	0.38 kB	2.4%
fir	22.8 kB	240	9.12 kB	40.0%
susan	90.8 kB	1253	206 kB	226.9%

increase in application size can be drastic (see susan which is 5.8 times the size of laplace but requires 542 times the amount of metadata).

Figure 5 shows the internals of our implementation of the PFcheck architecture. The instruction addresses (M bits wide) is sent into the CAM module which has M-bit wide entries for each of the N basic blocks. If there is a match, that means that this instruction address is a basic block base address – the one-hot ID value for that basic block is the output of the CAM on a match. Otherwise, the output of the CAM is all zeros indicating that the current instruction is inside a basic block. The output of the CAM is sent to an encoder that creates a log(N) wide signal that drives the address of the RAM module to get the prevID value for the current block. The entry in the prevID table is checked with the previously fetched ID that is stored in a register. If the bits do not match up, an interrupt signal is sent to the processor. In the case where the current instruction is not a basic block entry point, an interrupt will be also be generated if the current instruction does not directly proceed the previous instruction. This is equivalent to checking that PC does not equal $PC + 4$.

Table 2 shows how the area consumption and performance of the PFcheck architecture is depends on the configuration. For our experiments, we synthesized designs with varying amounts of basic block support and address bus width. Each design is labeled $N \times M$. Several trends are readily apparent. The BlockRAM and slice usage increase linearly with N. Decreasing the address bus width has less of an impact on area usage, and no impact on clock frequency. The limiting factor for this medium-sized FPGA was the number of BlockRAMs; we were not able to fit the 1024x32 on the device.

To test for correctness, we used PFencode to compile an application that contained a buffer overflow vulnerability. We attempted to write attack code on the stack and to overwrite the return address to point back to this buffer. While the architecture did not

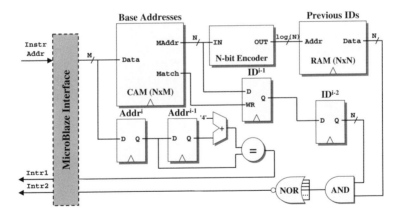

Figure 5. Internals of an implementation of the PFcheck architecture.

Table 2. PFcheck implementation results for a Xilinx XC2VP30 FPGA.

Config ($N \times M$)	64x16	64x32	128x32	256x32	512x32
Num Slices	450 (3.2%)	510 (3.7%)	840 (6.1%)	1615 (11.8%)	3031 (22.1%)
Num BRAMs	5 (3.7%)	9 (6.6%)	18 (13.2%)	36 (26.5%)	80 (58.9%)
Clock Freq	71.3 MHz	71.3 MHz	64.9 MHz	56.0 MHz	59.32 MHz

protect values on the stack from being overwritten, when the program attempted to return
to this malicious region an interrupt was triggered.

5. Conclusions and Future Work

In this paper we proposed and evaluated a reconfigurable architecture for verifying program flow integrity. We demonstrated the effectiveness of our approach with a implementation protecting a MicroBlaze processor running on a Xilinx ML310 FPGA board.

Further improvements are being made to the PFcheck architecture. We are currently
analyzing the performance overhead of writing the program flow metadata values to the
CAM and RAM. Also, we are investigating a paging architecture that will be able to
protect larger applications (in terms of number of basic blocks) without a loss in the
amount of security provided.

Acknowledgements

This work was supported in part by the National Science Foundation (NSF) under grant
CCR-0325207 and also by an NSF graduate research fellowship.

References

[1] 'Aleph One'. Smashing the stack for fun and profit. In *Phrack*, vol. 7, no. 49, Nov. 1996.
[2] J. Pincus and B. Baker. Beyond stack smashing: recent advances in exploiting buffer overruns. In *IEEE
     Security and Privacy*, vol. 2, no. 4, Jul. 2004, pp. 20–27.
[3] C. Cowan, C. Pu, D. Maier, H. Hinton, J. Walpole, P. Bakke, S. Beattie, A. Grier, P. Wagle, and Q. Zhang.
     StackGuard: automatic adaptive detection and prevention of buffer-overflow attacks. In *Proceedings of
     the 7th USENIX Security Symposium*, Jan. 1998, pp. 63–78.
[4] 'Bulba' and 'Kil3r'. Bypassing StackGuard and StackShield. In *Phrack*, vol. 10, no. 56, May 2000.
[5] C. Collberg, C. Thomborson, and D. Low. Breaking abstractions and unstructuring data structures. In
     Proceedings of the International Conference on Computer Languages (ICCL), May 1998, pp. 28–38.
[6] H. Chang and M. Atallah. Protecting software code by guards. In *Proceedings of the ACM Workshop on
     Security and Privacy in Digital Rights Management*, Nov. 2001, pp. 160–175.
[7] M. Corliss, E. Lewis, and A. Roth. Using DISE to protect return addresses from attack. In *Proceedings
     of the Workshop on Architectural Support for Security and Anti-Virus (WASSA)*, Oct. 2004.
[8] D. Kirovski, M. Drinic, and M. Potkonjak. Enabling trusted software integrity. In *Proceedings of the 10th
     International Conference on Architectural Support for Programming Languages and Operating Systems
     (ASPLOS-X)*, Oct. 2002, pp. 108–120.
[9] D. Lie, C. Thekkath, M. Mitchell, and M. Horowitz. Architectural support for copy and tamper resistant
     software. In *Proceedings of the 9th International Conference on Architectural Support for Programming
     Languages and Operating Systems (ASPLOS-IX)*, Nov. 2000, pp. 168–177.
[10] W. Shi, H-H. Lee, M. Ghosh, C. Lu, and A. Boldyreva. High efficiency counter mode security architecture
     via prediction and precomputation. In *Proceedings of the 32nd International Symposium on Computer
     Architecture (ISCA)*, Jun. 2005, pp. 14–24.
[11] J. Yang, Y. Zhang, and L. Gao. Fast secure processor for inhibiting software piracy and tampering. In
     Proceedings of the 36th International Symposium on Microarchitecture (MICRO), Dec. 2003, pp. 351–
     360.
[12] Trusted Computing Group, http://www.trustedcomputing.org, 2005.
[13] Xilinx. *MicroBlaze Processor Reference Guide*, available at http://www.xilinx.com, 2005.

Security and Embedded Systems
D.N. Serpanos and R. Giladi (Eds.)
IOS Press, 2006

Model-Based Validation of Enterprise Access Policies

Sandeep BHATT, William HORNE, Joe PATO, Raj RAJAGOPALAN
and Prasad RAO[1]
*Trusted Systems Laboratory, Hewlett-Packard Labs, 5 Vaughn Drive,
Suite 301, Princeton, NJ 08540*

1. Introduction

> *... IS buyers are mired in tuning technology
> knobs that bear little, if any, relationship to the
> business policies and procedures employed by the
> enterprise.*
>
> "Security Policy Automation in the
> Enterprise," Aberdeen Report, 2002

Consider managing security in an enterprise like HP. The HP network has thousands of switches, routers, applications and managed databases and hundreds of thousands of managed desktops, and many hundreds of terabytes of managed storage systems. This is the complex world into which new systems such as personal digital assistants, mobile phones with embedded servers have to interact with. These new systems are increasingly likely to have embedded java virtual machines, web servers, application servers, and databases, services which previously only used to reside on enterprise servers. An army of administrators is needed to manage the configurations of such an enterprise. Additional complications are introduced by the distributed geographic nature of the enterprise. End users in these enterprise systems participate in business processes that access resources across the entire enterprise.

Plenty of mechanisms for ensuring security exist at each layer of the enterprise. The network is protected by filters such as rules on firewalls, Access Control Lists (ACLs) on routers, Filters on Virtual Private Networks (VPNs). The server infrastructure is served by DNS, File Systems, and Directories all with their own ACLs. At the application layer web servers with their access control configuration files, application servers with their security policies and database servers with their grants tables attempt to enforce security. In short, each mechanism has its own concept of security – it controls access by different client to different resources possibly in different namespaces. Each such mechanism is also managed by a human administrator who has to set values for the appropriate filters to govern access to these resources. The natural question is how does an administrator configure these filters to achieve the desired security? Even

---

[1] Contact author. Prasad.rao@hp.com.

if an administrator configures one such mechanism to the best of his knowledge, how does he know that the net effect of all these configured mechanisms is the desired one?

To put it more precisely, the central question we address is: How do we coordinate the security configurations of all of these components to comply with high-level intent?

Current practice leaves much to be desired: IT departments write high level policy documents. Local administrators configure local systems in best faith attempt to conform to such policies. There exist few tools to verify the system as a whole works as intended by the IT department. Administrators resort to techniques such as penetration testing to attempt to discover policy violations. Unfortunately, these brute force mechanisms yield little or no business agility when it comes to change. Changes in policy take time to propagate to local level as manual processes are involved. As a result when new business alliances and mergers happen it is nearly impossible to know quickly and with certainty whether new security gaps have been created. Compliance checking is difficult because subtle interactions can lead to security vulnerabilities. As a result, frequently we only learn of security gaps caused by the combination of component configurations after they have been exploited. Manual processes also make it difficult to know if the enterprise is really as secure as it needs to be. Quite often we spend a lot of time and money on security measures, only to learn later and at great cost that the adversary was able to bypass these measures anyway. There is a need to make security operations more rigorous, less labor-intensive, and at the same time responsive to changing needs of business.

2. Vision and Approach

We address these issues in the vision presented in this paper. Firstly, we link business requirements to IT security by defining high-level security policies in terms of business goals. We use this notion of security policy to validate system configurations.

Secondly, we are building tools for system wide security. These tools assist enterprise planning by checking the system for policy violations before deploying. They facilitate management by pointing out gaps in security in the system as they occur.

Our approach is centered on modeling components (network, infrastructure, application) to capture input/output behavior with respect to configuration. These models focus on security aspects. In the analysis phase we compose components to reason about global behavior in order to compare global behavior to policy. We use the results of this analysis to report policy violations. Finally, we suggest configuration changes to bring system into compliance if necessary.

The conceptual architecture of our system is shown in Fig. 1.

3. Technical Details

In this section we introduce Datalog upon which we base our modeling language. Then we present a sketch of our approach to writing models, our policy language and validation. Space restrictions force us to be brief.

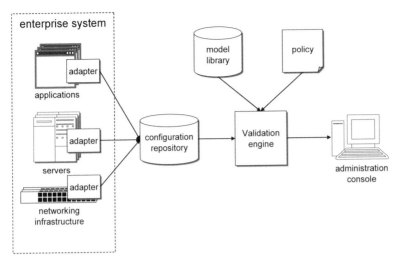

Figure 1. Conceptual System Architecture.

3.1. Models

Our modeling language is based on a subset of prolog known as Datalog. We will introduce datalog very briefly here – but this introduction will neither be formal nor complete. Datalog is a language of facts and rules. Datalog provides a logic based query language for the relational model. The complexity of answering a datalog query[2] runs in polynomial time.

Informally a Datalog predicate $p(a_1, \ldots, a_n)$, represents a relation p that maps the n-tuple $(a_1, \ldots, a_n)$ into $\{true, false\}$ depending on whether the tuple belongs to the relation. For example, a database relation is represented as

```
r("John Deere","277-1487").
r("Jane Doe","277-8765").
```

Additionally, a rule such as,

$$r_{head} \text{ :- } r_1, \ldots, r_n.$$

states that the predicate represented by the head is true, if each of the predicates in the body is true.

Using Datalog, we model an enterprise as a set of components, each of which is a *configured server*, $S_1 \ldots S_n$. For our purposes such configured servers include network devices, infrastructure, applications, etc. A model of a server consists of a predicate

```
allows(Server, Client, Op, Args)
```

The intuitive meaning is that when Client makes a request to Server of the form Op(Args) it will succeed. In our models, allows predicates can depend on other allows predicates. Following Datalog, in our models allows succeed if all the dependent allows succeed.

---

[2] Computing the well founded semantics model of a program [XSB].

3.2. Policy

Our policies are essentially on access control. First, let's consider policies that capture permitted actions

```
permit(Client, Server, Op, Args)
```

Permitted actions correspond to the set of services for which clients should have *direct* access. E.g. making sure employees have access to the services they need to do their job.

To be conservative, policies that capture prohibited actions, namely *denys,* have to be handled differently The set of allowed actions should be necessary and sufficient to support the permit policies – absolutely nothing else should be allowed. However, in order to create exceptions for an allow policy it is often necessary to have an explicit deny policy. Denies are specified using the same syntax permits

```
deny(Client, Server, Op, Args)
```

Denied actions correspond to the set of services for which clients should not have *direct* or *indirect* access, e.g. non-HR staff should not have access to salary information. There should be no sequence of actions starting from `Client` which ends with `Op` and `Args` being invoked on `Server`.

We use graph-theoretic transitive closure based mechanisms in order to compute policy compliance. Due to space restrictions, the details of these techniques are omitted here.

4. Related Work

There is a wide body of recent work that is related to this project from various aspects. We mention some of these below.

The "Smart Firewalls" prototype [SFW] developed previously by some of the authors, developed closed-loop, policy-based security management for the network layer, and provided the early motivation for the current work. The main distinction is that models for network layer access control devices are particularly simple – incoming packets either flow through without modification, or are blocked depending on the configured rules. Application models are more complex since they must capture message types and transformations.

The notion of policy based management has been around for some time. The most recent project that has the goal of policy-based management is the Ponder project [PON]. Policies in Ponder can be complex quantified statements on the attributes and methods of objects. In particular, security policies are typically restrictions on access to individual methods on objects. Ponder however does not address the ability to compose or end-to-end reasoning on the objects under consideration. As a result there is no concept of high-level policy and policy-based management is seen as a means largely to specify constraints on classes of objects rather than constraints on the behavior of the system as a whole.

Filtering Postures [FPOS] proposes using logic-based specifications of the requirements and binary decision diagrams to validate whether network layer devices such as firewalls, router ACLs and static routes are configured consistently.

Firmato [FRM] was the first analysis engine to generate rules for multiple firewalls that comply with high-level policy. Firmato generates firewall configurations given policies and topology but does not validate a given set of configurations.

The MulVal system [MVL] uses Datalog models to solve the problem of analyzing vulnerability reports to infer privilege escalations in a system. MulVal operates in two phases. In the first phase, a scanner consumes reports of vulnerabilities in common components (hosts, operating systems, network devices, applications) in a standardized XML format and searches the given network to find any components that are affected by these reports. In the second phase, MulVal logically deduces the privilege escalations (e.g. normal user becoming "root") that are possible due to these vulnerabilities using Datalog descriptions of the relationships between the components in question. Although MulVal addresses a complementary problem using similar ideas, they do not propose a formal modeling methodology.

Attack Graphs [JAJ, SHY] also model the cascading of attacks through a network but they do not have formal modeling methods. Unlike MulVal they do not deal with phenomena such as privilege escalation. Attack graphs analyze the potential impact of vulnerabilities on an environment without the accompanying context of enterprise security policies.

Transitive Closure-based reasoning: [NetKuang] which is based on [Kuang] proposed to find transitive vulnerabilities on networked computer systems created by poor system configuration using a rule-based approach. They use a backward-chained, goal-based expert system search on rules describing access structure as well as vulnerabilities. While Kuang is limited to analyzing a single host, NetKuang can analyze a LAN: the analyzer accesses hosts on the LAN using a customized network search algorithm. These works do not suggest a rigorous and general methodology that goes beyond vulnerability exploitation on hosts. To map the Kuang and NetKuang approaches to our terminology, these works are not based on policy and they make no attempts to validate permit policies – rather the approach is to find privilege escalations that constitute violations of deny policies.

Operating system vulnerabilities modeling [OSV]: This paper deals with the problem of modeling the transitive effects of bugs in operating system routines such as buffer overflow. This work has the ability to deal with sophisticated attacks such as phased attacks but at the cost of stateful modeling that makes the complexity of the logic exponential. The paper does not address networked environments.

In the commercial arena, SolSoft's policy manager [SOL] allows users to specify high-level network layer policies that are used to automatically generate configurations for firewalls, routers and switches for any desired topology.

TruSecure [TRU] offers an application layer security solution that claims to solve the problem of transitive access, but their solution uses best practices rather than formal methods.

5. Conclusions

In this paper we have presented a new vision for security management that is currently being researched and prototyped in HP Labs. This new vision will enable enterprise administrators and CIOs to directly execute their high-level security requirements on the enterprise environment and be assured that only required access to services is available. Our vision allows us to build tools that help validate existing security configurations against high-level requirements as well as plan configurations of environments so that we know that they are secure before they are deployed. This will take big step from the current manual and error-prone processes of security management. Our vision will also enable businesses to reduce the costs of security operations by making IT security more agile and responsive to changing business requirements.

References

[SFW] S. Bhatt, S. Rajagopalan, P. Rao. Automatic Management of Network Security Policy. MILCOM 2003.

[PON] N. Damianou, N. Dulay, E. Lupu, and M. Sloman. The ponder policy specification language. In Morris Sloman, editor, Proc. of Policy Workshop, 2001, Bristol UK, January 2001.

[FRM] Yair Bartal, Alain Mayer, Kobbi Nissan, and Avishai Wool. Firmato: A novel firewall management toolkit. In Proc. IEEE Computer Society Symposium on Security and Privacy, 1999.

[FPOS] J.D. Guttman. Filtering postures: Local enforcement for global policies. In Proc. IEEE Symp. on Security and Privacy, Oakland, CA, 1997.

[MVL] S. Govindavajhala and X. Ou. MulVal: Multiple Vulnerability Analyzer. To appear in Usenix Security Symposium, 2005.

[NetKuang] D. Zerkle, K. Levitt, "NetKuang—A Multi-Host Configuration Vulnerability Checker." *6th USENIX Security Symposium*. San Jose, California, July 22–25, 1996, pp. 195–204.

[Imm] N. Immerman. Descriptive Complexity, Springer 1999.

[JAJ] S. Noel and S. Jajodia. Managing attack graph complexity through visual hierarchical aggregation. Conference on Computer and Communication Security, 2004.

[Kuang] Robert W Baldwin Kuang. Rule-based security checking. Documentation in ftp://ftp.cert.org/pub/tools/cops/cops.tar.

[SHY] O. Sheyner and J. Wing. Tools for Generating and Analyzing Attack Graphs. *Proceedings of Formal Methods for Components and Objects*, Lecture Notes in Computer Science, 2004, pp. 344–371.

[OSV] C.R. Ramakrishnan and R.C. Sekar. Model-Based Analysis of Configuration Vulnerabilities. Journal of Computer Security, v. 10, pp. 189–209, 2002.

[SOL] Solsoft Policy Manager, SolSoft, Inc. www.solsoft.com.

[TRU] Enterprise Policy Management. White Paper. TruSecure, Inc. www.trusecure.com.

[XSB] P. Rao, K.F. Sagonas, T. Swift, D.S. Warren, and J. Freire. XSB: A System for Efficiently Computing Well-Founded Semantics. In J. Dix, U. Furbach, and A. Nerode, editors, Proceedings of the 4th International Conference on Logic Programming and Non-Monotonic Reasoning (LPNMR'97), number 1265 in Lecture Notes in AI (LNAI), pages 2–17, Dagstuhl, Germany, July 1997. Springer Verlag.

Security and Embedded Systems
D.N. Serpanos and R. Giladi (Eds.)
IOS Press, 2006

Research Issues in Homeland Security

Theodoros ZACHARIADIS*

Hellenic Aerospace Industry, Tanagra, Schimatari, Greece

Abstract. The diverse nature of European border defence is challenged by an equally diverse array of threats ranging from terrorists to drug smugglers, arms dealers, illegal explosives, and human traffickers. Moreover, political and societal developments have created a fluid security environment, where risks and vulnerabilities are more diverse and less visible. In this paper, we address the main Research & Technology initiatives at International and European Level and identify a number of research areas where innovative, technology-driven developments may provide short-term solutions. Aiming to enhance security of Greek and European citizens, HAI actively participates in a number of international forums, and invests in research activities. However, the only guaranteed way to preserve homeland security is to apply a universal, inspired, political, societal and educational programme, that will reduce the gap between countries, nations and closed, ideological groups.

Keywords. Surveillance, Security, WEAO, European Defence Agency

Introduction

Security has always been an important issue for Europe. In recent years however, there has been a growing awareness that security is not a permanent attribute [1]. As the gap between the developing and the developed countries continues to grow, there are millions of people searching for a better life in the USA, Canada, Australia and of course in Europe. The recent enlargement to the Europe Union to 25 countries has increased the external boarders to about 5000km of new sea borders and 4000 km of new land borders and brought about new challenges. Borders are monitored and protected by border patrol agents, video cameras, ground sensors, physical barriers, land vehicles and manned aircraft. However, the diverse nature of European border defence is challenged by an equally diverse array of threats ranging from terrorists to drug smugglers, illegal migrations, arms dealers, illegal explosives, and human traffickers. This is why border control has become a critical part of the security challenges and demands extra efforts to ensure a consistent high level of homeland security.

In addition, political and societal developments have created a fluid security environment, where risks and vulnerabilities are more diverse and less visible. New threats have emerged, which target European citizens life and interests. Terrorists' attacks, such as the ones of 9/11 in the USA, the Madrid railway attacks of March 2004 and especially the recent attacks in London's centre this July, underline that the major danger is not imported, but it is generated by citizens with wrong or misconceived ideological and political positioning, who were born and live inside the European Union boarders.

---

* Corresponding Author: Theodoros ZACHARIADIS, Electronics Systems Strategy & Development, Hellenic Aerospace Industry, Tanagra, Schimatari, Greece E-mail: tzachariadis@haicorp.com.

The only guaranteed way to preserve homeland security and prevent such terrorists' attacks is to face the generative causes that initiated them. However, this is a very long-term approach that incorporates brave political willingness, universal societal actions, intelligent promotion and more than everything inspired educational methodology. Looking for short-term, technology-driven solutions to enhance the European homeland security, there is an emerging need to coordinate the research community in order to address effectively and innovatively existing and future security challenges.

Aiming to enhance the protection of the Greek and European citizens and to play an important and efficient role in peace-keeping activities, Hellenic Aerospace Industry (HAI), as the largest Defence company in Greece, actively participates in a number of international forums, standardization bodies and research activities. In addition, following a developing strategic plan, HAI has endorsed a number of national and international strategic alliances and has established bilateral partnerships with prominent manufactures in Europe and USA.

In this paper, initially we address the main objectives and Research & Technology initiatives at International and European Level. Then, we present major research challenges in homeland security and we propose an Intelligent Surveillance System Architecture.

1. Security Objectives at European Level

Security is an evolving concept and presents many challenges that impact on a wide range of existing and emerging European policies and citizens' concerns, including the protection against terrorist threats. A white paper by the General Secretary Mr. Solana in Dec 2003 [2], proposes three strategic objectives for the European Union. These are:

a) *Addressing the new threats*: The Union needs to use a range of instruments to deal with the current threats such as terrorism, proliferation of weapons of mass destruction, failed states, regional conflicts and organized crime.

b) *Building security in Europe's neighbourhood*: The enlargement process resulted in a territorial increase of 34% and has to ensure that a consistently high level of security is established across its new, more diverse territory.

c) *Effective multinational co-operations*: In a world of global threats, no single European country will be able to tackle present or future complex security problems entirely on its own. The EU needs to have the most technologically advanced instruments for anticipating new security threats and dealing with them in a way that serves its interests and respects its values.

2. Security Research & Technology Initiatives

In addressing the new security challenges, innovative technology will play a key role. The European expertise and potential to research, develop and deploy a wide range of security technologies exists. However, in facing the complexity and diversity of the new threats, Europe should: a) increase cooperation between companies and countries, b) reduce duplication of effort, and c) achieve standardization and interoperability. In this respect, the following research organizations and activities in European level have been initiated.

2.1. Research Within the European Commission

In order to face the increasing need for security, the European Commission launched a Preparatory Action on "The enhancement of the European industrial potential in the field of Security Research," (PASR2005). The Preparatory Action provides an opportunity to undertake activities to identify and address critical issues in order to prepare the foundations for a comprehensive European Security Research Programme from 2007 onwards.

The aim of the PASR2005 activities have been [3]:

- *Improving situation awareness.* The aim of this activity has been to identify the main threats that could affect Europe, particularly borders and assets of global interest, by appropriate information gathering, interpretation, integration and dissemination leading to the sharing of intelligence.
- *Optimising security and protection of networked systems.* The aim of this activity has been to analyse networked systems, such as communications systems, utility systems, transportation facilities, or networks for (e-)business, and to show how to implement protective security measures against both electronic and physical threats.
- *Protecting against terrorism* (including bio-terrorism and incidents with biological, chemical and other substances). The aim of this activity has been to identify and prioritise the material and information requirements of governments, agencies and public authorities in combating and protecting against terrorism and to deliver technology solutions for threat detection, identification, protection and neutralisation as well as containment and disposal of threatening substances including biological, chemical and nuclear ones and weapons of mass destruction.
- *Enhancing Crisis Management* (including evacuation, search and rescue operations, active agents control and remediation). The aim of this activity has been to address the operational and technological issues that need to be considered from three perspectives: crisis prevention, operational preparedness and management of declared crisis.
- *Achieving interoperability and integrated systems for information and communication.* The aim of this activity was to develop and demonstrate interoperability concepts for (legacy) information systems in the domain of security, enabling the linking of existing and new assets in clusters to offer improved performance and enhanced adaptive functionality. To support interoperability, system providers need to involve end-users and standardization.

The Preparatory Action is expected to lead to a European Security Research Programme starting in 2007. Experience and knowledge gained from this phase will help to ensure that the future Research Programme will be optimally designed, and that it will contribute to the technological excellence and capabilities for the European Union.

2.2. Western European Armaments Organization (WEAO)

The WEAO was created in 1996 by countries-members of the Western European Armaments Group (WEAG). The broad umbrella of the WEAG Defence Research and Technology (R&T) activities cover sea, land, air and space platforms, going from components to the systems level, screening through electro-optics, modelling and simulation, radar and weapon systems. Specific requirements are addressed to adapt commercial applications and Commercial Off The Self (COTS) to Defence demands. All defence needs are considered under 13 Common European Priority Areas (CEPA) organized as follows:

- *CEPA 1: Modern Radar Technology* (inc. Electronic combat RF technology) *CEPA 2: Microelectronics* addressing dedicated military technologies.
- *CEPA 3: Advanced Materials and Structures* for specific military purposes and ensure their availability and cost-effectiveness.
- *CEPA 6: Advanced Information Processing and Communications* between European Industries and government institutions, for the fulfilment of Defence requirements.
- *CEPA 8: Advanced Electro-Optical systems and technologies* covering a broad area, from land to space applications, with a spectral range from UV to the far IR.
- *CEPA 9: Satellite Surveillance & Military Space technology targeting* areas such as: satellite on-board processing, antennas optimised for use in space, satellite clusters, data fusion, ballistic missile Defence etc.
- *CEPA 10: Underwater technology and naval hydrodynamics* addressing all aspects of underwater-applied science and hydrodynamics studies.
- *CEPA 11: Defence Modeling & Simulation technologies* allowing the armed forces to be prepared in a timely, cost-effective manner for any multinational operation, without having to resort to high-risk type of exercises under warlike conditions.
- *CEPA 13: Radiological, Chemical and Biological Defence*, initiating feasibility studies and providing technology demonstrators for new devices and equipment.
- *CEPA 14: Energetic Materials.* Covers all aspects of Energetic Materials including synthesis, characterization performance vulnerability, warheads and survivability.
- *CEPA 15: Missile, UAV and Robotic technology* covering all aspects, from seeker technologies through mission strategy, to control and actuation systems.
- *CEPA 16: Electrical Engineering.* Fulfilling military needs that are to be expected in view of operational requirements and sensor developments.

Hellenic Aerospace Industry participates in the most important CEPA steering committees namely CEPA 1, 2, 3, 6, 9, 11, 13 and 15.

2.3. European Defence Agency

The European Defence Agency (EDA) is a new organization, established by a Joint Action of the Council of Ministers on the 12th July, 2004, "to support the Member States in their effort to improve European defence capabilities in the field of crisis management and to sustain the European Security and Defence Policy (ESDP)" [4].

EDA aims to develop close working relations with existing arrangements, groupings and organisations such as the LoI (Letter of Intent) grouping, the OCCAR and the WEAG, targeting incorporation of relevant principles [5]. In practice however, this will result in incorporating and substituting their activities.

In the R&T direction, EDA aims to lead or manage initiatives in the following areas:

- *UAVs/ISTAR.* Technology demonstration work on long-endurance Unmanned Aerial Vehicles (UAVs), in the context of development of a wider ISTAR (Intelligence Surveillance, Target Acquisition and Reconnaissance) architecture.
- *Advanced European Jet Pilot Training.* Assuming leadership of the current collaborative effort involving 11 Participating Member States (plus Switzerland) to develop a common European system.
- *Command, Control and Communication.* Work to find solutions to current ESDP operational shortfalls, and to develop capacity and interoperability for the future.
- *Defence Test and Evaluation Base Rationalisation.* Development of proposals for budgetary savings by elimination of duplication of facilities in Europe.
- *Armoured Fighting Vehicles.* Collaborative technology development and/or procurement programmes, potentially facilitating industrial restructuring.
- *Commercial/Military Off-the-Shelf equipment.* Work to develop proposals for a European market in Commercial/Military Off-the-Shelf (COTS/MOTS) equipment, including feasibility study of an "electronic market place".

Moreover, EDA considers the following activities, as potential future areas of interest:

- *Naval Defence Technological and Industrial Base (DTIB).* Review of anticipated future demand and capacity, and current national strategies.
- *Air-to-Air Refuelling.* Review of European capability needs, national requirements and programmes, interoperability issues and potential for collaboration.
- *Chemical, Biological, Radiological and Nuclear (CBRN).* Review of all research activity in the CBRN direction.
- *Maritime surveillance.* Review of all activity underway in defence and security fora, with particular reference to the contribution of defence assets.

3. Challenges in Homeland Security

Homeland Security has completely changed, the last few years. Surveillance along with protection from all new methods and forms of terrorist attacks have dramatically complicated security and generated new research and technological challenges. Following the information chain, we may categorize them in the following groups.

3.1. Sensors & Information Gathering

The first step in effective homeland security is to gather and filter valuable information. There are already a number of sensor technologies including acoustics, electromagnetic, electro-optical, and infrared. Moreover, information may be captured by intelligent defence and surveillance systems, including the Vessel Traffic Service (VTS), deployed for traffic management, the "Automated Identification System" (AIS), largely used to display the picture of surrounding traffic, the military surveillance systems and patrol boats equipped with X-band coherent surface search radars, Interrogation Friend or Foe (IFF) secondary radar and target indication system and infrared/electro-optical sensors. These sensors and systems have dramatically evolved the last decades. Nevertheless, new innovative systems or products are still frequently announced, showing that research is underway. Moreover, two areas that create a centre of attention are:

- *Biometric Sensors.* Human identification (e.g. travellers, staff, drivers, pilots, skippers, passengers) based on biometrics is considered among the hottest areas in sensor research. Biometrics technologies including fingerprint, iris, face, voice recognition and abnormal behaviour attract a lot of research activities.
- *Unmanned Aerial Vehicles (UAVs).* UAVs are defined as powered aerial vehicles that do not carry a human operator, use aerodynamic forces to provide lift, can be expendable or recoverable, and can carry lethal or non-lethal payloads. Areas of research in UAVs/ ISTAR include remote control, Electro-Optical (EO) sensors, speed and loiter capabilities.

3.2. Secure Communications

Secure Communications is a very important area in Homeland Security. There are a number of wired (Leased Line, Optical, Ethernet) and wireless (HF, VHF, UHF, satellite) communication technologies. However, extended research is underway in areas like:

- *Software Defined Radio (SDR)* is being actively researched due to its potential to help realise reconfigurable radio systems whilst retaining common hardware platforms. SDR future systems will offer increased capability and flexibility and allow a single radio terminal to switch between different modes, bands, services and applications; that is a single device for ubiquitous information interaction.
- *Secure Tactical Ad-hoc Communications.* Ranging from still measuring sensors to groups of fighting supersonic aircrafts, secure tactical ad-hoc communications introduce a number of research issues like efficient routing, transmission with Quality of Service guarantees, power and energy savings.
- *Satellite Communications.* Bi-direction satellite communications utilising the DVB-RCS (Digital Video Broadcasting – Return Channel Service) will be one of the major alternatives for secure future communications. Research on tracking antennas, military satellite terminals, along with signal processing on the satellite are among the major efforts.

3.3. Interoperability

One of the main problems that current remote Surveillance systems face is Interoperability. Today there is not a single open standard to define how data should be represented, transmitted, delivered, handled, stored. Moreover, there is no standard communication interface and Application Programming Interface (API) to specify the data received by multiple sensors or generally from multiple information sources. The result is to have a number of isolated surveillance systems, with proprietary internal representations, which present their data in multiple different TV displays. Interoperability between surveillance systems from different manufacturers requires extended research and development, while even enhancement of a system with new state-of-the art sensors (radars, cameras, biometrics) from the same manufacturer may be quite resource consuming, if feasible at all.

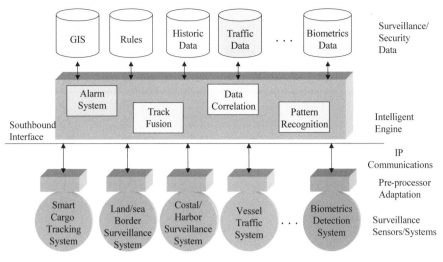

Figure 1. Proposed surveillance system.

3.4. Data Fusion and Classification

The target-tracking function has to collect data from sensors located in different places, both fixed and mobile, and combine them with stored in historic databases. Research is required in the ***Data Fusion*** function, which has to align all on-line data in space and time, in order to produce the Tactical Picture. Images and videos should be associated to the target they belong to, while algorithms have to be adapted to the scenario. The ***Pattern Recognition/ Classification/ Identification*** and the ***Situation Awareness*** functions have to establish the standard identity, the environment and other attributes for each target detected by the sensors. Moreover, research is required in the ***Scenario Modelling***, ***Simulation*** and ***Decision Making*** elements of the system in order to identify the threats, propose the action plans and in-time crisis management, and avoid both delays and/or overreactions.

4. Proposed Surveillance System Architecture

Based on the above research issues, the proposed surveillance and crisis management system is shown in Fig. 1.

As it is shown, multiple surveillance sensors/systems are adapted to a common Southbound Applications Programming Interface (API), while environmental, surveillance/security data in the form of GIS, Rules, historic and biometrics data are provided as input to the system. On the other hand, a number of intelligent modules, i.e. Pattern Recognition, Data Correlation and Track Fusion identify the targets, threats and situation, while alarm systems initiate the crisis management plans.

5. Conclusions

The long and diverse European boarders along with political and societal developments have created a fluid security environment, where risks and vulnerabilities are more diverse and less visible. Recent terrorists' attacks underline that the major danger is not imported, but it is generated by citizens, who were born and live inside the European Union boarders.

In this paper, we have identified a number of research issues, where innovative, technology-driven developments may provide short-term suppression of the problem. Aiming to enhance the protection of Greek and European citizens and to play an key role in peace-keeping activities, Hellenic Aerospace Industry actively participates in a number of international forums, standardization bodies, research and development activities. However, the only guaranteed way to preserve homeland security is to apply a universal, inspired, political, societal and educational long-term programme, that will reduce the gap between countries, nations and closed, ideological groups.

References

[1] Commission of the European Communities, "Concerning the adoption of the Programme of Work 2005 for the Preparatory Action in the field of Security Research," C(2005)259, 4th February 2005.
[2] J. Solana, "A Secure Europe in a Better World," European Security Policy, European Council, Thessalonica, 20/06/2003, ue.eu.int/ueDocs/cms_Data/docs/pressdata/EN/reports/76255.pdf.
[3] Commission of the European Communities, "On the implementation of the Preparatory Action on the enhancement of the European industrial potential in the field of Security research," Commission Communication, Brussels, 3.2.2004, COM(2004) 72 final.pdf.
[4] Council Joint Action 2004/551/CFSP of 12 July 2004 on the establishment of the European Defence Agency.
[5] European Defence Agency, "Steering Board sets direction for Agency's efforts to build european defence capabilities," Press Release, Brussels 21 June 2005, http://ue.eu.int/ueDocs/pressData/en/misc/85397.pdf.
[6] European Defence Agency, "2nd Meeting of the European Defence Agency's Steering Board," Press Release, Brussels, 22 November 2004.

Security and Embedded Systems
D.N. Serpanos and R. Giladi (Eds.)
IOS Press, 2006

Assurance in Autonomous Decentralized Embedded System

Kinji MORI [1]

Tokyo Institute of Technology

Abstract. Advancement in computer and communication technologies have resulted in an explosive growth in embedded systems. The market and users requirements have been rapidly changing and diversified. Under these evolving situations, the assurance to keep the continuous system operation of embedded systems is becoming more and more important. The Autonomous Decentralized System (ADS) has been proposed for resolving the on-line property to achieve the step-by-step expansion, maintenance and fault-propagation prevention for high-assurance. This architecture is effective to improve the reliability and reduce the development cost and product cycle time to market by data-driven mechanism. Moreover, the technologies have been applied in the IC card system for train fare-collection and the mobile network platform for intelligent transport service system.

Keywords. Embedded system, ADS(Autonomous Decentralized System), assurance, fault-tolerance, expansion, maintenance

1. Introduction

Distributed embedded systems with multiple processing elements are becoming common in various application areas ranging from multimedia to robotics, industrial control, and automotive electronics. Heterogeneous distributed architecture are required for such systems, where several processors, application-specific integrated circuits (ASIC), and field-programmable gate arrays (FPGA) are interconnected by various types of communication links, and multiple tasks are concurrently run on the system. Each task can be executed on a variety of software and hardware platforms with different costs [1,2]. In addition, the markets have been expanding rapidly and users requirements have been diversified and varied. However, the conventional architecture is either overdesigned or fails to meet the specified constraints. Therefore, finding an effective architecture to meet the heterogeneous requirements of hardware and software under this dynamic changing environment to achieve all realtime constraints are necessary.

As the breakthrough over the conventional systems, Autonomous Decentralized System (ADS) has been proposed in 1977 [3]. An autonomous decentralized system is defined as such a living thing which is composed of largely autonomous and decentral-

---

[1]Corresponding Author: Kinji Mori, Department of Computer Science, Tokyo Institute of Technology, 2-12-1 Ookayama, Meguro, Tokyo 152-8552, Japan. Tel: +81-3-5734-2664; Fax: +81-3-5734-2510; E-mail: mori@cs.titech.ac.jp.

ized components (subsystems). Their technologies have been developed in the various fields of transportation, factory automation, utility management, satellite on-board control, newspaper printing factory, information services, e-commerce, community service, and so on.

In this paper, the ADS concept and technologies are discussed and their applications to the IC card system for train fare collection: Suica and the mobile network platform for intelligent transport service system are shown to be effectively operated.

2. Background and Requirements

In the following years, the information technology will be strongly marked by the presence of embedded systems. Such systems are typically application specific systems containing software, hardware and communications channels tailored for a particular task. Nowadays, embedded systems are presented in almost all electronic devices even they are hardly noticeable. There exists a large variety of applications and functionality in which they are applied. In control systems, Program Logic Controllers (PLC) have been used for controlling processes such as temperature, mixture, position and velocity in a critical industrial systems. In consumer products, many further enhancements and numerous new home control, kitchen appliances and white-good products have been designed based on sensor/actuator signal processing by embedded systems. Mobile phones depends heavily on the use of standards implemented in embedded systems. In other professional areas like traffic control, car navigation, train control, plant control, etc., embedded systems may overpass the functionality that can not be provided by human beings [4].

In a beginning, embedded systems had been designed for satisfying an specific task or functionality in a single device. However, with the constant advance in the IT and the solution they provide while meeting a lot of constraints, the pervasion of embedded systems was derived. The possibility to share an embedded systems platform over many different applications in a domain makes them very attractive. For example, in home automation, a large extent specific hardware and/or software components, even for high-volume consumer-electronics applications, are connected in a network system in order to provide the functionality for living that each person is demanding. In this sense, gradually our society is becoming dependent on the proper functioning of embedded systems [5].

2.1. General Trends and User Needs

The embedded systems are characterized by the following properties:

Heterogeneous (software, hardware, mechanical components, optics, etc.) Embedded systems of various technological areas are designed under different hardware and software (Linux, Windows, Tron, etc.) platforms.

Complex (real-time requirements, low power, low cost, reliable, etc.) Embedded systems are mostly reactive systems, which means they react continuously to their environment at a speed imposed by the environment which lead often real-time capabilities. Low power and low cost are an inherent requirements for embedded systems. Reliability, robustness and safety constraints derive from situations where service continuation is impossible.

Flexible (time-to-market, personalized, online maintenance, online testing, etc.)
The time for the design and commercialization of an embedded system have to be done considering that the users requirements that derive from general trends in society related to aspects like individualization, globalization, mobility, fashion, etc., are always changing. Increasing individualization leads to more diversity in products and services, and therefore to the need for more flexibility in design. Growing needs for continuous service utilization and provision leads to online maintenance and testing. Moreover, exponential size increase continues in the embedded systems.

Communicative (networked, connected, sensors and actuators, etc.) Most of the current embedded systems are connected through a network and it is expected that in the future Internet plays also an important role. Sensors and actuators are also inherent components of embedded systems.

2.2. Technology Requirements

The increasing heterogeneity in software and hardware will require to shift to open standards. For example, Linux, an open-source operating system is garnering acceptance in the embedded world, multipurpose microprocessors are more likely to be used, etc.

In contrast with interactive systems that respond to external stimuli when they are ready with calculating their response at their own pace, embedded systems reactivity imposes often real-time capabilities. This results in special requirements for the hardware and software architecture of the platform to be used in which more decentralized control is required. Reliability, robustness and safety constraints derive from situations where service continuation is impossible and a certain degree of adaptive behavior, self-configuring and self-restoring should be possible.

The time-to-market (TIT) is one of the major requirements that embedding systems have to override by shortening it. Current hardware/software design and integration technologies must be developed in order to cope with such challenges. The individualization in the users preferences will force that the new embedded systems must be designed under the metrics of collaborative adaptive systems. The non-stop service utilization and provision will impose constraints on the design and implementation of embedded systems for supporting online maintenance and testing. Moreover, due to the gigantic size of the future systems, the design and implementation will be done on a step by step development considerations.

Since devices will become more and more connected in some kind of network, information management in the network will become a serious issue. Closely related to networking devices, they need to access information available in the network to do their job. While embedded systems nowadays access local data, in the future this data might be retrieved from elsewhere. Therefore, some technology that can envision Web-connectivity is required. Distributed and networked sensors and actuators will start to behave as intelligent agents. The complexity of these systems will increase and they will require increasing bandwidth for audio, video and wireless communication. Novel communication architectures and technologies will also be required.

3. Autonomous Decentralized System

3.1. ADS Concept

Autonomous Decentralized System (ADS) has been proposed to resolve the on-line property of on-line expansion, on-line maintenance and fault tolerance in a system, which means that the system can continue operation during partial expansion, maintenance and at the time of a partial fault [6]. The ADS is defined as the characteristics that each subsystem can control itself and coordinate with all of the other operating subsystems. Therefore the following two properties must be satisfied by each subsystem: Autonomous Controllability and Autonomous Coordinability.

3.2. ADS Architecture

Each subsystem has its own management system, the Autonomous Control Processor (ACP) to manage itself and coordinate with the others. The subsystem including its application software modules and ACP is an autonomous unit called "Atom". The self-contained subsystems including their respective ACPs are integrated into a system. In the ADS, all of the subsystems are connected only through the Data Field (DF); all data is broadcasted into the DF and the data itself logically circulates in the DF (see Fig. 1). The data moves around the application modules in the Atom and the DF in the Atom is called the Atom Data Field (ADF). In the DF, each data is attached with its "content code" which is uniquely defined with respect to the content of the data. To protect the operation of the subsystems from variation in the system, each subsystem broadcasts a message containing the content code instead of the receivers address. The application module is specified only by input and output content codes, and it is executed by the ACP only when all of the necessary data with the proper input content codes is received from the DF (Data-Driven Mechanism). The necessary content codes for the Atom are determined dependently on the application functions within it.

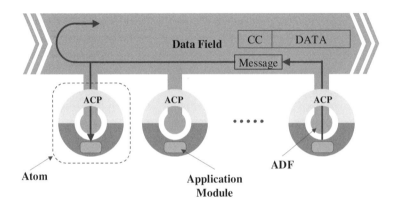

Figure 1. ADS Architecture.

4. Applications

4.1. SUICA

An embedded system which has successfully been developed and implemented utilizing ADS concept and architecture is the IC Card fare collection system (SUICA automatic fare collection gate systems), introduced by East Japan Railway Company in November 2001. This system is an integrated combination of fixed-line and wireless systems, where a contac/less IC card communicates by wireless with automatic fare collection devices (terminals) such as automatic fare collection gates machines (AFC gate machines), and the terminals communicate by fixed/line with center servers. The current number of card holders is approximately about 13 million and the number of transactions that are processed daily is in the order of 8 million which is expected to grow up to 30 million in a close future. In addition, the terminals and center servers are configured in autonomous decentralized architecture, so if trouble occurs, the trouble does not expand into the whole system. It is necessary for terminal AFC devices to provide high-speed processing and high-reliability because of the nature of railway transportation service. For these reasons, technologies and applications that can meet these requirements have been introduced.

4.1.1. Autonomous Decentralized IC Card System

In an IC card ticket system, the passengers go through gates with their IC cards in their hands. The transaction between and IC card and a terminal always depends on manual operations. At terminals each automatic fare collection device can execute autonomous high-speed processing communicating with IC cards in about 200ms. Also the data processed by terminals can be stored for a specific period, being connected in autonomous distribution architecture with center systems. Besides, the center system executes data processing autonomously to deal with the data from terminals that have been accumulated for a certain period of time. Moreover, the operation data for the terminals are received by the center server, so that any necessary measures can be taken on the center side. To enhance the reliability of the networked system as a whole, a style of accumulating a certain amount of data processed by terminal at each level was adopted. Finally, in order to secure the system expendability, the devices are configured in autonomous architecture so that it is easy to add different types of terminals, to connect with each other. See Fig. 2.

4.1.2. High Speed Data Processing Technology

When using IC cards, it is necessary to secure the security of their unique data, maintaining high speed processing. Suica cards are provided with respective keys for respective files, and R/Ws are provided with keys that enables simultaneous access to multiple files. Figure 3 shows the outline of the technology to process data at high-speed at the automatic fare gate for railway fare calculation. The passenger with a Suica commuter pass has to do is to pass this Suica card over the R/W at the ticket gate, and the necessary fare adjustment is automatically carried out. Since long time is necessary for complicated calculations, a technology that adapt to the particular users situation by a "before" and "after" calculation is proposed.

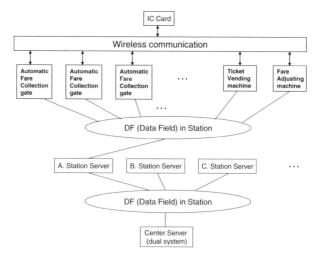

Figure 2. Autonomous decentralized IC card system.

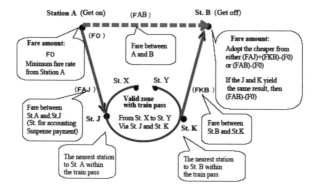

Figure 3. High speed data processing.

4.1.3. Autonomous Decentralized Processing Consistency Technology

The Suica system is composed of different kind of devices. Suica cards can be purchased from Suica automatic ticket vending machines. Stored fare (SF) value can be added to the Suica card with the fare-charging machine. Magnetized cards and tickets can be used at stations equipped with AFC gates in the same way as with the Suica card. Simplified AFC machines accepting only the Suica cards are installed at stations having no AFC gates. A technology is introduced with which each of the Suica cards is assigned a unique ID number, and all usage records are compiled in the Suica center server using the ID numbers through the installed network for control when the Suica cards are used. With the introduction of the technology, information for all IC cards can be consolidated into one information source for reliable and unified control of the IC card usage data by each card and for monitoring the unauthorized use of the IC cards.

4.2. Mobile Network Platform for ITS

The services of Intelligent Transport System (ITS), such as vehicle information and communication systems (VICS) and electronic toll collection (ETC), are typical applications of distributed embedded systems. The rapid growth of the Internet in recent years is driving the development of network services on a global scale. Amid these trends, the future progress of the vehicular society depends on further enhancing the ease-of-use of motor vehicles by providing Internet services to the people in the cars. The key to realizing these ends is the establishment of an ITS mobile network capable of handling motor vehicles as mobile terminals. The development is underway as a national project of Japan called the "Smart Gateway".

4.2.1. System Structure

The Smart Gateway system delivers information to the terminals in cars through radio base stations installed on the roadside (see Fig. 4). The Dedicated Short Range Communication (DSRC) method is used to deliver information to cars that are moving quickly through service areas consisting of microcells each having a 30m communication zone. The information delivered includes information to support safe driving such as traffic conditions as well as a variety of content-rich multimedia including Internet images and video [8].

The mobile network platform consists of a number of autonomous base stations (ABS). Based on the ADS architecture, each ABS is equipped with a Datafield Manager (DM), which handles message transmission to and from other ABSs via the network.

4.2.2. Autonomous Community Technology

Each ABS autonomously and dynamically forms a local community with other ABSs based on their physical locations and the kind of service to be provided to a mobile terminal (MT) without relying on the direction of others. For example, when an accident happened, the nearest ABS will dynamically form a community to forward this information to other ABSs. The size of the community is autonomously decided by each ABS according to the serious level of the accident.

Each ABS in a community shares the service progress and caches service content for an MT, and then autonomously provide services to an MT by recognizing its identifier and judging what kind of services to provide. This architecture ensures flexibility and high operating performance. The ABSs can be added and replaced gradually while the system is in operation. And when an ABS cannot transmit effectively to an MT be-

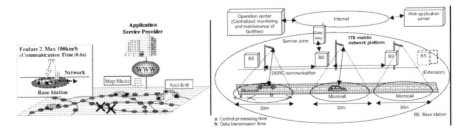

Figure 4. Mobile Network Platform for ITS.

cause of a communication failure, other ABSs can be able to continue the service. Moreover, the autonomous community technology ensures high-quality delivery and provides priority control among services. If some ABSs belong to several groups, they dynamically control the priority levels of services and deliver services to an MT based on these priority levels.

This model has been implemented in the DSRC base stations set up along a road and experimental trials are underway. Each base station consists of a DSRC board, and a compact PCI bus, and connects to the MT of a vehicle through DSRC wireless communication. A target board is also connected to an IEEE 802.3 network that is used to represent the roadside network. The CPU of the target board is an SH4 (200 MHz) processor and the real-time operating system (OS) is VxWorks 5.1.3.

5. Conclusions

Under the recent severe economic situation, the business in the various fields has been changing to produce new products and to supply new services. Moreover the life-cycle of these products and services have been getting short. As the technological trends, the openness and the down-sizing phenomena have been in progress, and the system is constructed by the multi-vender's machines.

The ADS concept is explained under the backgrounds not for the resource utilization, but for the easy-to-use and the easy-to-construct of the computing and controlling systems. This architecture shows that there exists no master and no direction among subsystems, and then the software productivity is much improved by building block manner of autonomous software modules. Moreover the applications in the distributed embedded systems of the ADS is described and its validity has been verified.

References

[1] B.P. Dave, G. Lakshminarayana, N.K. Jha: COSYN: Hardware-software co-synthesis of heterogeneous distributed embedded systems, *IEEE Transactions on Very Large Scale Integration (VLSI) Systems*, **vol. 7, no. 1**, (1999), 92–104.
[2] J. Liu, P.H. Chou: Distributed Embedded Systems for Low Power: a case study, *IEEE Proc. of Parallel and Distributed Processing Symposium*, April 2004.
[3] K. Mori et al.: Proposition of Autonomous Decentralized Concept, *Trans. IEE of Japan* **vol. 104C, no. 12**, (1984), 303–340.
[4] L.D.J. Eggermont et al.: Embedded Systems, *Vision on technology for the future PROGRESS*, Ludwig D.J. Eggermont edit., 2002.
[5] N. Subramanian and L. Chung: Architecture-Driven Embedded Systems Adaptation for Supporting Vocabulary Evolution, *IEEE Proc. of Principles of Software Evolution*, November 2000, 144–153.
[6] K. Mori: Autonomous Decentralized Systems: Concept, Data Field Architecture and Future Trends, *Proc. of ISADS'93*, Kawasaki, Japan, 1993.
[7] A. Shiibashi: Autonomous decentralized high-speed processing technology and the application in an integrated IC card fixed-line and wireless system, *Proc. ISADS'05*, Chengdu, China, April 2005.
[8] M. Hiraiwa, T. Aizono, A. Shimura: Implementation and Evaluation of Autonomous Decentralized System Based Mobile Communications for ITS Services, *Proc. of ISADS'03*, Pisa, Italy, 2003.

Security and Embedded Systems
D.N. Serpanos and R. Giladi (Eds.)
IOS Press, 2006

Vulnerabilities and Countermeasures for Embedded Processors

Shengqi YANG[a], Wayne WOLF[a], N. VIJAYKRISHNAN[b], Yuan XIE[b]
and Dimitrios SERPANOS[c]

[a]*Electrical Engineering Department, Princeton University, USA*
[b]*Computer Science and Engineering Department, Penn State University, USA*
[c]*Electrical and Computer Engineering Department, Patras University, Greece*

Abstract. In this paper, we presented vulnerabilities and countermeasures for embedded processors. Among all kinds of vulnerabilities and external attacks, we are most interested in power attacks, which infer program behavior from observing power supply current into an embedded processor core, are important forms of security attacks. In this work, we addressed a novel approach against the power attacks, i.e., Dynamic Voltage and Frequency Switching (DVFS). Results showed that this method hides processor state with 27% energy reduction and 16% time overhead for DES encryption and decryption algorithms. Furthermore, system leakage power, as an obstacle to power attacks in the future technology, was studied. Results showed that leakage power scaling makes the power analysis really difficult to be carried out and leaves crypto embedded processors secure without any kind of overheads.

1. Introduction

Computer system security is widely viewed as an important problem. Because computers are used to control infrastructure — electrical generation and transmission, transportation, etc. — and safety-critical equipment, many calls have been made to improve the security of computer systems built as part of these larger systems. But does embedded system security merely mean applying standard computer security measures to embedded processors?

In fact, embedded computers perform different tasks than general-purpose hardware and software are called upon to perform. As a result, embedded processors are exposed to new, different security risks and we must develop new techniques to guard against the threats that can be raised against embedded computers. While we may need to use most or all of the security techniques developed for general-purpose computing in order to safeguard embedded processors, embedded computers also need new security measures.

Embedded computers almost always perform real-time tasks. Real-time computing requires meeting deadlines — if a computation is not finished by the deadline, then the system fails. Not all real-time systems are safety-critical — a digital television, for example, must repaint the screen to meet the frame deadline. But the imposition of an external deadline makes embedded computing very different from traditional computing. Embedded computers must also operate on strict power budgets. All branches of computing must now pay attention to energy consumption, but embedded computers often operate under particularly strict energy and power consumption constraints. Finally, the hardware and software in embedded computing systems must be designed to simultaneously satisfy real-time, energy, and cost constraints, as well as the functional requirements. Traditional software design methodologies try to separate functional and non-functional requirements as much as possible, but embedded computing designers do not have that luxury.

There are, in fact, many systems that straddle the boundary between embedded and non-embedded computing. The personal digital assistant (PDA) provides a simple example: its user interface requires strict real-time programming, but its calendar and address applications are simple, 1960's-style databases. Industrial computers often perform real-time control when they interface to equipment, but also perform traditional client-server operations like inventory database management. As a result, embedded computers face some of the security problems of client-server systems, but client-server systems may also be infected with some of the vulnerabilities of real-time embedded systems.

As we will see in the remainder of this chapter, embedded computers are vulnerable to many types of threats relating to real-time operation and power consumption. These threats exist in isolated, non-networked systems. But connections to the Internet or dial-up connections make embedded computers much more vulnerable because they can be threatened by someone who does not have physical access to the equipment. Many computers that control infrastructure are already connected to the Internet or to dial-up connections. An increasing number of personal infrastructure items — cars, home appliances, etc. — also sport Internet connections. Network interfaces provide valuable features and services, but they also pose new threats and allow for coordinated attacks that greatly raise the stakes of embedded systems security.

2. Type of Threads

Wood and Stankovic [1] identified a number of possible attacks against sensor networks. They noted that some attacks are similar to those used in general-purpose networks while other attacks take advantage of the unique characteristics of sensor networks. They identified attacks at the major levels of network behavior: physical, link, network and routing, and transport. We cannot do justice to their analysis here, but we can give a few examples.

Radio networks are vulnerable to jamming attacks. It is relatively easy for an attacker to emit a jamming signal, but modern modulation methods like spread spectrum are less vulnerable to jamming. At the link layer, malicious collisions can be used to slow down a network. Attackers can also exhaust available bandwidth, which can be countered by rate limitations and reservations. At the network layer, geographically-biased routing and allocation schemes are vulnerable to homing attacks. Many sensor network systems take advantage of geographic knowledge to guide routing and distribute resources around the network. An attacker can watch traffic to learn the location of critical resources, then attack those critical nodes. Cryptography helps to hide the information needed for an attacker to home into critical resources.

Given that embedded computing systems operate in real-time and at low power levels, we expect two categories of attacks to be particularly important: **time-based attacks** and **energy-based attacks**.

In addition, we can expect new types of **physical proximity attacks** based on the adversary's ability to physically manipulate the computer.

We can identify several examples of each category of attack.

Time-based attacks on embedded computing systems can exploit the fact that the systems are sensitive to missed deadlines. A denial-of-service attack in a general-purpose system seeks to totally consume the target machine's computational capabilities. In a real-time embedded system, in contrast, we only have to disturb the timing enough to cause the system to miss a deadline. We call such an attack a **quality-of-service (QoS)** attack.

A QoS attack can aim at either the processor or at the network. As an example, consider automobile engine controllers. Automobiles have used embedded microprocessors to control their engines since 1980. Engine controllers perform sophisticated computations, such as Kalman filtering, to control the engine's spark and fuel. Without embedded engine controllers, automobiles could not meet today's fuel-efficiency and emissions requirements. In an automobile, for example, a network connects most of the electronic components; typical automobile networks have at least 50 nodes and some may have well over 100.

An engine controller could be attacked to cause it to miss deadlines for the spark or fuel control. Alternatively, one node on the car's network could be hijacked to either disturb the network timing itself or to attack another node on the network.

Automobile enthusiasts have hacked engine controller software since the earliest days of embedded engine controllers. These enthusiasts are primarily interested in improving the performance of their cars, usually at the expense of emissions standards. Such hacking may be illegal, since it violates emission standards, but it does not pose a serious safety threat to large numbers of people.

However, once cars are accessible from the Internet, engine controller hacking poses a serious threat. The hacker no longer is threatened by physical harm due to the consequences of the hack; the hacker may in fact want to inflict harm on others. Consider, for example, an engine controller virus that shut down all infected cars at the same time, such as rush hour. Such a virus would cause a huge number of accidents; it is arguably more dangerous if not all of the cars on the road suffer from the virus. Even the random hacking of cars by teenagers poses a serious threat to safety.

Energy-related attacks can take several forms. As Phil Koopman of CMU points out, many devices have batteries that operate certain portions of the electronics. Those batteries are designed to last for long periods of infrequent use, but an attacker could drain the battery prematurely.

Energy attacks can also manipulate power management utilities. Power management layers like ACPI provide software hooks to manage CPU and system power consumption. Power consumption is controlled by slowing down or turning off parts of the system. Power management can be used to attack the real-time characteristics of a system. Power management interfaces can also be used to burn excess energy by repeatedly turning components on and off.

Physical proximity attacks are not unknown in general-purpose computing, but servers generally rely on physical security as part of their protection. Embedded computers, unfortunately, cannot be totally isolated from their users. Steps can be taken to make it difficult for an adversary to obtain access to an embedded computer, but we cannot rely on such steps being totally effective.

A proximity attack can observe the computer, manipulate the computer, or both. Observing the computer may be sufficient to obtain cryptographic keys or simply to find vulnerable spots in the computer system's design. The attacker may not need physical proximity to make use of the information gleaned during observations. Manipulating the computer may cause it to use new data, run new programs, or to communicate with other computers in malicious ways.

A proximity attack may be aimed at the computer being observed. But the goal of an attacker may be to obtain design information that he/she can use to attack other nodes. These reverse-engineering attacks are common, for example, in satellite TV systems and we can expect them to occur in other industries as well.

In this work, we are most interested in protection of embedded processors against one popular and powerful attack, i.e., power attacks [2], which are considered as a fundamental class of attacks that are practically quite difficult to defend against. Simple Power Analysis (SPA) is based on measuring and analyzing power traces during cryptographic computations. Basically by using inspection, the attacker analyzes the trace and identifies executed instructions. Differential Power Analysis (DPA) is currently the most popular high order power analysis. This scheme utilizes power traces gathered from several runs and relies on the power consumption variation due to data dependency to break the key.

Various countermeasures against power attacks have been proposed to remove the symptoms that make a cryptoprocessor vulnerable to monitoring and analysis of side-channel information. The proposed defenses, for example, reduction of signal sizes [2] and introduction of noise to signals [3], mainly try to make it more difficult to measure. These techniques either make the sample size for the analysis significantly large, or try to break the ability of the attacker to correlate information which is used for statistical analysis to work. Most of the previously proposed circuit techniques impose significantly energy and hardware area costs. For instance, Ratanpal et al. [4] hide processor behavior by burning excess power.

In this work, we propose using Dynamic Voltage and Frequency Switching (DVFS) against all kinds of power attacks. Furthermore, leakage power consumption of a system as an obstacle for power attacks is studied as shown in Section 3.

3. Countermeasures Against Power Attacks

3.1. DVFS Against Power Attacks

Our novel power attack resistant DVFS cryptosystem, as shown in Fig. 1, is composed of processor core, DVFS feedback loop, and DVFS scheduler. The DVFS feedback loop [5] takes the value of desired Voltage/Frequency (V/F) as an object, which is stored in an internal register by the DVFS scheduler. DVFS feedback loop physically implements the desired supply voltage and operating frequency by using circuits such as ring oscillator, phase locked loop, etc, and finally outputs the supply voltage to the cryptoprocessor core. The DVFS scheduler unit randomly generates a voltage or frequency (V/F) value under certain limits and stores it in the register. This unit requires some timing information about the application program from the Operating System (OS), for example, the desired running time. In this work, we focus our attention on the microarchitecture of the DVFS scheduler unit.

In order to quantitatively measure the efficiency of our DVFS technique against power attacks, we define three metrics: Signal Trace Entropy (STE), Energy Overhead (EO) and Time Overhead (TO). STE measures the uncertainty of the signal trace moni-

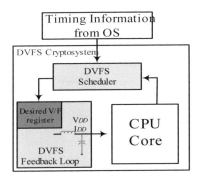

Figure 1. DVFS cryptosystem.

tored by the attacker over time. To calculate STE, we bin the signal values in a signal trace into equally N spaced containers, and count the number of signal values in each container, n_i. Then STE can be expressed as Eq. (1). Specifically in this work, we use Power Trace Entropy (PTE) and Time Trace Entropy (TTE) to represent the uncertainty of the power traces and the clock period traces, respectively. The power trace measures the power consumption for each clock cycle during the algorithm execution; while time trace gives the clock period for each clock cycle. For EO and TO, they measure the energy overhead and time overhead caused by using DVFS. We define *Vdd_normal* and *Fnormal* as the normal supply voltage and the normal operating frequency for the cryptoprocessor without DVFS. In general, they are the highest supply voltage and frequency. When the supply voltage is switched to a lower value *Vdd_scale*, the operating frequency *fscale* is scaled according to Eq. (2) where *Vth* represents threshold voltage. Finally, EO and TO can be expressed as Eqs. (3) and (4), respectively, where *TNCC* is the total number of clock cycles, and *Ci* is the capacitive load for *ith* clock cycle. For this work, we implement the DES encryption and decryption algorithms in software as benchmarks, and capture their energy consumption at each clock cycle when running on the processor core by using a customized version of the publicly available SimplePower [6].

$$ STE = -\sum_{i=1}^{N} \left(\frac{n_i}{\sum_{j=1}^{N} n_i} \log 2 \frac{n_i}{\sum_{j=1}^{N} n_i} \right) \tag{1}$$

$$ f_{scale} = \frac{(v_{dd\_scale} - V_{th})^{1.3}}{v_{dd\_scale}} F_{normal} \tag{2}$$

$$ EO = \sum_{i=1}^{TNCC} \frac{1}{2} C_i (v_{dd\_scale}^2 - V_{dd\_normal}^2) \tag{3}$$

$$ TO = \sum_{i=1}^{TNCC} \left(\frac{1}{f_{scale}} - \frac{1}{F_{normal}} \right) \tag{4}$$

DVFS scheduler algorithm
Input   : V_{dd_normal} , F_{normal}, TB, ETCC,   Signal_Done, RW_Enable **Output**   : V_{dd_scale}/f_{scale}
Algorithm : 1: *time_1*= **clock**() 2: generate random V_{dd_scale}/f_{scale} by using V_{dd_normal} , F_{normal} 3: assign V_{dd_scale}/f_{scale} to register in DVFSFL 4: initialize *timing, timing_space* to *zero* 5: determine High_limit_WT 6: **While** Signal_Done != 1 **Do** 7:   *time_3*=**clock**() 8:   generate a random number NCC < High_limit_WT 9:   **for** i=1:1:NCC 10:   NOP 11: **end for** 12: *time_2*= **clock**(); 13: *timing*= (*time_2-time_1*)/clocks_per_second_DVFSS 14: *timing_space* += *timing_space* 15: use *timing, timing_space*, TB, ETCC to determine the   lowest value of V_{dd_scale}/f_{scale}, 16: generate random V_{dd_scale}/f_{scale} > the lowest value 17: **if** RW_Enable==1 18:   assign V_{dd_scale}/f_{scale} to register in DVFSFL 19: **end if** 20: *time_4*=**clock**() 21: *timing_space*=(*time_4-time_3*) 22:**End While**

Figure 2. Implementation of DVFS scheduler unit. [7] (© [2005] IEEE).

The algorithm of the DVFS scheduler unit is shown in Fig. 2 [7]. The procedure takes *Vdd_normal*, *Fnormal*, *Signal_Done* and *RW_Enable* as inputs; the first two signals come from the OS and give initial values for the DVFS scheduler; the third signal is from the processor core which indicates whether the encryption/decryption finishes; and the fourth signal is sent out from DVFS feedback loop to reveal the status of the internal register which stores the desired voltage/frequency value. *TB* and *ETCC*, are input to the DVFS scheduler unit from the OS. Signals *TB* and *ETCC* are estimations of the timing budget and the total clock cycles for the application program when running on the processor core. Both of them can be generated by the OS after the application program is compiled.

For the DVFS scheduler unit, it first generates a random V_{dd_scale} or *fscale* and stores it in the register for the processor core using it to run the program. After that, it initializes and determines the *High_limit_WT*, which represents the high limit of the waiting time. This limit prevents the DVFS scheduler unit from a long random waiting time. For convenience, this waiting time limit can be calculated by the OS and input to the DVFS scheduler unit. Here we assign it a constant number. During the program running in the processor core, the DVFS scheduler unit iteratively generates random voltage/frequency values. In each iteration, it firstly waits a random time limited by *High_limit_WT*, then calculates some timing information, determines the lowest value (*LV*) for the next voltage/frequency generation, and produces a random voltage/frequency which is not lower than the *LV*. As a final step, it outputs the voltage/frequency value to the register. Variables *timing* and *timing_space* count the total elapsed time and the time elapsed for one iteration, respectively. They are used to calculate the *LV*.

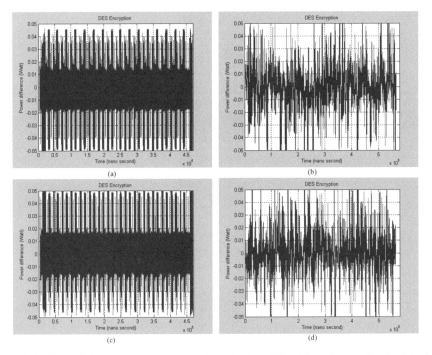

Figure 3. Difference between power traces generated using two different keys (vary in the first bit of the key) before using DVFS (a) and after using DVFS scheduler (b); Difference between power traces generated using two different plaintext (vary in the 10th bit of the plaintext) before using DVFS (c) and after using DVFS scheduler (d). [7] (© [2005] IEEE).

The primary goal of our DVFS-based scheme is hiding information. As a side benefit, our method consumes negligible amounts of energy. It does, however, introduce a modest performance penalty because it scales the operation frequency down at some time period. In order to reduce it, the DVFS scheduler unit first calculate the lower bound, i.e. LV, and then generates the suitable voltage/frequency. Eq. (5) shows how to calculate the lower bound for the scaled frequency. And the corresponding scaled supply voltage can be calculated by Eq. (2).

$$LV = \frac{(ETCC - \sum_i ti\min g\_space/f_{scale}(i-1))}{TB - (ti\min g + \Delta)} \tag{5}$$

where $f_{scale}(i-1)$ represents the scaled frequency randomly generated in the $(i-1)th$ iteration. The summation is done over the number of iterations and calculates the total time elapsed. Δ is an estimation of the time spent for steps from 16 to 21. The numerator gives the total clock cycles needed to finish the remainder workload, while the denominator gives the total time left for the application program to meet its deadline according to the time budget. Finally, this equation gives the lowest frequency for the processor to finish the application. The DVFS scheduler unit uses this number as a lower bound and generates a random frequency number which is higher than the bound.

Figure 3 compares two differential power traces generated by using two different keys and the same plaintext before using DVFS (Fig. 3 (a)) and after using DVFS

Table 1. Achieved performance for DES encryption and decryption by using DVFS scheduler.

DES	EO	TO	PTE	TTE
Encryption	−27.32%	16.15%	5.42%	6.02%
Decryption	−26.89%	16.01%	5.44%	6.05%

Table 2. Performance gain of DVFS cryptosystem over normal cryptosystem without DVFS.

Normal Cryptosystem	Energy	Time	PTE	TTE
DVFS Cryptosystem	−27%	16%	7.5%	∞%

scheduler (Fig. 3 (b)). And it illustrates the difference between two differential power traces generated by using two different plaintexts and the same key before using DVFS (Fig. 3 (c)) and after using our DVFS scheduler (Fig. 3 (d)). For Figs 3 (a) and (b), the secret keys vary in the first bit; while for Figs 3 (c) and (d) the Plaintexts vary in the tenth bit. These bit variations are randomly selected, and same profiles can be observed for other choices. Figures 3 (a) and (c) demonstrate that without DVFS significant information is leaked by using different key bits or different plaintext bits to run the algorithms and doing time correlation. When the DVFS scheduler is used, this information leakage is prevented as shown in Figs 3 (b) and (d).

Two factors contribute to this desirable property of our cryptosystem. (1) When the encryption/decryption program runs in our cryptosystem for the first time, operation A is executed at time t; while it is executed at time $(t+\Delta t)$ when the program runs again. Δt represents a time shift with positive or negative value. With high probability, it is not equal to zero. As a result, at a fixed time point for many power traces which are achieved by using different plaintexts or keys, different operations are carried out in the processor core. This makes time correlation, which is a very important step in power attacks, impossible. (2) Even if the same operation is executed at time t, the supply voltages for different runs may be different with much probability. This makes the power values at time t for different traces unequal and results in a random number for DPA bias signals. All the two aspects efficiently prevent the cryptosystem from the power attacks, such as SPA and DPA.

To test and quantify the efficiency of our cryptosystem against power attacks, DES encryption and decryption algorithms were run in this cryptosystem for one thousand times. Table 1 shows the energy overhead, time overhead, power trace entropy and time trace entropy for DES encryption and decryption algorithms. By adjusting the lowest value for $vdd\_scale/fscale$ in the algorithm to be a higher value, we can further reduce the time overhead. Experiments show that the TO range for encryption and decryption is about 17% to 5%.

Finally, we compare the performance of our DVFS cryptosystem and the cryptosystem without DVFS by using DES algorithm as a benchmark and summarize it in Table 2. As we can see, our novel cryptosystem obtains 27% energy reduction, 7.5% increase in power trace entroy, and ∞% increase in time trace entroy, with a timing overhead of 16%, compared with the cryptosystem without DVFS.

3.2. A Further Understanding of Chip Power

The power consumed by a silicon chip consists of not only dynamic power but also leakage power. Leakage power consumption is becoming more and more significant and comparable to dynamic power in the future technologies. However, dynamic power

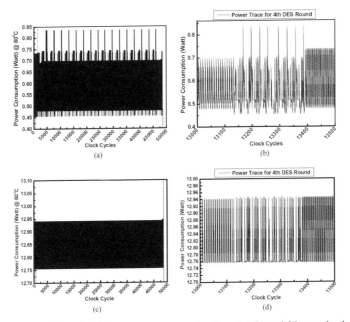

Figure 4. Power traces for embedded cryptoprocessor under 90nm (a) (b) and 25nm technologies (c) (d). (b) and (d) are partial power traces of the 4th DES encryption round.

is the only useful information for a power attacker in order to guess which operation is executed in the processor core. When the power attacker measures the power traces, it is impossible to separate the dynamic power from the leakage power which holds an almost random pattern and is really difficult to be filtered out by doing differential analysis because of its strong dependence not only on processor operation, but on execution environment, like temperature. As a result, whenever the leakage power, which can be viewed as a random big noise to the power traces, is comparable to the dynamic power, the information carried and revealed only by dynamic power might be lost because of the overwhelming leakage power noise. According to predictions by Yang et al. [8,9], this scenario will appear around and under 65nm technologies in which leakage power is comparable to dynamic power.

Figure 4 illustrates the power traces for the cryptoprocessor using 90nm technology Fig. 4 (a) and 25nm technology Fig. 4 (c). Both traces are measured under *353K*, considering both dynamic power and all significant leakage components. Partial power traces for the *4th* DES encryption round are shown in Fig. 4 (b) for 90nm technology and Fig. 4 (d) for 25nm technology. Under 90nm technology, the information of DES rounds is clearly revealed by tracing the power consumption which is dominated by dynamic power, as shown in Figs 4 (a) and (b). In contrast, this information is efficiently masked under 25nm technology because of the dominance of leakage power consumption which makes the dynamic power immeasurable, as shown in Figs 4 (c) and (d).

In the sense of power attack prevention, a big leakage power consumption, which always should be reduced from the viewpoint of low power design, is not too bad for it hides some side-channel information.

4. Conclusion

In this paper, we analyzed the vulnerabilities and countermeasures for embedded processors and specifically we presented a design of novel power attack resistant cryptosystem, which uses dynamic voltage and frequency switching to make the power traces show random property and prevent the power attackers from doing time correlation between different power traces. In the final section, we pointed out that the increasing chip leakage power consumption can become a very good obstacle to power attackers.

References

[1] A.D. Wood and J.A. Stankovic, "Denial of service in sensor networks," IEEE Computer, pp. 54–62, Oct. 2002.
[2] P. Kocher, J. Jaffe, and B. Jun, "Differential Power Analysis," in Proc.19th Intl. Advances in Cryptology Conference-CRYPTO'99, Aug. 1999, pp. 388–397.
[3] L. Benini, et al., "Energy-Aware Design Techniques for Differential Power Analysis Protection", in Proc. Design Automation Conf., June 2003, pp. 36–41.
[4] G.B. Ratanpal, R.D. Williams, and T.N. Blalock, "An On-chip Signal Suppression Countermeasure to Power Analysis Attacks", IEEE Trans. Dependable and Secure Computing, vol. 1, no. 3, pp. 179–189, July 2004.
[5] K.J. Nowka, et al., "A 32-bit PowerPC System-on-a-Chip with Support for Dynamic Voltage Scaling and Dynamic Frequency Scaling", IEEE Jour. Solid-Sate Circuit, vol. 37, no. 11, pp. 1441–1447, 2002.
[6] N. Vijaykrishan, M. Kandemir, M.J. Irwin, H.S. Kim and W. Ye, "Energy-Driven Integrated Hardware-Software Optimizations Using SimplePower", in Proc. International Symposium on Computer Architecture, June 2002.
[7] S. Yang, W. Wolf, N. Vijaykrishnan and Y. Xie, "Power Attack Resistant Cryptosystem Design: A Dynamic Voltage and Frequency Switching Approach", in Proc. Design & Test Europe Conf., March 2005, pp. 64–69.
[8] S. Yang, W. Wolf, N. Vijaykrishnan, Y. Xie and W. Wang, "Accurate Stacking Effect Macro-Modelling of Leakage Power in Sub-100nm Circuits", January 2005, pp. 165–170.
[9] S. Yang, W. Wolf, N. Vijaykrishnan, and Y. Xie, "Low-Leakage Robust SRAM Cell Design for Sub-100nm Technologies", in Proc. IEEE Asia and South Pacific Design Automation Conference, January 2005.

Security and Embedded Systems
D.N. Serpanos and R. Giladi (Eds.)
IOS Press, 2006

Agent-Based Modeling and Simulation of Malefactors' Attacks Against Computer Networks

Igor KOTENKO[1], Mihail STEPASHKIN[1] and Alexander ULANOV[1]
SPIIRAS, Intelligent Systems Laboratory, Russia

Abstract. The paper analyses state of the art in modeling and simulation of attacks against computer networks and presents authors' experience in applying multi-agent technology for attack simulation. The suggested approach for attack simulation is realized via automatic imitation of distributed computer network attacks on different levels of detail. The paper describes three attack simulation tools: Agent-Based Attack Simulator, Active Vulnerability Assessment System and Agent-Based Simulator of Distributed Denial of Service (DDoS) Attacks.

Keywords. Agent-based modeling and simulation, active vulnerability assessment, computer network attacks, penetration testing

Introduction

The necessity of attack modeling and simulation has arisen since the moment of appearance of the first incidents of penetration of computers and computer networks. Using the knowledge obtained from the generalization and formalization of computer systems' vulnerabilities and cases of attacks could considerably improve the efficiency of existent protection mechanisms. This is a strong argument in favour of serious study and research of the essence and the particular features of malefactors' attacks against computer networks.

This research cannot only be restricted by the generalization of the experience; it also has to be based on formal models of attacks and attack simulation tools. These models and tools could be very valuable in the design of security systems which are capable of operating with high-level notions like "identification of an attack scenario", "attack development forecast", etc. Such capabilities could enable the system to suppress the development of an attack on-line before the irreversible consequences occur. Attack simulation tools could also play an important role in the validation of security systems and policies. Such tools could be used as testing equipment, thus cutting the costs of and decreasing the time necessary for security policy validation.

The goal of research described in the paper consists in *analysis and development of a general approach, mathematical models, ontologies and software tools intended for agent-based modeling and simulation of attacks and active analysis of computer network vulnerabilities*. We developed formal models and techniques for attack modeling

---

[1] St. Petersburg Institute for Informatics and Automation, 39, 14th Liniya, St. Petersburg, 199178, Russia; E-mails: ivkote@iias.spb.su, stepashkin@computer.edu.ru, ulanov@iias.spb.su.

Table 1. Main directions and contents of relevant works.

Research directions	Main works
(1) Attacks and attack taxonomies	Lists of attack terms [5,18]; Lists of attack categories [44]; Attack results categories [5]; Empirical lists of attack types [28]; Vulnerabilities matrices [27]; Security flaws or vulnerabilities taxonomies [25]; Taxonomies of intrusions based on the signatures [26]; Incident taxonomies [18], etc.
(2) Attack languages	CASL [2], NASL [10], CISL [13], IDMEF [8], BRO [42], Snort [46], SNP-L [55], STATL [12], GasSATA [34], LAMBDA [7], AdeLe [35], Alert correlation [40], etc.
(3) Network attack modeling and simulation	State transition analysis technique [19,21]; Simulating intrusions in sequential and parallelized forms [4]; Cause-effect model [6]; Conceptual models of computer penetration [52]; Descriptive models of the network and the attackers [56]; Structured "tree"-based description [36,48]; Modeling survivability of networked systems [37]; Contingency analysis based on variations in intruder attack-potential [32]; Object-oriented Discrete Event Simulation [3]; Requires/provides model for computer attacks [54]; Situation calculus and goal-directed procedure invocation [14]; Game-theoretic approaches [31]; Models of attack propagation in networks [39]; Attack graphs for vulnerability analysis [20,50,53]; Modeling and inference of attacker intent, objectives, and strategies [30]; Multi-stage attack analysis [9], etc.
(4) Evaluating security systems	Methodology and software tools for testing [1,33,43]; Evaluations of intrusion detection systems [29]; Real-time test bed [11]; Dependability models for evaluation security [38]; Penetration testing of formal models of networks for estimating security metrics [51]; Global metrics for analyzing the effects of complex network faults and attacks [17]; Knowledge-based approach to network risk assessment [49]; Model checking for analysis of network vulnerabilities [45]; *Natural-deduction* for automatic generation and analysis of attacks against intrusion detection systems [47], etc.

and simulation taking into account the malefactor's intentions, the level of their knowledge and experience, and scenarios of network attacks specified on the macro and micro levels.

The rest of the paper is structured as follows. *Section 1* reviews relevant works and outlines suggested common approach for modeling and simulation of attacks. *Section 2* describes the models and architecture implemented in Agent-Based Attack Simulator (ABAS). *Section 3* outlines the peculiarities of Active Vulnerability Assessment System (AVAS) based on main decisions realized in ABAS. *Section 4* presents the architecture of and experiments fulfilled with Agent-Based Simulator of DDoS Attacks (ABSDA). *Section 5* outlines the main results of the paper and future work directions.

1. State of the Art in Modeling and Simulation of Attacks

The research papers relevant to attack modeling and simulation can be divided into the following groups: (1) Attacks and attack taxonomies; (2) Attack languages; (3) Research immediately coupled with network attack modeling and simulation; (4) Evaluating security systems and policies, vulnerability assessment tools (scanners), signature and traffic generation tools, security metrics, etc. This list is not exhaustive. Main directions and contents of relevant works are depicted in Table 1.

We think that an adequate approach for the investigation of remote distributed attacks on computer networks that has not been analyzed in depth is *agent-based modeling and simulation*. Our approach has applied the results of reviewed relevant works, but is evolving own theoretical and practical ideas about using formal models and multi-agent technology. We try to apply the idea that particular components of attack simulation system must be represented as a distributed system of autonomous adaptive software entities interacting via message exchange and making decisions in a cooperative and coordinated manner [22]. So, from implementation issue, a computer network attack can be considered as a sequence of coordinated actions of the spatially distributed malefactors. Each malefactor is mapped as an intelligent agent of the same architecture possessing the similar functionality. We use the teamwork interpretation of the malefactors' activity performing distributed attacks on the basis of combination of the joint intention and shared plans theories [22,24].

The attack simulation system should be based on mechanism of automatic construction and replaying of distributed attacks scripts by combining known attacks fragments, taking into account the malefactor's intentions, his level of experience, and knowledge of computer network attacked. Functioning of the attack simulation system is specified by the *attack model* defined as hierarchical structure that consists of several levels. While describing the developed model of attacks, we defined main notions of attack generation that are formalized in the problem domain ontology *"Computer network attacks"* [16]. In the developed formal model, the basic notions of the domain correspond to malefactor's intentions and all other notions are structured according to the structure of intentions. This is a reason why the developed approach is referred to as *"intention-centric approach"*. Three higher levels of the attack model correspond to an attacks scriptset, a particular script and script stages. The *attack scenarios level* defines a set of general malefactor's intentions (high level intentions or goals). This level corresponds to realization of series of scenarios which can be implemented by a group of malefactors. The *script level* defines only one malefactor's intention. The set of *script stages* can contain the following elements: reconnaissance, implantation (initial access to a host), gaining privileges, threat realization, covering tracks, and backdoors creation. Lower levels serve for malefactor subgoals refinement. The lowest level describes the malefactor's low level actions directly executing different exploits.

At the design stage, the attack simulation system operates with the *model of analyzed computer network*. This model is based on design specifications. At the maintenance stage, the attack simulation system interacts with a real *computer network*. This approach can be used at different stages of computer network life cycle, including design and exploitation stages.

2. Agent-Based Attack Simulator

The Agent-Based Attack Simulator (ABAS) [16] is built as a multi-agent system that uses two classes of agents: the agent of the first class (*"Network Agent"*) simulates an attacked computer network and the second one (*"Hacker Agent"*) – a hacker performing attacks against the computer network.

The agents are implemented on the basis of the technology supported by *Multi-Agent System Development Kit* (MASDK) [15]. The agents use different parts of the application ontology that is designed by use of the MASDK editor. The interaction between agents is supported by the communication component. While simulating an attack Hacker Agent sends a certain message to Network Agent. Network Agent analyzes the received message and forms a responsive message. This message is formed based on the Network Agent's knowledge base that represents the network configuration, information about possible existing attacks and reaction of the network on them.

The *behaviors of the agents* specified on the basis of state-machine models, which are interpretations of behavior specified formally by use of formal grammar framework. Hacker Agent acts on the basis of nested state machines. The state machine model of Network Agent is represented by a single state machine.

The main objective of the *experiments with the prototype of ABAS* was to evaluate the tool's efficiency for simulation of different attacks. We have investigated the prototypes possibilities for realization of two tasks: (1) checking a security policy at stages of design of network security system. This task is solved by simulation of attacks at a macro-level and research of responding a network model being designed; (2) checking security policy (including vulnerabilities recognition) of a real-life computer network. This task is fulfilled by means of simulation of attacks at a micro-level, i.e. by generating a network traffic corresponding to real activity of malefactors. These experiments were carried out for various parameters of the attack task specification and an attacked computer network configuration.

3. Active Vulnerability Assessment System

The main objective of the Active Vulnerability Assessment System (AVAS) consists in finding the vulnerabilities, calculating the security metrics and determining the security level of computer network and its components [23]. *The architecture of each vulnerability assessment component of AVAS* contains the following modules: user interface; module of malefactor's model implementation; module of attack scenarios generation; module of scenario execution; data and knowledge repository; module of data and knowledge repository updating; module of security level assessment; report generation module; network interface.

The module of malefactor's model realization determines a malefactor's skill level, a mode of actions and an attack goal. *The data and knowledge repository* consists of a knowledge base (KB) about analyzed system, a KB of operation rules, and a database (DB) of attack tools (exploits). This repository contains data and knowledge which are as a rule used by malefactor when he is planning and realizing attacks. *The knowledge base about analyzed system* includes data about the architecture and particular parameters of computer network (for example, a type and a version of OS, a list of opened ports, etc) which are needed for scripts generation and attack execution. This data usually can be received by malefactor using reconnaissance actions and methods of social engineering. *The database of operation rules* contains meta- and low- level rules of "IF-THEN" type determining AVAS operation on different levels of detail. Meta-level rules define attack scenarios on higher levels. Low level rules specify attack actions based on external vulnerability database. IF-part of each rule contains (meta-) action goal and (or) condition parts. The goal is chosen in accordance with a scenario type, an attack intention and a higher level goal (specified in a meta-rule of higher level). The condition is compared with the data from database about analyzed system. THEN-part contains the name of attack action which can be applied and (or) the link on exploit. Each rule is marked with an identifier which allows us to determine the achieved malefactor's goal. *The DB of attack tools (exploits)* contains exploits and parameters of their execution. A choice of a parameter is determined by the data in KB about analyzed system. For example, the program of ftp brute force password cracking needs to know the ftp server port which can be determined by port scanning.

The module of attack scenarios generation selects the data about analyzed system from the data and knowledge repository, generates attack scriptset based on using operation (functionality) rules, monitors scriptset execution and scriptset updating at runtime, updates data about analyzed system. *The module of scenario execution* selects an attack action and exploits, prognoses a possible feedback from analyzed computer network, launches the exploit and recognizes a response of analyzed computer network.

Network interface provides: (1) in case of operation with the model of analyzed system – transferring identifiers and parameters of attacks (or network packets under more detailed modeling and simulation), and also receiving attacks results and system reactions; (2) in case of interaction with a computer network – transferring, capturing and the preliminary analysis of network traffic. The preliminary analysis includes: (1) parsing of packets according to connections and delivery of information about packets (including data on exposed flags, payload, etc.) and connections; (2) acquisition of data about attack results and system reactions, and also values of some statistics reflecting actions of AVAS at the level of network packets and connections.

The module of security level assessment is based on developed taxonomy of security metrics. It is a main module which calculates security metrics based on results of attack actions. Examples of security metrics are number of total and successful attack scenarios, number of total and successful malefactor attacks on the certain level of taxonomy hierarchy, number of attacks blocked by existing security facilities, number of discovered and used vulnerabilities, number of successful scenario implementation steps, total score of confidentiality and criticality of assets that have been successfully attacked, number of confidential and critical assets that have been successfully attacked, etc.

The module of database and knowledge repository update downloads the open vulnerability databases and translates them into KB of operation rules of low level.

The AVAS prototype was implemented and the experiments were held based on the case-study developed.

4. Agent-Based Simulator of DDoS Attacks

The Agent-Based Simulator of DDoS Attacks (ABSDA) [22,24] is developed for *modeling and simulation of a wide spectrum of DDoS attacks and defense mechanisms* based on agents' teamwork formalism. In our approach it is offered that the agents' teamwork is organized by the team plan of the agents' actions. The mechanisms of the agents' interaction and coordination are based on three groups of procedures: (1) Coordination of the agents' actions (for coordinated initialization and termination of a common scenario); (2) Monitoring and restoring the agents' functionality; (3) Communication selectivity support (for choice of the most "useful" communications).

The prototype of ABSDA was developed by using the OmnetPP INET Framework [41] and C++. One of network fragments used for simulation is depicted in Fig. 1.

On the initial phase of simulation the attack and defense teams are created. The attack team contains several agents of class "daemon" and one agent of class "master". The defense team consists of four agents ("sensor", "detector", "filter" and "investigator"). The host under defense is "d_srv". Attack team tries to fulfill the DDoS attack, and defense team protects the attacked host. ABSDA allows imitating different classes of DDoS attacks and defense mechanisms. Experiments with the prototype have been

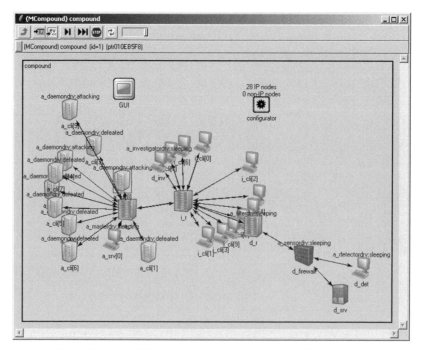

Figure 1. Example of the structure of computer network used for simulation.

conducted, including the investigation of attack scenarios against networks with different structures and security policies.

5. Conclusion

In the paper we described basic ideas of the agent-based modeling and simulation of network attacks. We developed the approach to be used for conducting experiments to analyze the efficiency and effectiveness of security policy against different network attacks. Software prototypes were developed. They allow imitating a wide spectrum of real life attacks. Experiments with the prototypes ware conducted, including the investigation of attack scenarios against networks with different security policies.

The further development of our modeling and simulation framework and software tools will consist of improving capabilities of the attack agents by expansion of the attack classes, implementing more sophisticated attack scenarios, and providing comprehensive experimental assessment of offered approach. Our future theoretical work is directed on development of formal basis for agent-based modeling and simulation of counteraction between attack and defense teams in the Internet.

Acknowledgement

This research is being supported by grant of Russian Foundation of Basic Research (№ 04-01-00167), grant of the Department for Informational Technologies and Computation Systems of the Russian Academy of Sciences (contract № 3.2/03) and partly funded by the EC as part of the POSITIF project (contract IST-2002-002314).

References

[1] D. Alessandri, C. Cachin, M. Dacier, etc., Towards a taxonomy of intrusion detection systems and attacks, *MAFTIA deliverable D3, Version 1.01, Project IST-1999-11583.* (2001).

[2] Custom attack simulation language (CASL), Secure Networks. (1998).

[3] S.-D. Chi, J.S. Park, K.-C. Jung, J.-S. Lee, Network security modeling and cyber attack simulation methodology, *ACISP 2001, Lecture Notes in Computer Science, Vol. 2119.* (2001).

[4] M. Chung, B. Mukherjee, R.A. Olsson, N. Puketza, Simulating concurrent intrusions for testing intrusion detection systems: parallelizing intrusions. *Proceedings of the 18th NISSC.* (1995).

[5] F.B. Cohen, Information system attacks: a preliminary classification scheme, *Computers and Security, Vol. 16, No. 1.* (1997).

[6] F. Cohen. Simulating cyber attacks, defenses, and consequences, *IEEE Symposium on Security and Privacy, Berkeley, CA.* (1999).

[7] F. Cuppens and R. Ortalo, Lambda: A language to model a database for detection of attacks, *Proceedings of RAID'2000.* (2000).

[8] D. Curry, Intrusion detection message exchange format, extensible markup language (xml) document type definition. *draft-ietf-idwg-idmef-xml-02.txt.* (2000).

[9] J. Dawkins, J. Hale, A Systematic approach to multi-stage network attack analysis, *Proceedings of the Second IEEE International Information Assurance Workshop (IWIA'04).* (2004).

[10] R. Deraison, The nessus attack scripting language reference guide, *http://www.nessus.org.* (1999).

[11] R. Durst, T. Champion, B. Witten, E. Miller, L. Spanguolo, Testing and evaluating computer intrusion detection systems, *Communications of ACM, 42(7).* (1999).

[12] S.T. Eckmann, G. Vigna, R.A. Kemmerer, STATL: An attack language for state-based intrusion detection, *Proceedings of the ACM Workshop on Intrusion Detection.* (2000).

[13] R. Feiertag, C. Kahn, P. Porras, D. Schnackenberg, S. Staniford-Chen, B. Tung, A common intrusion specification language (cisl), *Specification draft, http://www.gidos.org.* (1999).

[14] R.P. Goldman, A Stochastic model for intrusions, *Recent Advances in Intrusion Detection. Fifth International Symposium, RAID 2002, Lecture Notes in Computer Science, V. 2516.* (2002).

[15] V. Gorodetski, O. Karsayev, I. Kotenko, A. Khabalov, Software development kit for multi-agent systems design and implementation, *Lecture Notes in Artificial Intelligence, Vol. 2296.* (2002).

[16] V. Gorodetski, I. Kotenko, Attacks against computer network: formal grammar-based framework and simulation tool, *Recent Advances in Intrusion Detection. Fifth International Symposium. RAID 2002. Lecture Notes in Computer Science, Vol. 2516.* (2002).

[17] S. Hariri, G. Qu, T. Dharmagadda, M. Ramkishore, C.S. Raghavendra, Impact analysis of faults and attacks in large-scale networks, *IEEE Security & Privacy, September/October.* (2003).

[18] J.D. Howard, T.A. Longstaff, A common language for computer security incidents, *SANDIA Report, SAND98–8667.* (1998).

[19] K. Iglun, R.A. Kemmerer, P.A. Porras, State transition analysis: a rule-based intrusion detection system, *IEEE Transactions on Software Engineering, 21(3).* (1995).

[20] S. Jha, O. Sheyner, J. Wing, Minimization and reliability analysis of attack graphs, *Technical Report CMU-CS-02-109, School of Computer Science, Carnegie Mellon University.* (2002).

[21] R.A. Kemmerer, G. Vigna, NetSTAT: a network-based intrusion detection approach, *Proceedings of the 14th Annual Computer Security Applications Conference, Scottsdale, Arizona.* (1998).

[22] I. Kotenko, Agent-based modeling and simulation of cyber-warfare between malefactors and security agents in Internet, *19th European Simulation Multiconference. ESM'05.* (2005).

[23] I. Kotenko, M. Stepashkin, Analyzing vulnerabilities and measuring security level at design and exploitation stages of computer network life cycle, *MMM-ACNS-05, Lecture Notes in Computer Science, Springer Verlag, Vol. 3685.* (2005).

[24] I. Kotenko, A. Ulanov, Multiagent modeling and simulation of agents' competition for network resources availability, *Second International Workshop on Safety and Security in Multiagent Systems (SASEMAS '05). Utrecht, The Netherlands.* (2005).

[25] I.V. Krsul, Software vulnerability analysis, *Ph.D. Dissertation, Computer Sciences Department, Purdue University, Lafayette, IN.* (1998).

[26] S. Kumar, E.H. Spafford, A software architecture to support misuse intrusion detection. *Technical Report CSD-TR-95-009. Purdue University.* (1995).

[27] C.E. Landwehr, A.R. Bull, J.P. McDermott, W.S. Choi, A taxonomy of computer security flaws, *ACM Computing Surveys, Vol. 26, No. 3.* (1994).

[28] U. Lindqvist, E. Jonsson, How to systematically classify computer security intrusions. *Proceedings of the 1997 IEEE Symposium on Security and Privacy*, Los Alamitos, CA. (1997).

[29] R. Lippmann, J.W. Haines, D.J. Fried, J. Korba, K. Das. The 1999 DARPA off-line intrusion detection evaluation, *RAID'2000, Lecture Notes in Computer Science, Vol. 1907.* (2000).

[30] P. Liu, W. Zang, Incentive-based modeling and inference of attacker intent, objectives, and strategies. *ACM Transactions on Information and System Security, Vol. 8, No. 1.* (2005).

[31] K. Lye, J. Wing, Game strategies in network security, *International Journal of Information Security, February.* (2005).

[32] J. McDermott, Attack-potential-based survivability modeling for high-consequence systems, *Third IEEE International Workshop on Information Assurance, College Park, MD, USA.* (2005).

[33] J. McHugh, The 1998 Lincoln Laboratory IDS evaluation: a critique, *RAID'2000, Lecture Notes in Computer Science, Vol. 1907.* (2000).

[34] L. Me. Gassata, A genetic algorithm as an alternative tool for security audit trails analysis, *Proceedings of the first international workshop on the Recent Advances in Intrusion Detection (RAID'98).* (1998).

[35] C. Michel, L. Me, ADeLe: an attack description language for knowledge-based intrusion detection, *Proceedings of the 16th International Conference on Information Security.* Kluwer. (2001).

[36] A.P. Moore, R.J. Ellison, R.C. Linger, Attack modeling for information security and survivability, *Technical Note CMU/SEI-2001-TN-001. Survivable Systems.* (2001).

[37] S.D. Moitra, S.L. Konda, A simulation model for managing survivability of networked information systems, *Technical Report CMU/SEI-2000-TR-020.* (2000).

[38] D.M. Nicol, W.H. Sanders, K.S. Trivedi, Model-based evaluation: from dependability to security, *IEEE Transactions on Dependable and Secure Computing. Vol. 1, N. 1.* (2004).

[39] S. Nikoletseas, G. Prasinos, P. Spirakis, C. Zaroliagis, Attack propagation in networks, *Theory of Computing Systems,* 36. (2003).

[40] P. Ning, D. Xu, C.G. Healey, R.A.St. Amant, Building attack scenarios through integration of complementary alert correlation methods, *Proceedings of the 11th Annual Network and Distributed System Security Symposium (NDSS '04).* (2004).

[41] OMNeT++ homepage. *http://www.omnetpp.org.*

[42] V. Paxson, Bro: A system for detecting network intruders in real-time. *Proceedings of the 7th Usenix Security Symposium.* (1998).

[43] N. Puketza, M. Chung, R.A. Olsson, B. Mukherjee, A software platform for testing intrusion detection systems, *IEEE Software, Vol. 14, No. 5.* (1997).

[44] M. Ranum, A Taxonomy of Internet Attacks, *Web Security Sourcebook. John Wiley & Sons.* (1997).

[45] R.W. Ritchey, P. Ammann, Using model checking to analyze network vulnerabilities, *Proceedings SOOO IEEE Computer Society Symposium on Security and Privacy.* (2000).

[46] M. Roesch, Snort – lightweight intrusion detection for networks, *Proceedings of the USENIX LISA'99 conference.* (1999).

[47] S. Rubin, S. Jha, B.P. Miller, Automatic generation and analysis of NIDS attacks, *20th Annual Computer Security Applications Conference (ACSAC),* Tuscon, Arizona. (2004).

[48] B. Schneier, Attack trees: modeling security threats, *Dr. Dobb's Journal, December.* (1999).

[49] B. Shepard, C. Matuszek, C.B. Fraser, etc., A Knowledge-based approach to network security: applying Cyc in the domain of network risk assessment, *The Seventeenth Innovative Applications of Artificial Intelligence Conference on Artificial Intelligence (IAAI-05), Pittsburgh, Pennsylvania.* (2005).

[50] O. Sheyner, J. Haines, S. Jha, R. Lippmann, J.M. Wing, Automated generation and analysis of attack graphs, *Proceedings of the IEEE Symposium on Security and Privacy.* (2002).

[51] S. Singh, J. Lyons, D.M. Nicol, Fast model-based penetration testing, *Proceedings of the 2004 Winter Simulation Conference.* (2004).

[52] A.J. Stewart, Distributed metastasis: a computer network penetration methodology, *Phrack Magazine, Vol. 9, Issue 55.* (1999).

[53] L. Swiler, C. Phillips, D. Ellis, S. Chakerian, Computer-attack graph generation tool, *Proceedings DISCEX '01: DARPA Information Survivability Conference & Exposition II.* (2001).

[54] S.J. Templeton, K. Levitt, A requires/provides model for computer attacks, *Proceedings of the New Security Paradigms Workshop.* (2000).

[55] E. Turner, R. Zachary, Securenet pro software's snp-l scripting system, *White paper. http://www.intrusion.com, July.* (2000).

[56] J. Yuill, F. Wu, J. Settle, F. Gong, R. Forno, M. Huang, J. Asbery, Intrusion-detection for incident-response, using a military battlefield-intelligence process, *Computer Networks,* No. 34. (2000).

Security and Embedded Systems
D.N. Serpanos and R. Giladi (Eds.)
IOS Press, 2006

Current Problems in Security of Military Networks

Jaroslav DOČKAL and Pavel POKORNÝ
University of Defence, Czech republic
jaroslav.dockal@unob.cz

Abstract. This paper describes solution of practical problem how to change CADS (Data network of Army of Czech Republic) to be utilizable for own secure video-conferencing system. The entire configuration for intranet VPNs was practically tested.

Keywords. Security, military, MPLS/VPN, video-conferencing system

Introduction

Not more month ago Michael Lynn, a former employee with Internet Security Systems, spoke at the Black Hat conference about Cisco IOS vulnerabilities, be caused of stack and heap overflows. Vulnerabilities are in large software products something normal and also router operating systems grow into really large products. Of course, we use patches, ACLs and IDSs, we turn off any necessary processes and protocols etc., but there are everyday's obviosities. We do it but do not rely only upon it. The main for us is well-designed application and network.

In [1] we described first version of our solution is a modification of existing audio/video-conferencing software, which makes communication possible by secure connection without any other support from the operating system or network software. The suggested software is based on the multicast product Robust Audio Tool, which is used for voice transmission, and Videoconferencing Tool, which is used for picture transmission. We use also own modular crypto-library, which is easy to use and provides basic cryptographic functions such as various ciphers, hash functions, and random number generators.

We had several possibilities to solve it:
Authentication module:

- into client and server code,
- only into client code,
- only into server code,
- separate module on both sides.

Encryption module:

- into client code,
- separate module on client side,
- separate module on client and server side.

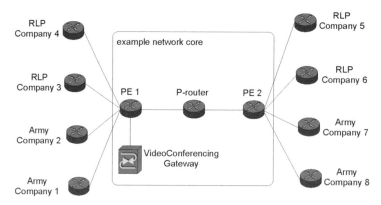

Figure 1. Videoconferencing Gateway in example network.

Finally we decided to fix authentication and encryption module on client side in separate daemon; on server side we locate only authentication module and it was integrated directly in server code. This solution was chosen because client software is under development contrary to server side with finished development. We pay for our solution with separate configuration in client side (multimedia data and all concerning encryption and authentication.

After finish our work programming work started measurement on network. When we made our experiments, we had not any problem because server was connected on backbone gigabit network and clients had connection 100 Mbps. But in our military network our video-conferencing system did not work properly and we started speculate how to change it. The next reason why to change our network was security reasons – we need to isolate packet streams, we asked for own IP address space, logical topology and network management. Solution for us was MPLS/VPN – disadvantaged of this technology was not for us any problem: MPLS VPNs do not use encryption – we have own encryption, multicasting is in MPLS complicated (see f.e. [6]) – we use unicast system based on mirror.

Using MPLS make possible to hide addressing structure of our MPLS core to the users. The address spaces between two VPNs are entirely independent (separation of addressing and routing). Of cause, customer's equipment (CE) needs to know address of the provider's equipment (PE); if we want to glue up this security hole, it is sufficient to deny telnet on the CE and PE router. On PE router we also can take another useful security measures: in ACL (Access Control List) allow routing protocol information only from CE router and configure MD-5 authentication for routing protocols.

To have a global on ACLs we started our work on ACL Generator, ACL Checker and Optimizer, and ACL Duplicities and Location Tester.

1. MPLS/VPN for the Czech Army

1.1. Overlapping Virtual Private Networks

Our military Network needs to extend its services with a videoconferencing service with will be provided by one gateway connected to the PE1 router, as shown in Fig. 1. The videoconference gateway is placed in a separate VPN to enhance the security of the newly created service.

Figure 2. VPN Connectivity Requirements in example network.

Both RLP (Air Navigation Services) and Army decided to use the service, but only central sites can use it, this means Army Company 2 and RLP center in. This requirement leads to an interesting problem: These two sites need to be in two VPNs: the corporate VPN to reach their remote sites and the Videoconference VPN to reach the Videoconferencing gateway. The connectivity requirements are illustrated in Fig. 2.

To support connectivity requirements similar to those in Fig. 2, the MPLS/VPN architecture supports the concept of sites, where a VPN is made up of one or multiple sites. A VPN is essentially a collection of sites sharing common routing information, which means that a site may belong to more than one VPN if it holds routes from separate VPNs. This provides the capability to build intranets and extranets, as well as any other topology.

The combination of the VPN IP routing table and associated VPN IP forwarding table is called VPN routing and forwarding instance (VRF). The relationship between the VPNs, sites, and VRFs can be summarized in the following rule, which should be used as the basis for any VRF definition in an MPLS/VPN network. All sites that share the same routing information (usually this means that they belong to the same set of VPNs), that are allowed to communicate directly with each other, and that are connected to the same PE-router can be placed in a common VRF. Using this rule, the minimum set of VRFs in the example network is outlined in Table 1.

To illustrate the interaction of per-VPN routing protocols with the MP-BGP used in the network core, consider the case of the Army VPN in the example network. Let's assume that the Company 2 and Company 8 sites are using OSPF to interact with the backbone, the Company 1 sites is using RIP, and the Company 7 site is using no routing protocol, there is a static route configured on the PE2 PE-router and the default route configured on the Company 7 router. The routing protocols used in Army VPN are shown in Fig. 3.

1.2. Route Targets

How does the router know which routes need to be inserted into which VRF? This dilemma is solved by the introduction of another concept in the MPLS/VPN architecture;

Table 1. VRFs in the PE-routers in the example Network

PE-router	VRF	Sites in the VRF	VRF Belongs to VPNs
PE 1	Army_central	Company 2	Army, Videoconference
	RLP_central	Company 3	RLP, Videoconference
	RLP	Company 4	RLP
	Army	Company 1	Army
	Videoconference	Videoconference gateway	Videoconference
PE 2	RLP	Company 5	RLP
		Company 6	
	Army	Company 7	Army
		Company 8	

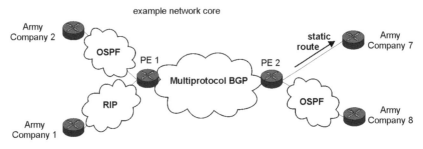

Figure 3. Routing Protocols Used in Army VPN.

the route target. Every VPN route is tagged with one or more route targets when it is exported from a VRF (to be offered to other VRFs). We can also associate a set of route targets with a VRF, and all routes tagged with at least one of those route targets will be inserted into the VRF. The route target is the closest approximation to a VPN identifier in the MPLS/VPN architecture.

The example network contains three VPNs and thus requires three route targets. The association between route targets and VRFs is outlined in Table 2.

1.3. Propagation of VPN Routing Information

The PE1 PE-router collects routing information from the Company 2 site using a per-VPN OSPF process. Similarly, the information from the Company 1 site is collected using a per-VPN RIP process.

The information gathered by various routing protocols in the PE1 PE-router is re-distributed into MP-BGP (PE2 PE-router is doing the same with information gathered from OSPF process as well as with static route). VPN addresses are expended with the route distinguishers at the moment of redistribution. The route export route target specified in the originating VRF is also attached to the route. The resulting 96-bit routing information is propagated by MP-BGP to the PE2 router. The redistribution of the

Table 2. Correspondence Between VRFs and Route Targets in example network

PE-router	VRF	Route Target Attached to Exported Routes	Import Route Targets
PE1	Army_central	Army, Videoconference	Army, Videoconference
	RLP_central	RLP, Videoconference	RLP, Videoconference
	RLP	RLP	RLP
	Army	Army	Army
	Videoconference	Videoconference	Videoconference
PE2	RLP	RLP	RLP
	Army	Army	Army

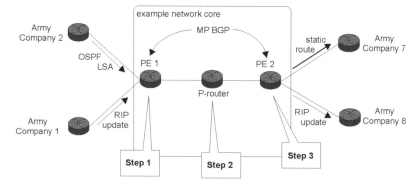

Figure 4. VPN Packet Forwarding – Preparatory Steps.

per-VPN routing information into MP-BGP is not automatic and must be manually configured on the router for each VRF unless this information was learned from the customer via BGP.

The PE2 router, after receiving MP-BGP routes, inserts the received routes into various VRF tables based on the route target attribute attached to each individual route. The route distinguisher is dropped from the 96-bit route when the route is inserted into the VRF, resulting yet again in a traditional IP route. Finally, the routing information received through BGP is redistributed into the OSPF process and is passed on to the Company 6 site.

1.4. VPN Packet Forwarding

Each VPN packet is labeled by the ingress PE-router with a label uniquely identifying the egress PE-router, and is sent across the network. All the routers in the network subsequently switch labels without having to look into the packet itself. The preparatory steps for this process are illustrated in Fig. 4.

Each PE-router needs a unique identifier (a host route – usually the loopback IP address is used), which is then propagated throughout the P-network using the usual IGP (Step 1). This IP address is also used as the BGP next-hop attribute of all VPN routes announced by the PE-router. A label is assigned in each P-router for that host

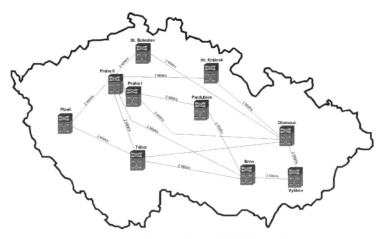

Figure 5. MPLS Backbone of CADS Network.

route and is propagated to each of its neighbors (Step 2). Finally, all other PE-routers receive a label associated with the egress PE-router through an MPLS label distribution process (Step 3). After the label for the egress PE-router is received by the ingress PE-router, the VPN packet exchange can start.

However, when the egress PE-router receives the VPN packet, it has no information to tell it which VPN the packet is destined for. To make the communication between VPN sites unique, a second set of labels is introduced. Each PE-router allocates a unique label for each route in each VPN routing and forwarding (VRF) instance. These labels are propagated together with the corresponding routes through MP-BGP to all other PE-routers. The PE-routers receiving the MP-BGP update and installing the received routes in their VRF tables and also installs the label assigned by the egress router in their VRF tables. The MPLS/VPN network is now ready to forward VPN packets.

When a VPN packet is received by the ingress PE-router, the corresponding VRF is examined, and the label associated with the destination address by the egress PE-router is selected. Another label, pointing toward the egress PE-router, is obtained from the global forwarding table. Both labels are combined into an MPLS label stack, are attached in front of the VPN packet, and are sent toward the egress PE-router.

All the P-routers in the network switch the VPN packet based only on the top label in the stack, which points toward the egress PE-router. Because of the normal MPLS forwarding rules, the P-routers never look beyond the first label and are thus completely unaware of the second label or the VPN packet carried across the network.

The egress PE-router receives the labeled packet, drops the first label, and performs a lookup on the second label, which uniquely identifies the target VRF and sometimes even the outgoing interface on the PE-router. A lookup is performed in the target VRF, and the packet is sent toward the proper CE-router.

1.5. Backbone for CADS MPLS Network

During the design of Multiprotocol Label Switching (MPLS) network for CADS (Data network of Army of Czech Republic) the current architecture of CADS was used and the real backbone was changed just a little to better support MPLS technology and to minimize the budget needed to transform the old CADS network. Figure 5 shows sug-

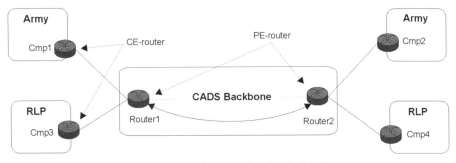

Figure 6. Example Intranet Topology in CADS.

gested MPLS core network for CADS. In this network there is no real P-router because all of the routers actually work also as PE-routers.

For the backbone routers I suggest that at least Cisco 7500 series routers be used. For the customer site routers, it is possible to use a lower series of Cisco routers such as the 3640 series.

1.6. MPLS/VPN Intranet Topology in CADS Network

One of the most important VPN topologies for the Army of Czech Republic that can be provisioned using the MPLS/VPN architecture is an Intranet between multiple sites that belong to the same sector or that belong to the same information system. This topology is the basic VPN network structure that provides any-to-any connectivity between sites using the peer-to-peer model. Using the same mechanisms you use to build the Intranet topology, you can add more advanced services and connectivity requirements such as adding videoconferencing service only for some parts of CADS.

Figure 6 shows an example of this type of topology. This is actually part of CADS network and configurations described further are patterns for configuring routers in the rest of CADS.

Example CADS MPLS/VPN backbone contains two VPNs: one for Army and one for Air Navigation Services (RLP). The Army VPN has sites in Company 1 and 2 (Cmp1 and Cmp2). The RLP VPN has sites in Company 3 and 4 (Cmp3 and Cmp4). Both VPNs provides any-to-any connectivity for their sites.

To provision this VPN service across the MPLS/VPN backbone it is mandatory to follow these steps:

1. Define and configure the VRFs.
2. Define and configure the route distinguishers.
3. Define and configure the import and export policies.
4. Configure the PE-to-CE links.
5. Associate the CE-interfaces to the previously defined VRFs.
6. Configure the Multiprotocol BGP.

1.7. Configuration of VRFs

The first step in provisioning a VPN service based on the MPLS architecture is to define and configure the Virtual Routing and Forwarding Instances (VRFs).

Table 3. Route Distinguisher Definitions.

VPN	Static ASN number	Unique Value	Route Distinguisher
Army	100	10	100:10
RLP	100	20	100:20

Each PE-router in the MPLS/VPN backbone is attached to a site that wants to receive routes from a specific VPN, so the PE-router must have the relevant VRF configuration for that VPN. Because in our example CADS network Router1 and Router2 PE-routers are both attached to both Army and RLP sites, the VRF configuration for these specific VPN customers must exist on both PE-routers.

We created the relevant VRFs and unique CEF forwarding and routing tables. However, the VRFs are not fully provisioned yet and do not contain any routes. It is necessary to configure the VRFs further to provide routes for the tables and to create associated MPLS labels. When entering the ip vrf vrf-name command, the router moves into the vrf configuration sub-mode. In this mode it is possible to configure the variables associated with this VRF, such as the route distinguisher and the import and export policies.

1.8. Configuring Route Distinguishers

Each VRF within the PE-router configuration needs to have an associated route distinguisher, which might or might not be related to a particular site or VPN membership of that site. In the most common case, where a site belongs only to one intranet VPN, it is technically possible, and recommended, to use a unique route distinguisher for the VPN.

Because in real life scenarios the customers who use the routes contained within the VRF also can attach to other MPLS/VPN service providers, it is important to use the ASN (Autonomous System Number) of the service provider as the first two bytes of the route distinguisher format to avoid using the same VPN-IPv4 addresses in separate MPLS/VPN domains; in our example it is number 100. Separate route distinguishers are not necessary for Intranet type of topology; therefore, in our CADS example the value of the route distinguisher is the same for each VRF that belongs to a particular intranet VPN. Table 3 shows the assigned values for each CADS VPN.

The same configuration is necessary for the CADS Router2 PE-router.

1.9. Configuration of Import and Export Policies

The last step in the configuration of each VRF is the addition of import and export policies for the VRF to use. These policies are used to populate routes into the VRF and to advertise routes out of the VRF.

If it is necessary to add more than one route target to any routes that are exported from or imported into the VRF, use the route-target export or route-target import command multiple times within the VRF configuration (Later will be used for adding Videoconferencing service).

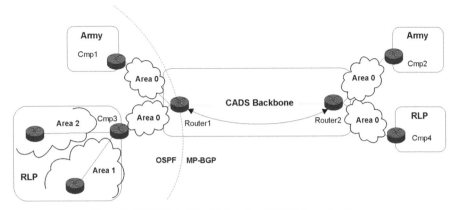

Figure 7. OSPF PE-to-CE with Area 0 and MPLS Super Backbone.

1.10. PE to CE Link Configuration

There are currently four separate ways that an MPLS/VPN backbone can receive routes from a VPN customer CE-router: BGP-4, RIP Version 2, OSPF, and static routing.

For the PE-CE configuration in CADS I selected Open Shortest Path First (OSPF) protocol option, because CADS already runs OSPF within each of their sites so it will not be necessary to redistribute OSPF information into other protocols such as BGP-4 or RIP Version 2.

Traditionally OSPF network consists of a backbone area (area 0) and a number of areas connected to this backbone through an Area Border Router (ABR). MPLS backbone for VPN with OSPF on the customer's site introduces a third level in the hierarchy of the OSPF model. This third level is called the MPLS VPN Super Backbone. The MPLS VPN Super Backbone also enables customers to use multiple area 0 backbones on their sites. Each site can have a separate area 0 as long as it is connected to the MPLS VPN Super Backbone. The result is the same as a partitioned area 0 backbone.

With this type of connectivity, the PE-router becomes an Autonomous System Boundary Router (ASBR) for the OSPF-MPLS/VPN backbone, although from the CE-router's perspective, it acts as an ABR when propagating inter-area routes between sites and the CE routers are ABR routers. Illustration of this architecture is shown in Fig. 7.

1.11. Association of Interfaces to VRFs

After defining all relevant VRFs on the PE-router, the PE-router has to know which interfaces belong to which VRF and, therefore, should populate the VRF with routes from connected sites. More than one interface can belong to the same VRF.

When the interface is associated with a particular VRF, its IP address is removed from the global routing table and from the interface and should be reconfigured after the interface is given membership to a VRF.

1.12. Configuration of Multiprotocol BGP

The final configuration step is to redistribute any routes that are contained within a particular VRF and that have been learned via MP-iBGP to other members of the VPN.

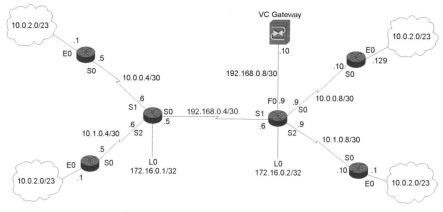

Figure 8. Address Schema of Tested Network.

This is achieved through the redistribution of routes from BGP into the relevant OSPF process.

The configuration of BGP requires several steps, and various configuration commands. It has to be configured for any PE-to-PE MP-iBGP sessions across the MPLS/VPN backbone. We need also to define and activate the BGP sessions between PE-routers.

The entire configuration for intranet VPNs was practically tested, on Fig. 8 you can see address schema of this topology.

2. Videoconferencing Service

On the router Router1 is created additional VRF for videoconference (VC) gateway:

```
!
ip vrf Video
rd 100:5
route-target export 100:5
route-target import 100:5
route-target import 100:6
route-target import 100:7
!
```

Only selected companies (commanding companies) have Access to the gateway and these are either in the VRF RLP_Commanders or in the VRF Army_Commanders. This means that separated VRFs for commanding companies also has to be created. The next configuration fragment (Army_Commanders on the PE-router Router1) shows VRF for Company with Access to VC Gateway created.

```
!
ip vrf Army_Commanders
rd 100:10
route-target export 100:10
route-target export 100:6
```

route-target import 100:10
route-target import 100:5
!

To select which computer from the commanding company site will have an access to videoconference gateway, use extended Access Control Lists (ACL) on the company's CE-router. Import and export policies on both PE-routers have to be configured properly so commanding companies can see only sites from its own VPN and videoconference gateway but cannot see the commanding companies from another VPN.

Conclusion

A scenario for our videoconference service was designed and implementation of these scenarios was described. Suggested videoconference service implementation will allow connecting selected sites through videoconferencing gateway but these sites will be still separated within the meaning of IP connectivity. Results of testing our videoconferencing system approved advantage of MPLS/VPN system.

We also as a "side effect" designed the new backbone for CADS. This architecture will provide secure and very scalable solution for private networks for different parts of Army of Czech Republic. What the next? We discuss two possibilities: CoS-based TE selection and fast OSPF (this solution is much simpler but we plan to test if rerouting time is sufficient.

Suggested solution simplifies the administrative work of administrators of CADS that is needed to manage all VPNs and also adding and removing sites from VPNs. MPLS technology is very scalable and this attribute makes MPLS the best choice for routing protocol in backbone of CADS network of the Czech Army.

References

[1] Tomas Boucek, Jaroslav Dockal, Petr Dusek, Tomas Konir: Secure videoconferencing system. SPI'2003 Conference, Brno.
[2] Peter Tomsu, Gerhard Wieser: MPLS-Based VPNs Designing Advanced Virtual Networks, Prentice Hall PTR, ISBN: 0-13-028225-1, 2002.
[3] MPLS Virtual Private Networks (VPNs; [Cisco IOS Software Releases 12.0 ST] – Cisco Systems [online]. Last revision 19.1.2005 [cit. 15.1.2005]. URL: http://www.cisco.com/en/US/products/sw/iosswrel/ps1612/products_feature_guide09186a00800e956e.html.
[4] Jim Guichard, Ivan Pepelnjak: MPLS and VPN Architectures, Cisco Press, ISBN: 1-58705-002-1, 2000.
[5] van Pepelnjak, Jim Guichard, Jeff Apcar: MPLS and VPN Architectures Volume II, Cisco Systems, ISBN: 1-58705-112-5, 2003.
[6] Internet draft draft-raggarwa-l3vpn-2547-mvpn-00.txt, Base Specification for Multicast in BGP/MPLS VPNs.

Security and Embedded Systems
D.N. Serpanos and R. Giladi (Eds.)
IOS Press, 2006

Multi-Agent Framework for Intrusion Detection and Alert Correlation

Vladimir GORODETSKY, Oleg KARSAEV, Vladimir SAMOILOV
and Alexander ULANOV

SPIIRAS, 39, 14-th Linia, St. Petersburg, 199178, Russia
{gor, ok, samovl, ulanov}@mail.iias.spb.su

Abstract. This paper presents multi-agent intrusion detection system (IDS) operating based on asynchronous data streams arriving from multiple heterogeneous sources. IDS is composed of many structured specialized classifiers each
trained to detect attacks of a fixed class. Alerts produced by classifiers having
the same specialization and operating in different feature representation spaces
are correlated at the upper layer. The top-layer classifier solves intrusion detection task: it combines heterogeneous alerts produced at a previous layer. The paper describes IDS architecture and emphasizes the reusability of some solutions
used in the developed IDS. The implemented multi-agent IDS is capable to detect three classes of attacks, *DoS*, *Probe* and *U2R* using input traffic.

1. Introduction

Since recently, intrusion detection task is of great concern and the subject of intensive
research and development. The common opinion is that this task solution requires as
much available information as possible to be used. Multiplicity and heterogeneity of
potential data sources, high-frequency dynamics and asynchronous nature of inputs
arriving from various sources make intrusion detection task very specific, complicated
and computationally intensive. Information ageing resulting from variety of frequencies of input data streams arriving from various sources is an important issue of real-
time Intrusion Detection System (IDS), practically ignored by the most of current research.

The IDS architecture is one more important aspect. This paper considers Multi-
Agent System (MAS) framework as a basis for IDS engineering. Indeed, this framework is specifically designed for intelligent distributed data processing (decision making, in particular) provides modularity and easy modifiability of MAS applications. A
strong argument in favor of the multi-agent framework is a maturity of the multi-agent
technology supported by a number of well grounded methodologies and software tools.
An attractive property of MAS technology is a potential reusability of the problem-
oriented solutions, proposed for decision making MAS at analysis, design, implementation and deployment stages and therefore may be used in multi-agent IDS.

The main subjects of this paper concern two above discussed issues, (1) asynchronous nature of data streams arriving to IDS from multiple heterogeneous sources and
(2) multi-agent architecture and technology of IDS. The rest of the paper is organized
as follows. Section 2 presents the IDS input data model, proposed structure of the in-

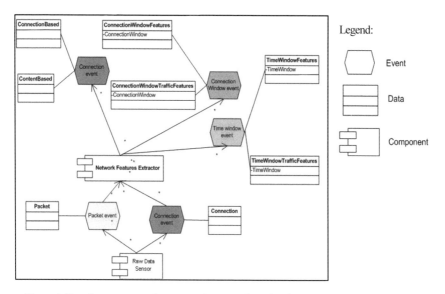

Figure 1. Raw data streams and preprocessing procedures forming secondary IDS data sources.

teracting classifiers designed for heterogeneous alert correlation and outlines dynamics of the IDS operation. Section 3 describes the proposed model of data ageing allowing on-line updating of the computer security status if IDS input is composed of asynchronous data streams. Section 4 provides a specification of the multi-agent IDS architecture described in terms of Gaia methodology [1] used for development of the multi-agent IDS prototype. Section 5 dwells upon results of the developed multi-agent IDS prototype testing using DARPA data [2]. Conclusion summarizes the paper contributions.

2. Data Model and Data Processing Structure in IDS

2.1. Input Data Model

Heterogeneity, high-frequency dynamics and asynchronous character of data captured by sensors of IDS are determinative for modeling its input data. In the below model the data streams resulting from preprocessing of the network traffic recoded in TCP dump are considered. Figure 1 illustrates the model of data and event streams accounted in the implemented IDS prototype. In this model, TCP dump of the network traffic is captured by the sensor, *Raw Data Sensor*. The latter produces primary events of two types: (1) *PacketEvent* triggered by incoming IP packet and obtaining *Packet* data, and (2) *ConnectionEvent* indicating completion of a connection and obtaining *Connection* data. These events and data arrive to *NetworkFeatureExtractor* intended for feature extraction from raw traffic data. *NetworkFeatureExtractor*, in turn, generates the secondary events, that are (3) *ConnectionWindowEvent* indicating completion of a time window containing a fixed number of connections; and (4) *TimeWindowEvent* indicating completion of the time window of a predefined duration. The latter events supervise operation of the feature extractors generating the following secondary data:

(1) *Connection-related* information used further for extraction of particular fea-
    tures specifying a connection. This information is stored in two files inter-
    preted as two data sources, i.e. *ConnectionBased* and *ContentBased*.

(2) *Time window-related* information representing certain statistics averaging cer-
    tain traffic data within sliding time window of predefined length and shift (in
    our case, within time window of 5 sec length sliding with 1 sec sift). This in-
    formation is used to extract the features composing two secondary data
    sources, *TimeWindowFeatures*, and *TimeWindowTrafficFeatures*.

(3) Connection window-related information representing certain statistics averag-
    ing traffic data within sliding window containing a predefined number of con-
    nections (in our case, containing 100 connections with 1 connection shift).
    This information is used to extract the features composing two other secon-
    dary data sources, *ConnectionWindowFeatures*, and *ConnectionWindowTraf-
    ficFeatures*.

Thus, traffic preprocessing procedures generate six secondary data sources containing over 100 features[1] generated based on DARPA data [2] containing mixture of normal and abnormal traffic caused by attacks of *DoS, Probe, U2R* classes.

2.1. Heterogeneous Alert Correlation Structure

Let us consider IDS correlating heterogeneous alerts, i.e. alerts notifying about various
classes of attacks. Such IDS is composed of a structure of specialized classifiers trained
for detection of attacks of particular classes, e.g., either *DoS*, or *Probe*, or *U2R*. In this
IDS, at the first layer, several classifiers are trained to detect the same attack class
based on data of various sources and/or various feature representation spaces. Each of
these specialized classifiers produces "*Alert*" if it detects an attack of its "own" class,
(e.g., "*DoS alert*"). At the second layer, alerts of the same type produced by source-
based classifiers are correlated and the result is sent to the top layer. The top-layer classifier solves intrusion detection task: it combines decisions of specialized alert correlation classifiers and produces decision in terms of a particular attack class if any.

The primary factor influencing on the IDS architecture is the structure of interaction of the source-based classifiers and meta-classifiers. Figure 2 presents an example
of such a structure. In it every data source is attached several classifiers trained to detect various attack classes and generate alerts in response to the "own" attack class.
Therefore alerts corresponding to *various classes* of attacks arrive to the meta-level.

Connection-based data source is attached three specialized classifiers, *DNS CB*,
R2U CB and *Probe CB* (Fig. 2). The first of them is trained to detect attacks of the
"*DoS*" class, the second one is trained to detect attacks of the *R2U* class and the latter
one is specialized to detect attacks of the *Probe* class. Let us emphasize that the above
mentioned classifiers of various specialization transmit alerts to various meta-
classifiers.

ConnectionWindowFeatures data source is attached two specialized classifiers,
R2U CW and *Probe CW* trained to detect the *R2U* and *Probe* attack classes respectively. They also send alerts to various classifiers of the meta-level.

ConnectionWindowTrafficFeatures data source is attached three specialized classifiers, *R2U CWT*, *Probe CWT* and *NormalCWT* trained to detect the *R2U, Probe* attack

---

[1] Preprocessing software and feature extractors were developed by the authors.

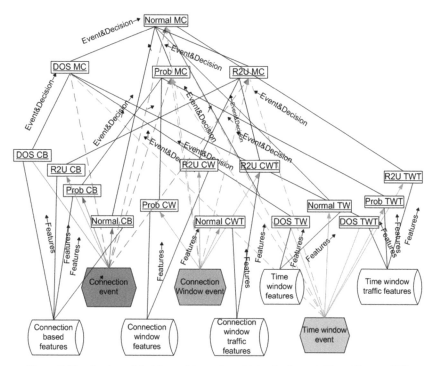

Figure 2. The structure of decision making and combining implemented in multi-agent IDS.

classes and identify *Normal* activity respectively. They send their alerts to different meta-level classifiers. *Time WindowFeatures* data source is attached three specialized classifiers, *DNS TW*, *R2U TW*, and *NormalTW* trained to detect the *DoS*, *R2U* attack classes and identify *Normal* activity respectively.

Time WindowTrafficFeatures source is attached *DNS TWT*, *R2U TWT*, and *ProbeTWT* classifiers trained to detect the *DoS*, *R2U* and *Probe* attack classes respectively.

At the meta-level, three specialized meta-classifiers are introduced. Each of them is responsible for combining decisions received from source-based classifiers trained for detection of a predefined type of attack. They operate in asynchronous mode making decision each time when an event and data from at least one source-based classifier arrive. A peculiarity of the decision making structure given in Fig. 2 is that one more decision combining layer, a top layer, is used in it. It combines the inputs arriving from specialized meta-classifiers thus solving the intrusion detection task.

3. Models of Data Ageing

Due to the fact that averaged frequencies of various data streams may be noticeably different, the data arriving to meta-level possess finite life time: after certain time period elapsing from the moment when the data are produced these data become less useful or completely useless for assessment of the current computer security status.

According to alert correlation strategy used in IDS, decision of each meta-classifier is updated at any time instant when new input ("event") produced by a source-based classifier arrives and, therefore, the meta-classifier updates its decision based on the newly and previously received decisions of the specialized classifiers i.e. based on the data having different ages and therefore different relevancies to the current computer security status. Thus, *data ageing* is one of the important peculiarities of the alert correlation system in question. Let us discuss the models of data ageing.

Two data ageing models were explored. The *first* of them assumes that each data item is assigned a certain "age" at the moment of the computer security status update and if this data "age" is less than a fixed threshold (individual for each data source) then these data are used "as they are". Otherwise, these data are assumed *missing*:

$$D_i(t_{k+1}) = \begin{cases} D(t_k), & if \ t_k \le t_{k+1} \le t_k + T_i^{Ag} \\ \varnothing, & otherwise \end{cases}$$

where $D_i(t)$ -stands for the decision of a classifier attached to *i-th* data source and produced at time instant t; t_k stands for the time instant at which the decision arrives into meta-classifier; T_i^{Ag} stands for the threshold value of life time of the decision D_i produced by the source # i; and $\varnothing$ stands for the missing value.

This model was experimentally investigated, and the results were fully described in [3]. An advantage of this model is that it is rather simple. An approach to solution of such task and sound algorithm of decision making if some data are missing are described in [4]. A drawback of this model is that it can found out too rough.

The second model assumes that the learning mechanism has to automatically determine dependence of informative power of a decision produced by a source classifier on its "age". In other words, this model assumes that each input of an alert correlation classifier is assigned an additional numerical attribute $\Delta_i(t_1, t_2) = t_2 - t_1$, the "age" of input from *i*-th source-based classifier produced at the time instant t_1 if it is used by alert correlation procedure at the time instant t_2. Thus, when *i-th* source-based classifier produces and sends its decision to meta-layer at instant t_β^i its age is $\Delta_i(t_\beta^i) = 0$. If this decision is used later, at a time instant t_α, the attribute $\Delta_i(t_\alpha^i, t_\beta^i) = (t_\alpha - t_\beta^i)$.

The last model of data ageing is used in IDS considered below. Let us note that for this model no specific learning technique for decision combining is necessary.

4. IDS MAS Technology and Reusable Solutions

4.1. MASDK Software Tool

MAS technology that is specifically designed for large scale distributed intelligent systems. Currently it is about its industrial maturity, while providing designers with a range of well grounded methodologies and software tools proposing reusable solutions at analysis, design, implementation and deployment of MAS applications. For multi-agent IDS, these reusable solutions can support a fair part of development activity, thus, noticeably decreasing the development time and cost. Other group of reusable solutions is appropriate specifically for IDS as common for many such applications. Figure 3 illustrates particular development activities based on Gaia methodology [1].

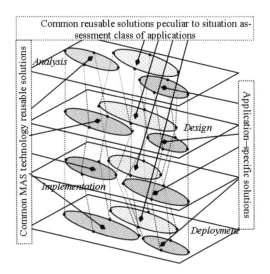

Figure 3. Layers of MAS development in Gaia methodology and classes of reusable solutions of each layer.

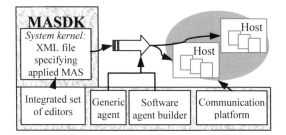

Figure 4. MASDK 3.0 components and their interaction.

According to it, MAS development is divided in four stages:[2] (1) analysis, (2) design, (3) implementation and (4) deployment.

Analysis assumes development of MAS application meta-model of high level of abstraction, i.e. engineering of ontology, discovery of MAS tasks, roles and their functionalities, description of services provided by the roles and high-level scheme of role interactions in particular task' solving [1]. *Design* stage addresses the *formal specification* of the analysis stage solutions and specification of particular MAS agents' classes. *Implementation* is intended for a development of the software code while *deployment* is aimed at determining the locations of MAS components within computer network.

Let us outline the software means of particular MAS software tool, MASDK 3.0 [5] based on the Gaia methodology. MASDK 3.0 software tool consists of the following components (Fig. 4): (1) *system kernel* that is a data structure for XML-based representation and storing of formal specification of MAS application; (2) *integrated* multitude of the graphical *editors* supporting user's activity aimed at formal specification of MAS application; (3) library of C++ classes constituting what is usually called *Generic agent* implementing common reusable components of agents; (4) communica-

---

[2] Gaia methodology considers only two stages of MAS development that are analysis and design.

tion platform to be installed in computers network where MAS should be deployed, and (5) builder of software agent instances, generating source C++ code and executable code of software agents as well as deploying software agents within previously installed communication platform.

The technology of MAS specification in *System Kernel* is supported by graphical editors structured in three levels. Editors of the *first level* support description of MAS application at the meta-level realizing the analysis stage of Gaia methodology. This set of editors includes (1) *application ontology* editor, (2) editor for conceptual *description of roles, agent services, names of agent classes,* and schemes of *roles' interactions,* (3) editor of *roles interaction protocols.* Editors of the *second level* support *design stage* of Gaia methodology aimed at specification of agent classes: (1) editor for specification of *behavior meta-models* of agent classes; (2) editor for state machine-based specification of *agent functions and behavior scenarios*; (3) editor for specification of software agents' *private* components of the *ontology* inheriting the notions of shared application ontology. Editors of the *third level* support MAS implementation stage and aimed at: (1) C++ implementation of the set of *application-specific components* and *functions* specified at design stage; (2) specification of *configuration of the computer network* where the designed MAS is to be deployed; (3) specification of *instances* of agent classes and their addresses within the network, and (4) specification of initial states of *mental models* of agent instances. The designed XML specification together with the application-specific components coded in C++ and reusable components of *Generic Agent* are automatically compiled into executable code via use of XSLT technology.

Thus, MASDK 3.0 provides the developer with a number of reusable solutions common for practically any MAS. Analysis of reusable solutions of this type is omitted in the paper because this is beyond the paper scope. Generally speaking, MASDK 3.0 software tool provides the developer with a number of standard templates stored in *Generic agent* and graphical means to fill these templates out in user friendly style.

Some of these templates partially filled out at design of multi-agent IDS appeared to be common for various IDS and that is why such at least partially filled out templates can be reused in other IDS as ready solutions. They are described in the following subsection.

4.2. IDS Architecture and Reusable Solutions

Although several reusable solutions were developed for multi-agent IDS, due to limited paper space only two of them are discussed below: meta-model of multi-agent IDS and the solution supporting the asynchronous inputs handling of IDS in heterogeneous alert correlation. Other solutions are partially described in [6].

Analysis stage of a multi-agent IDS development assumes roles discovering, roles' interaction protocols and allocation of the discovered roles to the agent classes. Based on the analysis of the roles and the protocols common for many IDS, the following IDS application independent roles and atomic protocols are discovered (Fig. 5):

Roles

- *DataSensor* – source of raw data; performs raw data preprocessing, feature extraction, transmission of the primary events and generation of the secondary events (see Section 2);
- *ObjectDataReceiver* – acceptor of the classification object features;

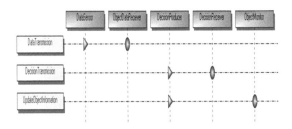

Figure 5. Reusable Roles and Protocols.

- *DecisionProvider* – source of decisions produced upon the security status;
- *DecisionReceiver* – receiver of the decisions produced by *DecisionProviders*;
- *ObjectMonitor* – receiver of information presenting an object to be classified.

Protocols

- *DataTransmission* – the protocol transmitting the features-related information;
- *DecisionTransmission* – the protocol transmitting the decisions produced upon the computer security status;
- *UpdateObjectInformation* – the protocol performing updating of the information concerning the computer security status.

The aforementioned protocols are basic ones. Let us list the auxiliary ones.

- *AttackLogTransmission* – the protocol performing transmission of the attack log (the true labels of the attacks needed for the designed system testing);
- *OptionsProtocol* – the protocol performing adjusting of initial options determining the regime of the system operation.

Agent classes and roles allocated to them

The agent classes are allocated the roles they have to perform. The following agent classes are generic for many multi-agent IDS:

- *NetLevelAgent* – an agent class performing the *DataSensor* role (raw data pre-processing and extraction of the events and secondary features);
- *BaseClassifiers* – an agent class assigned the *DecisionProvider* role responsible for source-based alerts; it assesses the security status when it receives an event from the source it is attached to. In particular the IDS application considered here, this agent class is replicated into the following instances of software agents:
  - *DOS_CB*: produces decisions using *ConnectionBased* features when it receives the event *ConnectionEvent*; trained to detect the *DoS* attack class;
  - *DOS_TW*: produces decisions using *TimeWindowFeatures* features when it receives the event *TimeWindowEvent*; trained to detect *DoS* attack class;
  - *DOS_TWT*: produces decisions using *TimeWindowTraficFeatures* features when it receives the event *TimeWindowEvent*; trained to detect *DoS* attack class;

      ○ *Prob_CB*: produces decisions using *ConnectionBased* features when it receives the event *ConnectionEvent*; trained to detect the attacks of the class *Probes*;

      ○ *Prob_CW*: produces decisions using *ConnectionWindowFeatures* features when receives *ConnectionWindowEvent* event; trained to detect *Probes* attacks;

      ○ *Prob_TWT*: produces decisions using *TimeWindowTraficFeatures* features when it receives the event *TimeWindowEvent*; trained to detect *Probes* attacks;

      ○ *R2U_CB*: produces decisions using *ConnectionBased* features when it receives the event *ConnectionEvent*; trained to detect the attacks of the class *R2U*;

      ○ *R2U_CW*: produces decisions using *ConnectionWindowFeatures* features when it receives the *ConnectionWindowEvent* event; trained to detect *R2U* attacks;

      ○ *R2U_CWT*: produces decisions using *ConnectionWindowTraficFeatures* features when it receives the *ConnectionWindowEvent* event; trained to detect *R2U* attacks;

      ○ *R2U_TWT*: produces decisions using *TimeWindowTraficFeatures* features when it receives the event *TimeWindowEvent*; trained to detect the *R2U* attacks.

- *Metaclassifiers*: an agent class performing the roles *DecisionReceiver* and *DecisionProvider*; it is responsible for combining decisions produced by its child classifiers (Fig. 2). This class of agents is replicated into the following instances:

      ○ *DOS_MC*: an agent instance correlating alerts of the source-based classifiers trained to detect the *DoS* attack class;

      ○ *Prob_MC*: an agent correlating alerts of the source-based classifiers trained to detect the *Probes* attack class;

      ○ *R2U_MC*: an agent instance correlating alerts of the source-based classifiers trained to detect the *R2U* attack class;

      ○ *Normal MC*: an agent instance analyzing alerts arriving from the metaclassifiers (if any) and correlating heterogeneous alerts.

- *SystemMonitor* – an agent class assigned the role *ObjectMonitor*; it provides visualization of the information about security status of the host depending on time.

The above represented roles, protocols and agent classes (*NetLevelAgent, BaseClassifiers, Metaclassifiers* and *SystemMonitor*) are the instances of reusable solutions of multi-agent IDS. The roles are specified in terms of services[3] they have to provide. The services, in turn, are delivered in terms of state machines. Behavior of each agent class determined by the roles assigned to it is specified in two layers. At the upper layer the interaction structure of the state machines representing particular services of agent class roles is specified. At the lower layer each above mentioned state machine speci-

---

[3] Term "*agent service*" was introduced in Gaia methodology. It is understood as agent class behavior either within a certain protocol, or in reply to the user commands, or as a result of agent class proactive behavior, or in monitoring of external environment.

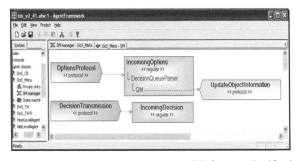

Figure 6. Services of the agent classes responsible for meta-classification.

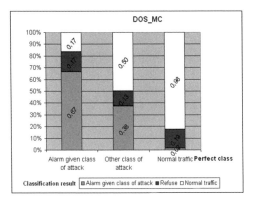

Figure 7. Evaluation of the performance quality of the *DOS_MC* meta-classifier.

fies a certain service in details. Such specifications developed for the above mentioned agent classes are the representatives of reusable solutions for multi-agent IDS.

An example of agent class behavior specification for *Metaclassifiers* agent class is given in Fig. 6. This example is selected due to the fact that this agent class implements one of specific IDS procedures, processing of the asynchronous alerts arriving from the source-based classifier. Figure 6 illustrates the upper level of this agent class specification. It presents the services this agent class delivers and their interactions.

Various meta-classifiers (see Fig. 2) differ (1) in their rule bases used for alert correlation, (2) in the lists of the source-based classifiers forming their inputs and also (3) in the lists of the receivers of the decisions produced by different alert correlation agents. The basic services of these agents are reusable. Detailed specification of the state machines implementing the aforementioned services is omitted due to the paper space limits.

5. Experimental Results

The heterogeneous alert correlation IDS MAS designed according to the above described principles and architecture was implemented using MASDK 3.0 [5]. All classifiers composing the proposed homogeneous alert correlation structure were trained using VAM [7] and GK2 [4] algorithms and tested using DARPA data [2].

Some testing results are illustrated in Fig. 7. This figure presents information about performance quality (probabilities of correct classifications, false alarms and signal missing) of the alert correlation classifiers received from the classifiers trained to detect the attacks of particular classes. Data used in training procedures as "counter class" include basically normal traffic. The situation when the meta-classifier refuses to classify input data occurs when the difference between the sums of the weights of rules voting in favor of *Alert* and *Normal* decision is less than the experimentally selected threshold. Analysis showed that, as a rule, such kind of situation actually corresponds to some other class of attacks. Figure 7 illustrates the performance quality of the alert correlation meta-classifier destined for detection of the *DoS* class of attacks. An important observation is that even if the source-based classifiers operate not too precisely, at the meta-layer, where the decisions of the specialized classifiers are combined, the quality of the *DoS* attack detection as a rule increases.

6. Conclusion

The paper contribution is twofold. *The first* of them is the proposed input data model accounting for high-frequency dynamics and asynchronous nature of input, i.e. the data properties of the primary importance. For such a model of IDS input, the paper proposes heterogeneous alert correlation scheme which in some sense has analogy in biological immune systems: specialized classifier→immune cell, attack class→antigen. The major idea of the approach is to organize IDS system as a structured set of classifiers trained to detect the attacks of a fixed class and thus produce alerts if "own" attack class is detected. These decisions asynchronously arrive to the second layer responsible for correlation of the alerts of the same type. The top-layer classifier solves intrusion detection task: it combines heterogeneous alerts of specialized alert correlation classifiers while producing decision it terms of particular attack class. The proposed model of data ageing allows combining alerts arriving asynchronously. *The second* paper contribution concerns the proposed multi-agent architecture and a number of reusable solutions making IDS MAS development process easier and faster.

Acknowledgement

This research is supported by grant #1993P of European Office of Aerospace R&D and by grant #04-01-00494 of the Russian Foundation for Basic Research.

References

[1] M. Wooldridge, N. Jennings, D. Kinny, The Gaia Methodology for Agent-Oriented Analysis and Design, Journal of Autonomous Agents and Multi-Agent Systems, Vol. 3, No. 3, 285–312 (2000).
[2] http://www.ll.mit.edu/IST/ideval/data/1998/1998_data_index.html.
[3] V. Gorodetsky, O. Karsaev, V. Samoilov, On-Line Update of Situation Assessment Based on Asynchronous Data Streams. 8th International Conference on Knowledge-Based Intelligent Information & Engineering Systems, LNAI, vol. 3213, Springer, 2004, pp. 1136–1142.
[4] V. Gorodetsky, O. Karsaev, V. Samoilov, Direct Mining of Rules from Data with Missing Values, Studies in Computational Intelligence, T.Y. Lin, S. Ohsuga, C.J. Liau, X.T. Hu, S. Tsumoto (Eds.). Foundation of Data Mining and Knowledge Discovery, Springer, (2005) 233–264.
[5] V. Gorodetsky, O. Karsaev, V. Samoilov, V. Konushy, E. Mankov, A. Malyshev, Multi-Agent System Development Kit, R. Unland, M. Klusch, M. Calisti (Editors), "Multi-Agent Technology and Software Tools", Whitestein Publishers. Accepted for publication (2005).

[6] V. Gorodetsky, O. Karsaev, V. Samoilov, A. Ulanov, Asynchronous Alert Correlation in Multi-Agent Intrusion Detection Systems, Lecture Notes in Computer Science, vol. 3685 (2005).
[7] V. Gorodetski, V. Skormin, L. Popyack, Data Mining Technology for Failure Prognostics of Avionics, IEEE Transactions on Aerospace and Electronic Systems, volume 38, # 2, pp. 388–403 (2002).

Security and Embedded Systems
D.N. Serpanos and R. Giladi (Eds.)
IOS Press, 2006

Securing Home and Building Automation Systems Using the zPnP Approach

Ran GILADI

Department of Communication Systems Engineering, Ben-Gurion University, Israel

Abstract. Home and building automation systems are becoming mainstream. Homeowners and building managers can now orchestrate and monitor applications and services. These systems are based on embedded systems distributed in the building and in all the controlled devices. However, embedded systems and their interconnection infrastructure, plus the ability to communicate with these systems remotely pose a serious security threat. While viruses in a PC or cellular phone can be inconvenient, a virus or Trojan horse in building functions can become a serious problem, and even prove fatal. This paper models and analyses these systems and proposes security model and measures, based on the security components from what we term as the zPnP approach [11], to make home and building automation systems safer.

Introduction

Intelligent building is based on a concept according to which building components and functions, utilities, electrical circuits, HVAC (heating, ventilating, and air-conditioning), lights, communications, audio and video are all controlled and monitored by a computerized system. We term this system Home and Building Automation System (H&BAS). With these systems one can achieve security, energy saving, and a comfortable environment to the building's inhabitants. H&BAS research and commercialization is an emerging trend. Although much research has been invested in H&BAS as well as numerous industrial projects, neither common practice, nor standardization effort was emerged. H&BAS uses special purpose networks that contain their own entities, protocols, and functions. Currently there are hundreds of controlled network standards and implementations that are used for H&BAS, some being more widespread than others. H&BAS networks can have either a centralized or a distributed architecture. Distributed networks are based on autonomous entities, embedded systems, and in general are more robust than centralized networks. Most widespread commercial systems are based on distributed networks, and in this paper we focus on these kinds of systems.

When discussing H&BAS, one has to pay particular attention to pervasive and ubiquitous computing, which are the underlying computing infrastructure behind home automation. Much research has been invested on pervasive, ubiquitous and intelligent building computing. Security issues, however, have not been explored in depth [3], especially not in the context of H&BAS. Several researchers and practitioners have noted that security in this new computing paradigm is a real problem. Stajano [18], for example, points to cyber-criminals and computer villains who exploit new, ingenious attacks that are otherwise impossible to implement in traditional computing environments.

The benefits and the hazards in H&BAS can be illustrated by the following scenario, inspired by SUN's introduction to the Jini home automation project [7]: *Your alarm clock which set itself automatically based on your work schedule and rings to wake you up. Obviously, it will let you sleep if you marked your PC calendar for a day off. While drinking your morning's coffee (it was hot and ready right on time) the TV broadcasts your most important messages (e-mails, SMS, etc.) and other filtered, interesting, newscasts from last evening, pausing when you walk away from the TV. Later, when entering your office, you are automatically authorized to enter the floor, and your office and PC wake up. If anyone else enters your room or touches your PC without your explicit permission, the PC and the door automatically lock themselves and notify security. While working, you might get an SMS message, asking you to approve a grocery purchase that your home generated; the detailed generated grocery list is in your e-mail.*

This is not fiction, and more extraordinary scenarios exist in environments such as health care, entertainment, surveillance, and other services. However, a contrary situation might also be possible, one which not has yet been described (except perhaps in some nightmarish science fiction movie or an episode from X-Files): *Just as you left home for work, an SMS was sent to a burglar, telling him that the house is at rest, no activities are taking place, apart from these indicating a "clear" space for him. He sends an SMS message back, deactivating the alarm, opens the back-door blind and enters the house. From previous pictures he took from your surveillance video camera he knows precisely where to find what he is looking for, not before letting these video cameras transmit some phantom pictures, just in case you'll feel like watching your living room.*

This is also not fiction, and other even more frightening scenarios can be envisioned, such as someone being locked inside a room, toying with your heating or lighting systems, or any other activities that could put you even in physical danger. A virus in your PC or cellular phone is at most annoying, but a virus in your home infrastructure can be a material danger. Threats can result not just from a virus, or a Trojan horse, but from any other malicious code, not intended to be there or to function the way it does, or simply a code that can jeopardize the building's inhabitants from any reason. Security threats in H&BAS will become a crucial issue as these systems become widespread, and as standardization of these systems make them open, known, and accessible.

To address these problems, this paper propose a general framework of security based on the security components from what we term as the zPnP approach [11], to be implemented by embedded systems of the H&BAS.

The paper proceeds as follows: In the next section an overview of home and building automation systems is described. A security analysis of H&BAS follows with Section 2. Section 3 describes the security components of the zPnP system we suggest. A summary and conclusions will this paper.

1. Home and Building Automation Systems (H&BAS)

A brief description of the H&BAS model is required here in order to fathom its security flaws. A more detailed description of this model can be found in [11].

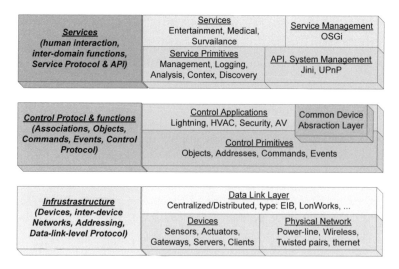

Figure 1. H&BAS three layer functional model.

Home and building automation systems (H&BAS) is modeled functionally into three layers (each layer can be further subdivided into two sublayers, as shown in Fig. 1): infrastructure (physical devices and network), control (function, information model and protocol) and services (i.e., human interaction, adaptive control, auto configuration, self-healing and inter-systems or inter-domains functions).

The infrastructure layer is the physical layer containing the devices and the inter-device network architecture and protocols. Devices usually consist of sensors and actuators, but other devices that participate in the network can also be present, such as special purpose controllers, communication gateways, servers and clients attached directly or indirectly into the network for various tasks (set-up, monitor, etc.). Networks can be based on various wireless technologies, power line interfaces, or dedicated twisted pairs, which run some media access protocol (usually a variation of CSMA or plain Ethernet) at rates of thousands bps to about a Mbps. Common implementation of such infrastructures are [21]: X10 [23], EIB [5], and LonWorks [13].

The control layer is the main layer carrying the control tasks, as programmed by the control system's tools and facilities. In this layer a configuration tool of the appropriate infrastructure instance is used to define and download all the objects in the control domain, as well as names and addresses, associations, commands, responses, triggers, etc., thus creating a static, pre-programmed and inflexible functioning control application. The control application can be targeted at just one control application (i.e., lightning, HVAC, etc.) or a combination of several. When used by upper layer entities (services), there must be some kind of "common device application layer" (CDAL) [21] in the control layer for integrating and interfacing heterogeneous control systems.

The upper layer is the service layer, where the "real intelligence" of the smart home or building is applied. This layer contains in its lower sublayer all the service primitives, functions and APIs required for the services to be best utilized. This may contain primitives such as logging, event reporting, connection establishment, security, discovery, mapping, parsing, user interface functions, analysis tools and context correlations. In addition, standard management tools and APIs can be used for building ap-

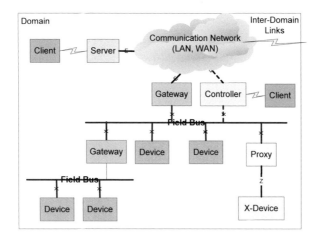

Figure 2. H&BAC physical model.

plications and services, like UPnP [4,15,20,21], Jini [4,7,21], or SNMP [10]. The upper sublayer is the actual application or service, or it can be a standard interface to services, like OSGi [4,21].

H&BAS can be also modeled by the physical building blocks and interrelations of all its components, i.e., the devices (e.g. sensors and actuators), the inter-device network (the field bus), the control devices and servers, gateways (including routers, repeaters, and bridges), external interfaces, etc. (Fig. 2). This modeling is important in identifying the points that should be protected against attackers.

It is important to distinguish between centralized, or master/slave systems, and distributed ones. In distributed systems, most or all control operations are carried by peer-to-peer communication, which is mandatory. Although there still exist servers which carry specific control tasks or services, their primary function is set-up and configuration, and they are not required for the operational mode of the control network. These servers can therefore participate in security tasks as offline trusted third parties (as will be described below). The centralized systems contain a central server that not only set-ups and configures the entire system, but is also mandatory for its operation. No direct communications is carried out between peers in a centralized network, and the slave devices, even "smart" ones, have to be protected in an entirely different security model than those participating in the distributed network. The central server in this category of systems can act as a security policy server or group controller and key server (GCKS), as defined in multicast security (MSEC) RFCs [1,6,22].

2. Security Analysis of H&BAS

H&BAS should be evaluated according to its confidentiality, authentication, non-repudiation, and integrity properties [14], and interruption, interception, modification, or fabrication attacks [19]. Some properties may be more important than others, but all should be addressed.

Current control networks used for H&BAS are not secured. By examining the physical H&BAS model (Fig. 2) one can identify its weaknesses for passive and active attackers. Anyone can essentially tap these networks and sniff the ongoing traffic, or

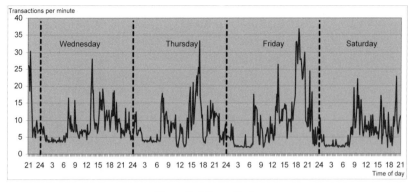

Figure 3. A House Beat.

insert his own commands into the network. In some cases (for example, where the network has extensions outside physical protected premises) it is even possible to add or replace devices on the network, or modify their software. Remote access to gateways that are connected to these networks can also be analyzed by sniffers, and information can be retrieved, manipulated, replayed or fabricated. Passive attackers can also learn about specific activities going on inside the building, or rate of activities ("building beat"), just by simple tapping and sniffing the messages that are results of the control and event transactions (Fig. 3). This is possible even if encrypted control messages are used, simply by counting the messages (or encrypted messages), or the traffic load on the home network.

An active attacker can intercept messages and replay them later after learning their impact, or understanding their functions (even if they are encrypted, if timestamping or sequencing mechanism is not used). The attacker can also interrupt messages like these dealing with alarms (again, even if they are encrypted), or can fabricate messages that cause actions he or she wants to be executed (this is harder if the messages are encrypted). An active attacker can replace devices, or alter their content (program, circuitry, etc.) in such a way that the devices will function in a different way than what they initially were designed to.

3. Security Implementation in zPnP Systems

3.1. zPnP Architecture

We designed a zero plug and play (zPnP) architecture for home and building automation systems that will enable easy deployment, programming and functioning of H&BAS [11]. The zPnP architecture provides a means for every application and every device to interoperate in a native, easy to implement manner. The principles of zPnP rely on the Internet-0 concept ([8,12]) and the UPnP scheme [4,15,20]. In UPnP every device contains XML descriptions of its identification, capabilities, services, and allowed actions. These descriptions and actions are transferred over HTTP over UDP and TCP over IP. The UPnP scheme includes some assisting mechanisms (e.g., discovery and event notifications). In zPnP a simpler implementation of each of the UPnP layers is used, i.e., Internet-0 for the IP layer, SCP instead of TCP/UDP, a lighter version of the HTTP server, and coded content instead of XML format. zPnP contains security measures in the basic networking layer, which assures confidentiality and authentications of and between the participants.

3.2. zPnP Security

In order to implement an effective security system, we analyzed the H&BAS model with respect to potential threats. The H&BAS model has four vulnerable points: a) the devices themselves, i.e., the embedded systems and hardware; b) the inter-device network; c) the external services and links (via cellular, WAN, Internet and other similar links); and d) servers and clients that are running and using applications that manipulate or query the H&BAS.

Protecting servers and clients are beyond the scope of this work. As far as H&BAS concerns, however, servers and clients can be isolated from any non-H&BAS application or network, or they can be protected by conventional means.

The security principle we designed for zPnP is based on its distributed nature, and requirements for scalability, multilevel and ubiquitous operation. Since we cannot assume that there is a "master" server or any other centralized entity for ongoing security management tasks (zPnP is fully distributed), we have to establish all security policy, key management and group control operations during the set-up and configuration phase. We know that during this phase: a) we have a configuration and set-up tool that we can use as a trusted third party (the "initiator" or "Root" as defined in [22]), and b) we can assume that during this phase access and key distribution can be authenticated easily by interactive operation or secured channels. Using one common symmetric key for all participants, and possibly a few others for subgroups to support multilevel security, will fulfill the scalability requirement, as well as the lack of on-line key management, group controller, or policy server. These common symmetric keys can be established in the set-up and configuration phase, by the set-up and configuration tool described above. Some security operations, however, should be carried out by an off-line trusted third party entity, as we shall describe in the following (e.g., re-keying, code attestation). It is possible to use the set-up and configuration tool from time to time to perform the periodical required security tasks.

3.2.1. Device Level Security

It can be assumed that the devices initially (at the set-up phase) function properly and pose no security threats. Vulnerabilities in the device level security can develop later, during their operation. They result from the communication of the devices with other entities in the H&BAS (exposed to attackers), from the programming of the devices or from a malfunction, which might create faults in the behavior of the devices or exposure to security threats.

The communication of the devices with other entities in the H&BAS should be handled by inter-device network protection as described in the following (assuming other entities are functioning properly).

The content of the embedded devices' program memory should be verified periodically (e.g., code attestation [16,17]). This verification assures that the devices are functioning as they should, i.e., no attempt was made to tamper their programs, thereby their functionality. Secure misbehavior detection [17] can assist in protecting bad programming or malfunction devices. Fault programming or device malfunction can be monitored periodically by a service that checks irregularities or unlikely patterns in the device's behavior. These periodical verifications can be carried out by an entity that is not mandatory in zPnP ongoing operation, for example, the set-up and configuration tool or server. This entity, however, should be a trusted third party, and used from time to time in order to validate network security.

3.2.2. Inter-Device Network Security

An inter-device network security model has to be designed for hundreds of devices and participants, communicating peer-to-peer, with no online central management or trusted third party. There is no "session" in H&BAS; once set-up, the devices start a long-term "session" with all other devices, with no termination of this "session".

The communication between zPnP devices has to be broadcasted since it is impossible to maintain multicast groups just for those participating in an event or control group (it depends on the event and the initial programming). Only higher level control tasks or services can reduce the number of participants to several subgroups.

These requirements and the fact that no directories or key management servers can be assumed, indicate the necessity for one common symmetric key ("Net Key" [22]) to implement basic communication between zPnP devices. More symmetric keys for subgroups can be defined, to support multilevel security for higher level control or service requirements. It should be noted, however, that most current group multicast security mechanisms [1,6,22] use pairwise keying, which is impractical for zPnP.

3.2.2.1. Key Establishment Protocol

The Shamir's no-key protocol [14], or three-pass algorithm is the preferred transport protocol for our requirement, since it assumes no a priori keying material, uses only symmetric technique, and protects from passive attackers. This protocol, however, has no entity authentication.

Device authentication can be achieved by using Shamir's no-key protocol during the set-up and configuration phase of the H&BAS, which is usually an interactive procedure. During this set up, the installer has to press a button on the installed device in a timely manner, synchronized with the set-up and configuration tool (the initiator), to allow the device to be uniquely identified by the initiator for address establishment, program and parameters download, and security material exchange. Apart from the security material exchange, this interactive dialog is common practice in most H&BASs (EIB [5], LonWorks [13]). The fourth principle in Internet-0 [12], by the way, suggests to retrieve the security key from the device, in addition to the device MAC address, when pushing this button.

The procedure of key establishment for zPnP is as follows:

a) The set-up and configuration tool (the initiator) is connected to the H&BAS.
b) The participating devices are connected to the H&BAS, and sequentially enter an interactive initialization process as follows.
c) Using Shamir's no key protocol, the initiator transports the net key (K) to the device in three messages, followed by a fourth message that contains the device MAC address disclosed and encrypted (if the system uses one, or random address otherwise, for confirming the key to the initiator), followed by a fifth message that contains the encrypted assigned logical address:

    1. Initiator $\rightarrow$ device: K^{α} mode p
    2. Initiator $\leftarrow$ device: $(K^{\alpha})^{\beta}$ mode p

3. Initiator → device: $(K^{\alpha\beta})^{\alpha(-1)}$ mode p
4. Initiator ← device: E_K(MAC Address), MAC Address
5. Initiator → device: E_K(Logical Address)

It is extremely important to execute Shamir's no-key protocol only while the installer is involved interactively. If the initiator or the device receive during this handshake any unexpected message or unsynchronized message (two messages received while waiting for a message in this sequence), or expected response is delayed, the participants should immediately stop the key transport, since there might be a security threat by an active attacker or a malfunction device.

d) After the key and the address are transported, the rest of the initialization process (program download) continues, encrypted.

3.2.2.2. Secured Messaging

Once the key is established and the H&BAS become operational, all the devices can use the net key to communicate the commands, events and responses, as they do in non-secured H&BAS. However, several issues must be dealt with, in order to support the required security and to increase the security level, such as multilevel support, re-key, randomized fields, time stamping and hiding the beat.

Multilevel: Some devices may require a different or higher level of security, for mission critical functions, sub grouping of some sensitive devices, etc. The communication protocol is upgraded to include such requests by specific protocol op-codes, called by a device (usually a controller, server, the set-up and configuration tool, and alike). Following these protocol op-codes the involved devices may initiate the pair-wise Shamir's no-key protocol to establish another key at a desired level using the established addresses of the required devices. Choosing between keys will be the application's responsibility.

RE-key: Another protocol op-code is reserved for re-key requests made by the initiator for the purpose of refreshing the keys (security might be compromised by using long term keys for similar messages). Re-keying is done by resetting the devices and initiating the key establishment protocol, including address establishment and key transport, or it is done by simple broadcasting of re-key requests, using the existing key (which is vulnerable to known key attacks).

Blurring & Sequencing: Since H&BAS messages usually have a fixed format, improved security can be achieved by adding variable random length fields to the messages, randomly filled. In addition, null messages with no meaning whatsoever should be produced and transmitted, to blur the H&BAS beat if some passive attacker counts messages or measures the control network load. All messages must be timestamped in order to avoid replay attacks. Sequencing is also possible, but a global message counter that numbers the messages must be used.

3.2.3. External Services and Links

This is probably the most vulnerable place in the H&BAS, and most of the potential attacks will be targeted here. It is outside the buildings physically, most of these connections are on the open, using public networks, e.g., Internet or WANs, and therefore more accessible to attackers. Such links and communication means are usually familiar, and there are many tools and methods for compromising these links.

There are many ways to protect these external links, however, based on the vast experience and tools that were designed specifically against these kinds of attacks, e.g., Internet standards like SSL (Secure Socket Layer) and its successor TLS (Transport Layer Security), SSH (secure Shell), and Internet applications that use these security protocols like HTTP/S (Hypertext Transfer Protocol using SSL), FTPS (File transfer Protocol over SSL) and SFTP (SSH based FTP) and many more. There are also many research studies that investigate how to make these external links secure, even specifically for H&BAS ([2,9]).

Even secured Internet servers can suffer from attacks, not so much to compromise security maybe, but more to interrupt availability (Denial-Of-Service, for example). In H&BAS connectivity might be critical issue, and these kinds of attacks should be minimized. This and the necessity to support external links with lean zPnP devices led us to design a specific protocol for use by external applications.

The protocol we designed is based on a silent encrypted UPD session, somewhat similar to the Reliable Transport Layer (RTL) combined with the Security Layer placed above the UDP suggested in [2]. The server or the device is silent and does not respond unless the right encrypted pattern enters the agreed UDP port, thereby preventing any attacker from discovering the port by standard port scanning tools. Sliding window and keepalive protocols are implemented to ensure data integrity and session continuity and recovery.

4. Summary

Home and building automation systems (H&BAS) have become common practice, with many applications and services. Their main functions are control and monitor in lightning, HVAC, security, and entertainment (AV usually). Most applications are energy saving, surveillance, and improving buildings' inhabitants "quality of life" (adjusting temperature, light, music, communications, etc.).

These systems are composed of tens to thousands of embedded devices and systems, communicating together to carry the control, events, and response messages across the system. In addition, external systems can be attached, some for monitoring, some for applications and some for control. The entire system can bring many benefits to the humans that use them, or actually, live inside them. However, their malfunction, in any component, for any reason, by anyone, malicious or accidental, can be very harmful. We analyzed the weaknesses in these systems, and proposed a security concept and implementation that is based on the zPnP approach for H&BAS, that reduce dramatically these threats. The zPnP security measures were designed so that easy implementation of them can be done on commercial systems like EIB [5] or Lon-Works [13].

References

[1] Baugher, M., Canetti, R., Dondeti, L. and Lindholm, F., "MSEC Group Key Management Architecture", *IETF MSEC WG draft*, 2004.
[2] Bergstrom, P., Driscoll, K. and Kimball, J., "Making Home Automation Communications Secure", IEEE Computer, Vol. 34, No. 10, pp. 50–56, 2001.
[3] Campbell, R., Al-Muhtadi, J. and Naldurg, P., "Towards Security and Privacy for Pervasive Computing", in Okada, M., Pierce, B.C., Scedrov, A., Tokuda, H. and Yonezawa, A. (Eds.), *Software Security – Theories and Systems, Lecture Notes in Computer Science*, No. 2609 Springer, 2003.

[4]   Dobrev, P., Famolari, D., Kurzke, C. and Miller, B.A., "Device and Service Discovery in Home Networks with OSGi", *IEEE Communications Magazine*, Vol. 40, No. 8, pp. 86–92, 2002.

[5]   EIB – European Installation Bus association: http://www.eiba.org.

[6]   Hardjono, T. and Weis, B., "The Multicast Group Architecture", *RFC 3740, IETF*, 2004.

[7]   Home – The Jini™ Home Automation Project, *http://home.jini.org.*

[8]   Krikorian, R. and Gershenfeld, N., "Internet 0 – inter device internetworking", *BT Technology Journal*, Vol. 22, No. 4, pp. 278–284, 2004.

[9]   Herzog, A. and Shahmehri, N., "Towards Secure E-Services: Risk Analysis of a home Automation Service", *Proceedings of the 6th Nordic Workshop on Secure IT-Systems (Nordsec)*, pp. 18–26, Lungby, Denmark, 2001.

[10] Giladi, R., "SNMP for Home Automation", *International Journal of Network Management*, Vol. 14, No. 4, pp. 231–239, 2004.

[11] Giladi, R., "Home and Building Automation System Using zPnP Architecture", *Technical Report, CSE, BGU*, 2005.

[12] Gershenfeld, N., Krikorian, R. and Cohen, D., "The Internet of Things", *Scientific American*, Vol. 291, No. 4, pp. 76–81, 2004.

[13] LonWorks, ANSI/EIA 709.1 Control Networking Standard, http://www.echelon.com.

[14] Menezes, A., van Oorschot, P. and Vanstone, S., *Handbook of Applied Cryptography*, CRC Press LLC, 1997.

[15] Miller, B., Nixon, T., Tai, C. and Wood, M., "Home Networking with Universal Plug and Play", *IEEE Communications Magazine*, Vol. 39, No. 12, pp. 104–109, 2001.

[16] Seshadri, A., Perrig, A., van-Doorn, L. and Khosla, P., "SWATT: Software-based ATTestation for Embedded Devices", *IEEE symposium on Security and Privacy*, Oakland, CA, 2004.

[17] Shi, E. and Perrig, A., "Designing Secure Sensor Networks", *IEEE Wireless Communications*, Vol. 11, No. 6, pp. 38–43, 2004.

[18] Stajano, F., *Security for Ubiquitous Computing*, Halsted Press, 2002.

[19] Stallings, W., *Network Security Essentials – Applications and Standards*, Prentice Hall, Englewood Cliffs, NJ, USA, 2000.

[20] UPnP – http://www.upnp.org.

[21] Valtchev, D. and Frankov, I., "Service Gateway Architecture for a Smart Home", *IEEE Communications Magazine*, Vol. 40, No. 4, pp. 126–132, 2002.

[22] Wallner, D., Harder, E. and Agee, R., "Key Management for Multicast: Issues and Architectures", *RFC 2627, IEFT*, 1999.

[23] X10 – http://www.x10.com.

180

Security and Embedded Systems
D.N. Serpanos and R. Giladi (Eds.)
IOS Press, 2006

REWARD: A Routing Method for Ad-Hoc Networks with Adjustable Security Capability

Zdravko KARAKEHAYOV and Ivan RADEV
Technical University of Sofia, Bulgaria

Abstract. This paper describes REWARD, a novel routing algorithm for wireless sensor networks. The algorithm is adjustable and can wage counter attacks against either single black holes or teams of malicious nodes. The proposed routing technique is suitable for network nodes that can tune their transmit power. REWARD forwards packets using geographic routing. The algorithm utilizes two types of broadcast messages, MISS and SAMBA, to organize a distributed data base for detected black hole attacks. The method has different levels of security which can be set according to the local conditions. In order to determine the effectiveness of REWARD we developed ANTS, a simulation environment which models the operation of a wireless sensor network.

Keywords. Distributed sensor networks, Secure routing, Low-power design

Introduction

The transition from desktop computing to embedded systems is associated with price, power and timing constrains. A special class embedded systems, termed distributed sensor networks (DSN), are characterized by extra requirements: small size and sufficient battery lifetime. Distributed sensor networks can be alternatively labelled mobile ad-hoc networks (MANET). While the term DSN is associated with data acquisition applications, MANET emphasises mobility and the lack of infrastructure. Distributed sensor networks can be scalable to thousands of nodes that cooperatively perform complex tasks. The interaction between the nodes is based on wireless communication. Wireless sensor networks (WSN) is yet another synonym.

1. Location

A deployment may leave numerous nodes located in a large geographical region. Most typical roles require nodes to know their own positions. Sensor readings are of interest if only bound to a known location. A known distance between a sender and a receiver and their locations help to communicate power efficiently. In this case, the transmit power can be adjusted according to the distance and the environmental conditions.

Routing algorithms may require or benefit from available node locations. It is fairly common to select the next hope node minimizing the distance to the destination node. Finally, applications such as target/event tracking utilize location to the extreme.

Assume that the event is a moving light shadow edge. Each node is aware of a set of neighbor locations. A method has been developed to identify the nodes which will not be immediately approached by the event and can be turned off to save energy [1]. The method is based on the dual space transformation. Points from the primal space are transformed into lines in the dual space. Lines from the primal space are transformed into points in the dual space. As a result, the dual space is partitioned into cells. Nodes identify which cell contains the event-point and which nodes-lines form the cell. Since the event can not intersect a specific node-line, before it crosses one of the cell boundaries, the node can stay turned off as long as none of the boundary nodes senses a transition. This method may provide a substantial power reduction for a large sensor field. However, if nodes that line the perimeter around the event misbehave and declare a transition, it will force several other nodes to wake up and waste energy [2]. The chance for battery replacement is practically non existent and the battery attack emerges as a significant threat.

2. Aggregation

When data is collected from numerous sensors in a dense network, there is a high probability for redundancy. Data redundancy will result in unnecessary and replicated transmissions. Aggregation, based on correlated data of neighboring nodes, helps to reduce the total volume to be routed. Consequently, there are nodes which receive two or more data streams and then aggregate them into a single stream. This approach, however, makes the network more vulnerable. If the packets through a malicious node are simply consumed or lost, the attack against the network is termed black hole [3]. To work around this problem longer routes must be employed or perhaps more streams. Inevitably, the corrective actions will increase the power consumption.

3. Computation

Assume that the functionality is partitioned into tasks. The movement of nodes imposes deadlines on the tasks execution times.

3.1. Compile-Time Scheduling

The tasks cannot be pre-empted. Each task is characterized by its execution time and deadline. The execution time is measured in number of clock cycles, NC. Assume that the processor has two modes: an active mode and a power saving mode. The task deadline T_{DL} accommodates both the active period T_{ACT} and the power-saving period T_{PS}

$$T_{DL} = T_{ACT} + T_{PS} \tag{1}$$

In both CPU modes the power consumption scales linearly with the clock frequency.

$$P_{ACT} = k_{ACT} \times f^{CLK} + n_{ACT} \text{ and } P_{PS} = k_{PS} \times f^{CLK} + n_{PS} \tag{2}$$

If $n_{ACT} > n_{PS}$, the energy per task has a minimum for

$$f^{CLK,OPT} = \sqrt{\frac{n_{ACT} - n_{PS}}{k_{PS}}} \sqrt{\frac{NC}{T_{DL}}} \tag{3}$$

If $n_{ACT} \leq n_{PS}$, the clock frequency must be selected as low as possible.

A tool named CASTLE (crystal annealing software tool for low energy) has been developed to provide computer assistance in calculating the optimal clock frequencies. CASTLE has potential for further reduction of energy if the sequence of tasks and possible overlaps are specified. After a search through all combinations, CASTLE finds the most beneficial trade-off consistent with the specification. Currently, CASTLE employs the AT91M55800 microcontroller built-in multiplication and division factors for the oscillator frequency, but it could be easily extended to support other variable-frequency processors [4].

3.2. Run-Time Scheduling

While the compile-time scheduling does not fully exploit the potential for power reduction under changing conditions, a run-time scheduling would provide adaptability. An operating system will be responsible for the dynamic scheduling. Moreover, the operating system will act as a power manager, adjusting the supply voltage and the clock frequency. An algorithm has been developed for low-power, run-time scheduling [5]. The algorithm, named LEDF, maintains a list of all ready for execution tasks. Again, the tasks cannot be pre-empted. The CPU is capable of operating at different voltages and clock frequencies. The supply voltage and the clock rate are controlled by the operating system. The LEDF algorithm is an integrated part of the operating system. On the top of the ready list is the task with the earliest deadline. The first step is to test if this task can meet its deadline at the lowest clock rate (lowest voltage). If this clock rate is too low, the next higher possible value is considered. When the current task deadline is met, an additional test is performed. The algorithm checks if the other tasks from the ready list can meet their deadlines at the highest clock rate. If any task will miss its deadline, the rate in focus is insufficient and the next higher speed for the current task is considered. As soon as the deadlines of all other tasks in the ready list can be met at the highest speed, the clock rate (voltage) is accepted and the task begins execution. When the task completes execution, the algorithm again selects the task with the nearest deadline to be off and running. Inevitably, the CPU must spend energy to sort the tasks in the ready list and verify both tests. The LEDF algorithm has a computational complexity of $O(n \log n)$ for n tasks and a processor with two clock rates.

4. Communication

There are two possibilities for communication in the field of ad-hoc networks: radio-frequency radiation and optical communication. The energy used to send a bit between two radios over a distance d may be written as

$$E = A \times d^n \tag{4}$$

where A is a proportionality constant and n depends on the environment [6]. Rewrite Eq. (4) for NH number of hops [7]. Also, include the energy for receiving E_R and energy for computation E_C. The energy has a minimum for

$$\text{NH}_{\text{OPT}} = d \times \sqrt[n]{\frac{A(n-1)}{E_R + E_C}} \tag{5}$$

At the radio level all packets are broadcast. This feature of the inter-node radio behavior can be used to take advantage in two directions. First, routing can be improved if instead of choosing a single route ahead of time, the path through the network is determined based on which nodes receive each transmission [8,9]. Second, security can be improved if nodes listen to their neighbor transmissions to detect black-hole attacks [10,11].

5. REWARD

REWARD is a routing method that allows a wireless ad-hoc network to organize a distributed data base for detected black hole attacks. The data base keeps records for suspicious nodes and areas. Routing in a dense network would allow alternative paths to avoid suspicious nodes and areas. The algorithm utilizes two types of broadcast messages, MISS and SAMBA. The MISS message is not related to a specific protocol and can be used after any route discovery procedure. In contrast, nodes are capable of providing suspicious locations via SAMBA messages only if they apply REWARD as a routing algorithm.

5.1. MISS Message

Assume that a demand-driven protocol performs a route discovery procedure. When the destination receives the query, it sends its location back and waits for a packet. If the packet does not arrive within a specified period of time, the destination node broadcasts a MISS (material for intersection of suspicious sets) message. The destination copies the list of all involved nodes from the query to the MISS message. Since the reason for not receiving the packet is most likely a black-hole attack, all nodes listed in the MISS message are under suspicion. Nodes collect MISS messages and intersect them to detect misbehaving participants in the routes. The detected malicious nodes are excluded from the routing.

5.2. REWARD with Replication

The initial idea for REWARD (receive, watch, redirect) was associated with replication. Figure 1 shows the sequence of multihop transmissions under REWARD.

After five transmissions the destination receives two packets with identical data. Each node's transmissions are directed to both immediate neighbors, one node forward and one node backward. If a node attempts a black-hole attack and drops a package, it will be detected by the next node in the path. The watcher waits for a predefined time period, transmits the packet changing the path and broadcasts a SAMBA (suspicious area, mark a black-hole attack) message. The SAMBA message provides the location of the black-hole attack.

5.3. REWARD Against a Single Malicious Node

Figure 2 shows an example. Each node tunes the transmit power to reach both immediate neighbors. The nodes transmit packets and watch if the packets are forwarded. If a

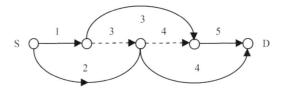

Figure 1. Two identical packets are sent to the destination.

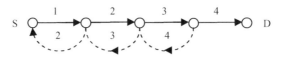

Figure 2. Transmissions must be received by both neighbors.

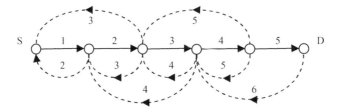

Figure 3. REWARD against two black holes.

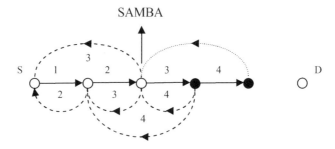

Figure 4. REWARD detects the second black hole.

malicious node does not act as a forwarder, the previous node in the path will broadcast a SAMBA message.

5.4. REWARD Against a Team of Black Holes

REWARD is a scalable method capable of waging counter attacks against a different number of black holes. Figure 3 shows an example routing with the assumption that a team of two malicious nodes would attempt a black hole attack. In this case the algorithm requires the nodes to listen for two retransmissions.

Figure 4 indicates the exact positions of the black holes in the path. The first malicious node forwards the packet using the required transmit power to deceive two nodes backward. The second malicious node drops the packet, however the attack is detected by the last node before the black holes. The missing transmission is shown by a dot line in Fig. 4. An extra black hole in the path would mask the attack.

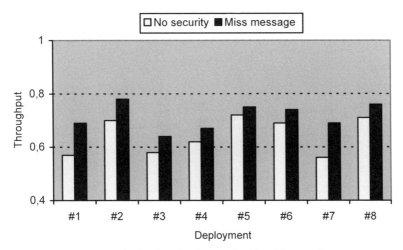

Figure 5. The fraction of packets received for eight examples.

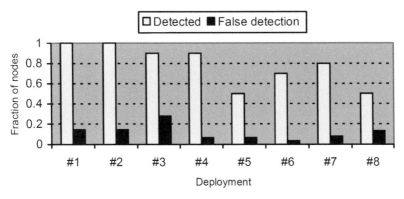

Figure 6. Detected malicious nodes against false detection.

5.5. Routing Through a Suspicious Area

REWARD employs security levels which correspond to the number of malicious nodes that can be detected [11]. When a packet approaches a suspicious area, the security level is gradually increased. Leaving the suspicious area, the algorithm declines the security level. Consequently, the energy overhead associated with security is declined as much as possible.

6. ANTS Simulator

ANTS (ad-hoc networks traffic simulator) is a tool developed to simulate the functionality of ad-hoc networks. We assume that all nodes are stationary throughout the simulation. The simulator allows to vary with the number of nodes, locations, battery capacity and communication range. Figure 5 shows simulation results of the throughput, 100 packets routing for eight example deployments. Figure 6 shows the fraction of malicious nodes detected against false detection, nodes excluded from the network as ma-

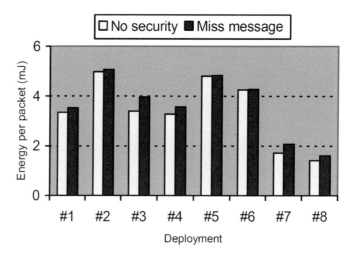

Figure 7. Energy per packet in both modes.

licious when in fact they are not. MISS messages are broadcasted within areas which include all nodes involved in the corresponding routing. Figure 7 attempts to show how MISS messages increase the power consumption due to more uninterrupted routes and the MISS broadcasting itself.

7. Conclusion

In this paper we discuss security and power efficiency of wireless ad-hoc networks. The routing algorithm in focus, REWARD, take advantage of the broadcast inter-radio behavior to watch neighbor transmissions and detect black hole attacks. As soon as network nodes misbehave, the method begins to create a distributed data base which includes suspicious nodes and areas.

The sets of suspicious nodes emerge locally by intersecting MISS messages. The locations of detected black hole attacks are broadcast via SAMBA messages.

References

[1] J. Liu, P. Cheung, L. Guibas and F. Zhao, A dual-space approach to tracking and sensor management in wireless sensor networks, Palo Alto Research Center Technical Report P2002-10077, 2002. Available at www2.parc.com/spl/projects/cosense/pub/dualspace.pdf.

[2] Z. Karakehayov, Design of distributed sensor networks for security and defense, In *Proceedings of the NATO Advanced Research Workshop on Cyberspace Security and Defense: Research Issues*, edited by J.S. Kowalik, J. Gorski and A. Sachenko, Springer, NATO Science Series II, Vol. 196, 2005, 177–192.

[3] H. Deng, W. Li and D.P. Agrawal, Routing security in wireless ad hoc networks, *IEEE Communications Magazine*, October, 2002, 70–75.

[4] Atmel Corporation, *AT91 ARM Thumb Microcontrollers, AT91M55800A*, 2002. Available at www.atmel.com.

[5] V. Swaminathan, Y. Zou and K. Chakrabarty, Techniques to reduce communication and computation energy in wireless sensor networks, in *Handbook of Sensor Networks: Compact Wireless and Wired Sensing Systems*, edited by Mohammad Ilyas and Imad Mahgoub, CRC Press LLC, 2005.

[6] J.M. Rabaey, M.J. Ammer, J.L. Silva, D. Patel and S. Roundy, PicoRadio supports ad hoc ultra-low power wireless networking, *IEEE Computer*, Vol. 33, July, 2000, 42–48.

[7] Z. Karakehayov, Low-power design for Smart Dust networks, in *Handbook of Sensor Networks: Compact Wireless and Wired Sensing Systems*, edited by Mohammad Ilyas and Imad Mahgoub, CRC Press LLC, 2005.

[8] S. Biswas and R. Morris, Opportunistic routing in multi-hop wireless networks, *ACM SIGCOMM Computer Communication Review*, Vol. 34, Issue 1, January, 2004, 69–74.

[9] M. Witt and V. Turau, BGR: Blind geographic routing for sensor networks, In *Proceedings of the Third International Workshop on Intelligent Solutions in Embedded Systems,* Hamburg, Germany, May, 2005.

[10] S. Marti, T.J. Giuli, K. Lai and M. Baker, Mitigating routing misbehavior in mobile ad hoc networks, In *Proceedings 6th Int. Conference Mobile Computing Networking (MOBICOM-00)*, New York, August, 2000, ACM Press, 255–265.

[11] Z. Karakehayov, Using REWARD to detect team black-hole attacks in wireless sensor networks, In *Proceedings of the Workshop on Real-World Wireless Sensor Networks*, REALWSN'5, Stockholm, June, 2005.

Security and Embedded Systems
D.N. Serpanos and R. Giladi (Eds.)
IOS Press, 2006

On the Security of the GSM Cellular Network

Elad BARKAN and Eli BIHAM

*Computer Science Department, Technion – Israel Institute of Technology,
Haifa 32000, Israel*

Abstract. In this paper we report on the current status of the security of GSM (generation 2.5). We review main attacks on GSM, and present an improvement for withstanding reception errors.

Keywords. GSM, Security, A5/1, A5/2, Cryptanalysis

1. Introduction

GSM is the most widely used cellular system in the world, with over a billion customers around the world. The system was developed during the late 1980s, and the first GSM network were deployed in the early 1990s. GSM is based on second generation cellular technology, i.e., it offers digitalized voice (rather than analog, as used in prior systems).

GSM was the first cellular system which seriously considered security threats. One example is a secure cryptographic hardware in the phone (the SIM - Subscriber Identity Module), which was introduced in GSM. Previous cellular systems had practically no security, and they were increasingly the subject of criminal activity such as eavesdropping on cellular calls, phone cloning, and call theft.

The security threat model of GSM was influenced by the political atmosphere around cryptology at the 1980s, which did not allow civilians to use strong cryptography. Therefore, the objective was that the security of GSM would be equivalent to the security of fixed-line telephony. As a result, only the air-interface of GSM was protected, leaving the rest of the system un-protected. The aim of the protection on the air-interface is to provide two kinds of protections: protect the privacy of users (mostly through encryption), and protect the network from unauthorized access to the network (by cryptographic authentication of the SIM).

The privacy of users on the air-interface is protected by encryption. However, encryption can start only after the mobile phone identified itself to the network. GSM also protects the identity of the users by pre-allocating a temporary identification (TMSI - Temporary Mobile Subscriber Identity) to the mobile phone. This temporary identification is used to identify the mobile phone before encryption can commence. The temporary identification for the next call can be safely replaced once the call is encrypted.

Authentication of the SIM by the network occurs at a beginning of a radio conversation between the mobile phone and the network. After the phone identifies itself (e.g., by sending its TMSI), the network can initiate an authentication procedure. The procedure, is basically a challenge-response scheme based on a pre-shared secret Ki between the mobile phone and the network. In the scheme, the network challenges the mobile phone with a 128-bit random number $RAND$; the mobile phone transfers $RAND$ to the SIM, which calculates the response $SRES = A3(Ki, RAND)$, where $A3$ is a one-way function; then, the mobile phone transmits $SRES$ to the network, which compares is to the $SRES$ value that it pre-calculated. The encryption key Kc for the conversation is created in parallel to the authentication by $Kc = A8(Ki, RAND)$, where $A8$ is also a one-way function. The remainder of the call can be encrypted using Kc, and thus, the mobile phone and the network remain mutually "authenticated" due to the fact that they use the same encryption key. However, encryption is controlled by the network, and it is not mandatory. Therefore, an attacker can easily impersonate the network to the mobile phone using a false base station with no encryption. In general, it is not advisable to count on an encryption algorithm for authentication, especially in the kind of encryption that is used in GSM.

The exact design of A3 and A8 can be selected by each operator independently. However, many operators used the example, called *COMP128*, given in the GSM memorandum of understanding (MoU). Although never officially published, COMP128's description was found by Briceno, Goldberg, and Wagner [1]. They have performed cryptanalysis of COMP128 [2], allowing to find the pre-shared secret Ki of the mobile phone and the network. Given K_i, A3 and A8 it is easy to perform cloning. Their attack requires the $SRES$ for about 2^{17} values of $RAND$. The required data for this kind of attack can obtained within a few hours over-the-air using a fake base station.

The original encryption algorithm for GSM was A5/1. However, A5/1 was export restricted, and as the network grew beyond Europe there was a need for an encryption algorithm without export restrictions. As a result, a new (weakened) encryption algorithm A5/2 was developed. The design of both algorithms was kept secret (it was disclosed only on a need-to-know basis, under an non-disclosure agreement, to GSM manufacturers). In 2002, an additional new version A5/3, was added to the A5 family. Unlike, A5/1 and A5/2, it's internal design was *published*. A5/3 is based on the block-cipher KASUMI, which is used in third generation networks. A5/3 is currently not yet deployed in GSM, but deployment should start soon.

The internal design of both A5/1 and A5/2 was reverse engineered from an actual GSM phone by Briceno [3] in 1999. The internal design was verified against known test-vectors, and it is available on the Internet [3].

After the reverse engineering of A5/1 and A5/2, it was demonstrated that A5/1 and A5/2 do not provide an adequate level of security for GSM. However, most of the attacks are in a known-plaintext attack model, i.e., they require the attacker not only to intercept the required data frames, but also to know their contents before they are encrypted. The first known-plaintext analysis of A5/1 was performed by Golic [4] in 1997, when only a rough structure of the cipher leaked. He proposed two attacks that demonstrated that A5/1 is not as strong as it could have been. In 2000, the second attack of Golic was significantly improved by Biryukov, Shamir, and Wagner [5], in some scenarios the improved attack can find the key in less than a second. However, the attack requires a storage of four 74-gigabyte disks and a lengthy precomputation. Later that year, Biryukov and Shamir generalized this attack [6]. At the same time, a different approach was taken by Biham and Dunkelman [7]. Their attack requires about 20500 data frames (about 95 seconds of conversation) and recovers the key with a time complexity of about 2^{40} A5/1 clockings.

Another line of attacks on A5/1 started in 2001, when Ekdahl and Johansson [8] applied ideas from correlation attacks to A5/1. Their attack requires a few minutes of known-plaintext, and finds the key within minutes on a personal computer. One advantage of this attack is that it requires no preprocessing and no large storage. In 2004, Maximov, Johansson, and Babbage [9] observed a new correlation and used it to improved the attack. Given about 5000 frames (about 9.2 to 23 seconds of known-plaintext), their attack recovers the key within 0.5–10 minutes on a personal computer. In 2005, the attack was further improved by Barkan and Biham [10], using conditional estimators and weaknesses of one of A5/1 internal registers. The improved attack can work with 1500 frames of data (about 6.9 seconds of conversation) and can find the key within one to two minutes on a personal computer. They also describe a source for known plaintext in GSM, that can provide the 1500 required frames of known plaintext from about 3 minutes worth of ciphertext.

As for A5/2, it was cryptanalyzed by Goldberg, Wagner and Green [11] immediately after the reverse engineering. This attack on A5/2 works in a negligible time complexity and it requires only two known-plaintext data frames which are exactly $26 \cdot 51 = 1326$ data frames apart (about 6 seconds apart). Another attack on A5/2 was proposed by Petrović and Fúster-Sabater [12]. This attack works by constructing a systems of quadratic equations whose variables describe the internal state of A5/2 (i.e., equations of the form $c = \bigoplus_{i,j} a_i \cdot a_j$, where $a_i, a_j, c \in \{0, 1\}$, a_i and a_j are variables and c is a constant). This attack has the advantage that it requires only four know-plaintext data frames (thus the attacker is not forced to wait 6 seconds), but it does not recover the encryption key, rather, it allows to decrypt most of the remaining communications.

The latest attacks on A5/2 were proposed by Barkan, Biham, and Keller in 2003 [13]. First, they describe a very efficient known-plaintext attack on A5/2 (less than one second on a personal computer to find the encryption key). Then, they use a flaw in the way GSM uses its error-correction code: the data to be transmitted is first subjected to the error-correction code, and only then it is encrypted and transmitted (instead of first being encrypted and then subjected to the error-correction code). Using this flaw, they convert the known-plaintext attack to a ciphertext-only attack on GSM, i.e., now the attacker needs only to tap the encrypted communications, and is able to find the encryption key. They use flaws in the protocol to mount an active attack on A5/1 networks, allowing to find the encryption key in A5/1 networks in less than a second.

In the remainder of this paper, we review the main ideas behind the Barkan, Biham, and Keller attack [13], and present an improved attack method for withstanding reception errors.

2. Main Ideas of the Barkan, Biham, and Keller Attacks

2.1. Short Overview of A5/2

The internal state of A5/2 is composed of four linear-feedback shift registers (LFSRs), R1, R2, R3, and R4, of lengths 19-bit, 22-bit, 23-bit, and 17-bit, respectively. At each data frame, the registers are initialized using Kc and a publicly known frame number, and

A5/2 is run to produce an output that is called keystream. The data frame is encrypted by a bit-wise XOR with the keystream. Therefore, given a plaintext and a ciphertext, we can calculate the keystream as their bit-wise XOR.

To produce an output bit of the keystream, R4 is clocked, and according to its value, R1, R2, and R3 are clocked, in such a way that either the three registers are clocked, or two of the registers are clocked and the other register stands still. Then, an output bit is calculated according to the values of R1, R2, and R3. The process is repeated to generate additional output bits.

The first step of the initialization process is linear in Kc and the frame number (i.e., it can be calculated by multiplying the value of Kc and the frame number by a binary matrix, using modulo 2 additions). The second (weird) step of the initialization process is forcing one bit of each register to be 1. This step reduces the effective size of the internal state of A5/2 from $19 + 22 + 23 + 17 = 81$ bits to $18 + 21 + 22 + 16 = 77$ bits.

2.2. Main Ideas of the Known-Plaintext Attack on A5/2

Given a value for R4, every keystream bit can be written as a quadratic expression of the internal state of R1, R2, and R3 right after initialization. For example let $x_0, \ldots, x_{18}$, $y_0, \ldots, y_{21}, z_0, \ldots, z_{22}$ be variables representing the bits of R1, R2, and R3, respectively. Then, the first bit of the keystream is $k_0 = x_{12}x_{14} \oplus x_{12} \oplus x_{12}x_{15} \oplus x_{14}x_{15} \oplus x_{15} \oplus x_{18} \oplus y_9y_{13} \oplus \ldots \oplus z_{16}z_{18} \oplus z_{22}$. Due to the linearity of the initialization of the A5/2, the keystream bits of different frames can still be written using the same variables of the first frames. Thus, each data frame adds equations without increasing the number of variables. After collecting about 450 equations (less than four data frames), the linear terms can be found (by linearizing the system and solving it, e.g., using Gauss elimination). Then, the initialization process is reversed to find Kc. The attack requires to try all the 2^{16} possible values for R4, until a consistent solution is found. Most inconsistencies are detected and discarded during the Gauss elimination. The remaining solutions are verified by trial encryption.

In a faster implementation, the 2^{16} possible equation systems are calculated in advance. Since the systems are overdefined, we use the redundancy to filter R4 values that are inconsistent. For each candidate value $R4'$ of R4, we construct a consistency-check matrix $T_{R4'}$, such that for the correct value of R4 and the keystream k it holds that $T_{R4'} \cdot k^T = 0$, where 0 is the zero vector.

With 16 equations of consistency check, on average two candidates for R4 remain after this filtering. For these two candidates, the key is calculated by solving the equation systems, and verified using trial encryptions. The whole attack completes on a personal computer in less than a second, and consumes a few tens of MBs of memory (for storing the consistency-check matrices).

2.3. Main Ideas of the Ciphertext-Only Attack on A5/2

GSM must use error correction to withstand reception errors. However, in the GSM protocol the message (consisting of four frames of data) is first subjected to an error-correction code, which doubles the size of the message from 228 bits to 456 bits. Only then, the coded message is encrypted and transmitted. Let P be the 228-bit message before error correction. Then, error correction can be modeled as a multiplication of P by a matrix G of size 456×228, i.e., $M = G \cdot P$, where M is a 456-bit vector.

The message is encrypted using the keystream k. Therefore, the transmitted message is $C = M \oplus k = G \cdot P \oplus k$.

The corner stone for the ciphertext-only attack is the parity check matrix H of the error-correction code. For H it holds that $H \cdot G = 0^{228}$, where 0^{228} is a vector of 228 zeros, and the rank of H is 228. When H is applied on the ciphertext C, we get that $H \cdot C = H \cdot G \cdot P \oplus H \cdot k = 0 \oplus H \cdot k = H \cdot k$. Therefore, the contribution of the transmitted message is eliminated, and we obtain an equation system that only involves the bits of the keystream k: $H \cdot k = H \cdot C$.

To complete the ciphertext-only attack, each bit of the keystream is replaced by its quadratic expression, thus, we obtain a quadratic system of 228 equations. By considering another ciphertext message, we obtain 228 additional equations, which together with the former equations constitute 456 equations. This number of equations is sufficient to employ an attack similar to the one of the case the known-plaintext attack.

The ciphertext only attack requires twice as many frames as the known-plaintext attack, and works with the same time and memory complexity, i.e., in less than a second on a personal computer.

Note that the systems of equations $H \cdot k = H \cdot C$ is independent of the key stream generation algorithm. Therefore, it can also be constructed in case of A5/1. However, solving it in the case of A5/1 is very complex. One interesting ciphertext-only attack on A5/1 considers $H \cdot k$ as the output of a random random function whose input is Kc and the frame number (alternatively, the input can be the internal state of A5/1). Inverting this random function, reveals the key. A time/memory/data tradeoff [6] can be used to invert $H \cdot k$ back to the internal state in a time faster than exhaustive search.

2.4. Main Ideas of the Active Attack on A5/1 Networks

The main observation is that once the authentication is complete, Kc is determined, regardless of whether A5/1 or A5/2 is employed. Therefore, the following attack succeeds whenever the mobile phone supports A5/2.

The attacker performs a man-in-the-middle attack. It impersonates the network to the mobile phone (using a fake base station), and the mobile phone to the network. During authentication the network sends *RAND*, and the attacker forwards *RAND* to the mobile phone. The SIM of the mobile phone calculates *Kc* and *SRES*, and returns *SRES* to the attacker. The attacker does not immediately forward *SRES* to the network (the network timeout allow 12 seconds of delay). Instead, it asks the mobile phone to start encryption using A5/2. The mobile phone starts encryption, as the request appears as a legitimate request of the "network" (which is actually the attacker). The mobile phone sends an acknowledgment message which is already encrypted. The attacker then uses the ciphertext-only attack, and in less than a second recovers *Kc*. Only then, the attacker forwards *SRES* to the network. When the network asks the attacker to encrypt using A5/1, *Kc* is already known, and thus, the attacker can encrypt and decrypt the conversation. The result is that the attacker communicates with the network using A5/1, but with the mobile phone using A5/2.

The attacker can listen to the conversation by continuously forwarding messages between the mobile phone and the network (the attacker needs to decrypt the messages and re-encrypt them using the other cipher). Furthermore, the attacker can change the information that passes, or completely take over the conversation, replacing the mobile phone. The attacker can also perform call theft by initiating a connection with both the network and mobile phone, and using the mobile phone as an oracle for *SRES* and *Kc*.

2.5. Improving the Attacks to Withstand Reception Errors

A possible problem in a real-life implementation of the above attacks is the existence of radio reception errors. A single flipped bit might fail an attack (i.e., the attack ends without finding K_c). Once the attack fails, the attacker can abandon the problematic data, and start again from scratch. But in a noisy environment, the chances are high that the new data will also contain errors. An alternative approach that we present in this section is to correct these errors.

Two kinds of reception error can occur: flipped bits, and erasures. A flipped bit is a bit that was transmitted as "1" and received as "0", or vice versa. Erasures occur when the receiver cannot determine whether a bit is "1" or "0". Many receivers can report erased bits (rather than guessing a random value).

A possible inefficient algorithm to correct reception errors is to exhaustively try all the possibilities for errors. For flipped bits, we can first try to employ the attack without any changes (assuming no error occurred), and if the attack fails we repeat it many times, each time guessing different locations for the flipped bits. We try the possibilities with the least amount of errors first. The time complexity is exponential in the number of errors, i.e., about $\binom{n}{e} A$, where A is the time complexity of the original attack, n is the number of input bits, and e is the number of errors. The case with erasures is somewhat better, as we only need to try all the possible values for the erased bits. The time complexity is thus $2^e A$, where e is the number of erasures. In the un-optimized known-plaintext attack, an erased plaintext bit translates to an erased keystream bit. Each keystream bit contributes one equation, thus, we can simply remove the equations of the erased keystream bits. If not too many erasures occur, we still have sufficiently many equations to perform the attack. However, in the optimized attack, we pre-compute all the equation systems, and thus we cannot remove an equation a posteriori. We could pre-compute the equation systems for every possible erasure pattern, but it would take a huge time to compute, and it would require huge storage. Therefore, another method is needed.

In the rest of this section, we present an (asymptotically) better method to apply the optimized attack with the presence of erasures. For simplicity, we focus on the optimized known-plaintext attack on A5/2, but the optimized ciphertext-only attack can be similarly improved.

Assume that e erasures occur with their locations known, but no flips. We view the keystream as the XOR of two vectors, a first vector that contains the undoubted bits of the keystream (with the erased bits set to zero), and a second vector that has a value for the erased bits (with the undoubted bits set to zero). Let r be the first vector. Let r_i be the ith possibility (out of the 2^e possibilities) for the second vector, where i is the binary value of the concatenated erased bits. Thus, given the correct value for i, the correct keystream is $k = r \oplus r_i$.

We find the correct value for i without an exhaustive search. Recall the consistency-check matrices $T_{R4'}$. The linear space spanned by $T_{R4'} \cdot r_i$, where $i \in [0, \ldots, 2^e - 1]$, has a maximum dimension of e (if the columns of $T_{R4'}$ are linearly independent the degree is exactly e, for simplicity we assume that this is indeed the case). We denote this linear space by $\vec{T}_{R4'}$.

We reduce the problem of finding the correct i to a problem of solving a linear system. For each $R4'$, we compute $T_{R4'} \cdot r$. Clearly, for the correct $R4'$ value and for the correct r_i value, $T_{R4'} \cdot (r_i \oplus r)$ is a vector of zeros. Therefore, for the correct r_i, $T_{R4'} \cdot r_i = T_{R4'} \cdot r$. Thus, the problem of finding the correct i is reduced to finding the r_i that solves this equation.

An efficient way to solve such a system is as follows: First find e vectors that span the space $\vec{T}_{R4'}$. Such e vectors are given by $b_j = T_{R4'} \cdot r_{2^j}$, where $j \in \{0, 1, 2, \ldots, e-1\}$. Then, we define a new matrix B whose columns are the vectors b_j: $B = (b_0, \ldots, b_{e-1})$. Finally, we find the correct i by requiring that $B \cdot i = T_{R4'} \cdot r$, and solving the system (e.g., using Gauss elimination) to find i. If inconsistencies occur during the Gauss elimination, we move on to the next candidate of R4, otherwise we assume we found the value of R4 and the keystream, and use the attack to recover K_c (which is verified using a trial encryption). Note that if the degree of $\vec{T}_{R4'}$ is smaller than e, then Gauss elimination might result in more than one option for i. In such case, the number of options for i is always less or equal to 2^e.

The number of needed rows in $T_{R4'}$ in order to correct e erasures is about $16 + e$: For each of the 2^{16} candidate values of $R4$ the e erasures span a space of at most 2^e vectors, thus, there are about 2^{16+e} candidate solutions. Therefore, the number of rows in $T_{R4'}$ needs to be about $16+e$ in order to ensure that only about two consistent solution remain.

The time complexity of correcting the erasures for a single candidate of R4 is composed of first calculating the matrix B and $T_{R4'} \cdot r$, and then solving the equation system $B \cdot i = T_{R4'} \cdot r$. Calculating B and $T_{R4'} \cdot r$ is comparable to one full vector by matrix multiplication, i.e., about $456(16 + e)$ bit-XORs. The Gauss elimination takes about $O((16 + e)^3)$ bit-XOR operations. The processes is repeated for every possible value of R4. Thus, the time complexity is about $2^{16}(456(16+e) + (16+e)^3)$ bit-XOR operations. Assuming that ten erasures need to be corrected, the total time complexity is about 2^{31} bit-XOR operations, i.e., about three and a half times the complexity of the optimized known-plaintext attack without reception errors. A naive implementation for correcting ten erasures would take about $2^{10} \approx 1000$ times longer to execute than the optimized known-plaintext attack. It can be seen that the benefit of the method grows as the number of erasures increases because the method's time complexity is polynomial in the number of erasures, compared to an exponential time complexity in the case of the naive method.

3. Summary

In this paper, we reviewed the main attacks on GSM, and we described the main ideas behind the attacks of Barkan, Biham, and Keller [13]. Then, we introduce a new method that improves these attacks to withstand reception errors. Thus, the attacks are made robust to operate even in a noisy radio environment.

References

[1] Marc Briceno, Ian Goldberg, David Wagner, *An implementation of the GSM A3A8 algorithm*, http://www.iol.ie/ kooltek/a3a8.txt, 1998.
[2] Marc Briceno, Ian Goldberg, David Wagner, *GSM Cloning*, http://www.isaac.cs.berkeley.edu/isaac/ gsm-faq.html, 1998.

[3] Marc Briceno, Ian Goldberg, David Wagner, *A pedagogical implementation of the GSM A5/1 and A5/2 "voice privacy" encryption algorithms*, http://cryptome.org/gsm-a512.htm (originally on www.scard.org), 1999.

[4] Jovan Golic, *Cryptanalysis of Alleged A5 Stream Cipher*, Advances in Cryptology, proceedings of Eurocrypt'97, LNCS 1233, pp. 239–255, Springer-Verlag, 1997.

[5] Alex Biryukov, Adi Shamir, David Wagner, *Real Time Cryptanalysis of A5/1 on a PC*, Advances in Cryptology, proceedings of Fast Software Encryption'00, Lecture Notes in Computer Science 1978, Springer-Verlag, pp. 1–18, 2001.

[6] Alex Biryukov, Adi Shamir, *Cryptanalytic Time/Memory/Data Tradeoffs for Stream Ciphers*, Advances in Cryptology, proceedings of Asiacrypt'00, Lecture Notes in Computer Science 1976, Springer-Verlag, pp. 1–13, 2000.

[7] Eli Biham, Orr Dunkelman, *Cryptanalysis of the A5/1 GSM Stream Cipher*, Progress in Cryptology, proceedings of Indocrypt'00, Lecture Notes in Computer Science 1977, Springer-Verlag, pp. 43–51, 2000.

[8] Patrik Ekdahl, Thomas Johansson, *Another Attack on A5/1*, IEEE Transactions on Information Theory 49(1), pp. 284-289, 2003.

[9] Alexander Maximov, Thomas Johansson, Steve Babbage, *An improved correlation attack on A5/1*, proceedings of SAC 2004, LNCS 3357, pp. 1–18, Springer-Verlag, 2005.

[10] Elad Barkan, Eli Biham, *Conditional Estimators: an Effective Attack on A5/1*, proceedings of SAC 2005, pp. 1–19, Springer-Verlag, 2005.

[11] Ian Goldberg, David Wagner, Lucky Green, *The (Real-Time) Cryptanalysis of A5/2*, presented at the Rump Session of Crypto'99, 1999.

[12] Slobodan Petrović, Amparo Fúster-Sabater, *Cryptanalysis of the A5/2 Algorithm*, Cryptology eprint Archive, Report 2000/052, http://eprint.iacr.org, 2000.

[13] Elad Barkan, Eli Biham, Nathan Keller, *Instant Ciphertext-Only Cryptanalysis of GSM Encrypted Communications*, Advances in Cryptology, proceedings of Crypto 2003, Lecture Notes in Computer Science 2729, Springer-Verlag, pp. 600–616, 2003.

Security and Embedded Systems
D.N. Serpanos and R. Giladi (Eds.)
IOS Press, 2006

August 2005

Telecommunications Fraud & Electronic Crime in Fix and Mobile Embedded Systems

Michalis MAVIS[1]

Head of OTE (Hellenic Telecom Organization) Security and Fraud Control Division, v. Chairman of the Hellenic Fraud Forum

Abstract. Telecommunications fraud and Electronic Crime is moving from the fix networks (PSTN, ISDN) towards the mobile networks (GSM, 3G-UMTS, WiFi, WiMax, Blue-tooth, etc) and the content. Mobile phones are now becoming targets of malicious code, like the PCs are already, as of many years ago. When mobile phones are used as tools for value added services, the risk is obvious. Security countermeasures embedded in those systems are the only solution, against all those threats and risks.

Keywords. Security, telecom fraud, electronic crime

Introduction

Today's environment is mainly characterized by the convergence of Telecom, IT and entertainment technologies. Even though in many countries broadband penetration is very low, in some countries (especially in Asia) communications speed exceeded 10MB/sec in local loop so that users may watch even TV programs on their pc, by using their fast Internet connection. Mobile communications and technologies long or short range (e.g. 3G, WiMax – WiFi, Bluetooth) are widely used.

On the other hand Internet Protocol (IP), VoIP and video/TV over IP will be standard and more widely used in the near future infrastructures.

New services are evolving every day making our lives easier, but leave a lot of space to electronic crime and telecommunications fraud.

In this paper we will concentrate on specific security related threats found on fix and mobile systems. It should be noticed that presenting all related security vulnerabilities requires very extensive work and is out of the scope of this paper.

What is clear today is that crime and fraud is moving towards content and especially to mobile systems. According to FIINA (Forum for International Irregular Network Access) Telecom Operators and Service Providers are loosing around 60 B€ (Euros) every year due to telecommunications fraud and electronic crime.

---

[1] Michalis Mavis used to work as crypto engineer in NATO – Brussels, between the years 1989 and 1993. Email: mmavis@ote.gr.

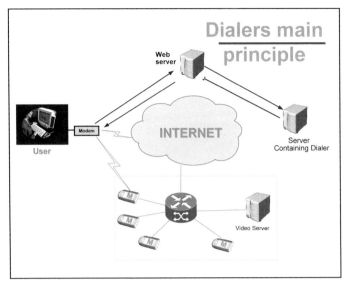

Figure 1. How diallers work.

1. Some Security Concerns in Fix Networks

Lots of managers view security as another feature of the infrastructure – something you install, configure and administer, like a remote management application. But, security is neither a feature nor a product. Security is a non-feature requirement. Features in applications, for instance, are designed to allow input A to produce output B. Security is the mechanism that enables that activity to happen safely.

The well known telephone infrastructure (PSTN, ISDN) has been very resistant to security attacks and has not suffered from significant problems since the introduction of the signalling system SS7, used to establish and manage telephone calls. Users of the telephone infrastructure have no direct access to SS7 signalling, and the local exchange provides a very robust firewall between the edge signalling protocols supporting telephony services and the core SS7 signalling network.

However, the recent rapid growth in VoIP service offerings raises important concerns about security. The openness of IP networks in general, and the security risks that have been well documented in the Web world, suggest that VoIP networks are inherently vulnerable to a range of potential attacks. Service providers need to understand the vulnerabilities of VoIP networks and take appropriate measures to counter them in order to maintain a high level of confidence among users of VoIP services.

A VoIP broadband access network must address three key security issues:

- Invasion to privacy
- Denial of service
- Theft of service

A VoIP broadband access network must be designed to address security threats. For each interface, the following must be considered. Authentication and non-repudiation, Access control, Integrity and confidentiality.

Service providers deploying VoIP networks have experienced few security problems to date, but as VoIP services become more widely available the level of risk is bound to rise. It is only a matter of time before we start to see concerted attacks on VoIP networks, but service providers who have been prudent in putting the appropriate security measures in place have little to fear.

2. Internet Related Security Concerns

To give a total view of the Internet related security problems is a very extensive work. Just to give a first feeling of the continuous cyber-war, we refer to the British NISCC (National Infrastructure Security Co-ordination Centre located in London-UK) recent publication [1]. According to the document produced by the Centre, on 16th June 2005:

- UK Government and companies are targeted by trojianised email attacks.
- The attackers aim appears to be covert gathering and transmitting of commercially or economically valuable information.
- Trojans are delivered either in email attachments or through links to a website.
- The emails employ social engineering, including spoofed sender address and information relevant to the recipient's job or interests to entice them into opening the documents.
- Once installed on a user machine, trojans may be used to obtain passwords, scan networks, exfiltrate information and launch further attacks.
- Anti-virus software and firewalls do not give complete protection. Trojans can communicate with the attackers using common ports (e.g. HTTP, DNS, SSL) and can be modified to avoid anti-virus protection!

On the other hand as Internet use is becoming more familiar to a growing number of people all over the world, security threats like spyware, adware, pharming, phising and diallers are becoming common problems to most of them. Lets try to give some explanations and definitions about those threats:

2.1. Spyware: The word *spyware* elicits an immediate reaction from anyone who has surfed the Internet in the past couple of years. Pop-up advertisements, suddenly sluggish Internet connections, and strange icons that mysteriously appear on your desktop and refuse to be removed are all associated with a type of program called spyware. Although less common, these simple annoyances can cross the line into clearly malicious behaviour. For example, the program may search for and steal confidential information such as user names and passwords for fraudulent purposes. Those programs have the ability to scan systems or monitor activity and relay information to other computers or locations in cyberspace. Among the information that may be actively or passively gathered and disseminated by spyware are passwords, log-in details, account numbers, personal information, individual files, or other personal documents. Spyware may also gather and distribute information related to the user's computer, applications running on the computer, Internet browser usage, or other computing habits.

Spyware frequently attempts to remain unnoticed, either by actively hiding or by simply not making its presence on a system known to the user. These types of programs can be downloaded from Web sites (typically in shareware or freeware), email messages, and instant messengers.

2.2. Adware: Programs that facilitate delivery of advertising content to the user through their own or another program's interface. In some cases, these programs may gather information from the user's computer, including information related to Internet browser usage or other computing habits, and relay this information back to a remote computer or other locations in cyberspace.

Adware can be downloaded from Web sites (often in shareware or freeware), email messages, and instant messenger programs.

2.3. Pharming: Basically, pharming involves interfering with the name resolution process on the Internet. When a user enters an address (such as www.deutche-bank.com) this needs to be converted into a numeric IP address as 169.14.45.187. This is known as name resolution, and the task is performed by DNS (Domain Name System) servers. These servers store tables with the IP address of each domain name. On a smaller scale, in each computer connected to the Internet there is a file that stores a table with the names of servers and IP addresses so that it is not necessary to access the DNS servers for certain server names.

Pharming consists in the name resolution system modification, so that when a user thinks he or she is accessing to bank's Web page, he or she is actually accessing the IP of a spoofed site. Pharming exploit the old problem of DNS cache poisoning. There are new attacks, which make DNS cache poisoning trivial to execute against a large number of nameservers running today.

2.4. Phishing owed its success to social engineering techniques, but since not all users take the phishing bait, its success was limited. Also, each phishing attack was aimed at one specific type of banking service, further reducing the chances of success.

2.5. Diallers or Internet "dumping" or modem hijacking takes place when, unknown to the user, a malicious program transfers the user from the current internet service provider (ISP), which is usually accessed using an un-timed local call, to a premium rate telephone number. The user is unaware that this has happened until they receive their next telephone bill. Internet dumping is more likely to happen through adult content sites. Worldwide operators have received many complaints about Internet dumping. Internet users have found that, while they surfed the net or went to non-adult sites, diallers had downloaded themselves, or the user—who may have thought it was some other piece of software, inadvertently downloaded them.

There has been a sharp rise in the number of e-commerce-related disputes, according to a European Consumer Centre Network, a body which acts on behalf of European consumers. In its 2004 Report [2], it dealt with around 193 e-commerce cases (a rise of 150 percent over the previous year).

3. Countermeasures

The solution against those kinds of fraud lies, as ever, in anti-virus and anti-spyware security solutions. Pharming attacks depend on an application in the compromised system (this could be an exe file, a script, etc.). But before this application can run, obviously it needs to reach the operating system. Code can enter the system through numerous channels; in fact, in as many ways as information can enter the system: via e-mail (the most frequent), Internet downloads, copied directly from CD or floppy, etc. In

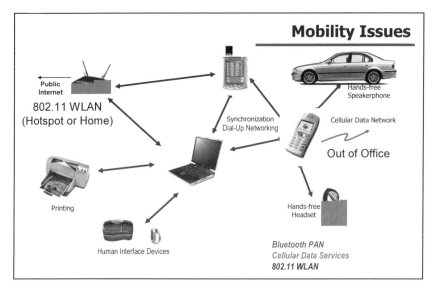

Figure 2. Mobile gadgets are open to many security threats.

each of these information entry points, the anti-virus has to detect the file with the malicious code and eliminate it, provided it is registered as a dangerous application in the anti-virus signature file.

Unfortunately, the propagation speed of malware today is head-spinning, and there are more malicious creators offering their source code to the rest of the hacker community to create new variants and propagate even more attacks. The virus laboratories don't have enough time to prepare the malware detection and elimination routines for new malicious code before they start spreading to PCs.

Despite the efforts and improvements from virus labs, it is physically impossible for them to prepare an adequate solution in time against some of these threats that can spread in just a few minutes. The solution against these kinds of threats should not, therefore, depend, at least not in the front line of protection, on a reactive solution based on viral identifier files but rather systems that detect the actions that theses threats carry out. In this way, every time there is an attempted attack on the computer's DNS system (as in the case of pharming applications), the attack is recognized and blocked along with the program carrying out the attack.

4. Threats Against Mobile Phones

As more mobile gadgets come equipped with sophisticated software and new netwrok features, they are becoming vulnerable to the nuisances that affict personal computers – from spam to spyware to financial fraud. Mobile viruses are only recently starting to represent a serious problem. Mobile devices such as cellphones and hand-helds are new frontier for the world's malware writers and hardware hackers. Although 3G operators are concentrating on delivering content for adults, a new report suggests they should also consider introducing television clips for children.

According to the research firm IDC, mobile television has largely been aimed at adults, with sports clips, news bulletins, entertainment updates and so called 'mobisodes' all being introduced in a bid to whet the appetites of mobile phone users. Some of those mobisodes or mobile games consist a serious threat to the mobile phone users. Malicious code is some times resident in this piece of softare and may cause various problems, like the following:

- Block – destroy mobile phone completely.
- DoS attack to the mobile phone.
- Attack the battery.
- Steal – delete internal memory (address book).
- Make calls. Send spam SMS via victims' phones.
- Make PRS (very expensive) calls.
- Monitor (spy) conversation!
- When mobile phone is connected to a pc, hack the pc.

One difficulty in fixing the vulnerabilities is a limitation in most cell phone software that makes it impossible to download patches over the cellular network itself. Instead, a cell phone user must bring each phone to a service centre where the updated operating system can be placed into the device with a flash-memory card. Experts are considering the need to an over-the-air way to update thesc units after infected or install patches before infection. Considering the complex inter-working situation within the mobile terminals, the network and the application servers, it is necessary a correlative reacting system to effectively protect both the terminals and the network from attacks, which should address not only the prevention policies, but also policies that will be performed if virus or worms have been found in the mobile network.

As example knowing that some mobile terminal are infected with virus or worms, the network side should have a way to control the behaviour of these terminals, thus to prevent the virus from spreading in the whole network, or at least keep the spreading in a configurable limitation. For the detected potentially dangerous application, the network side should take block or restriction performance so as to keep the network in a relatively immune status.

Increasingly, mobile phones and similar devices connected to the mobile networks are available with enhanced features, including colour screens, picture messaging, video cameras and Internet browsers and can be used to access a growing variety of content. These advanced features are accompanied by a growing ability within the mobile operators to offer faster data connections over the 3G networks.

Analysts expect spending on adult contents for cell phones to top $1 Billion worldwide in 2005. Two new studies from Juniper Research conclude that Gambling and Adult based content have the potential to generate revenues in excess of 6 b€ by 2006.

The dangers and risks associated with using 3G or Mobile Internet services can be reduced through effective education of the safe and appropriate behaviours to adopt when using this new technology.In common with general Internet safety recommendations, children and young people should be taught the importance of keeping personal information private, of the appropriate behaviours to use when online, the need to critically evaluate any information they find, and the importance of seeking advice from an adult if they see any content or are contacted in a way which makes them feel uncomfortable.

Figure 3. Games downloaded in mobile phones may contain malicious code.

5. Conclusions

A security awareness program is necessary because lack of awareness on information security may produce a lot of problems to idividuals and companies.

Although the security risks cannot be totaly eliminated, increasing awareness of information security will spread knowledge and thus increase understanding of information security concept and objectives.

Telecommunications Fraud & Electronic Crime in fix and mobile embedded systems is moving towards content and in new services. Security awareness is a must, in order to avoid bad consequences.

Fraud and Crime scenarios become more and more complex, especially when mobile phones are used on value added services (casino games, mobile banking etc.) and fighting need knowledge in many technology areas.

Security improvements will both increase compliance and reduce risks, making security breaches less likely and/or less costly, in other words real bottom-line business benefits.

References

[1]   NISCC Briefing 08/2005 (16 June 2005) – Targeted Trojan Email Attacks.
[2]   European Consumer Centre Network – 2004 Report.

Security and Embedded Systems
D.N. Serpanos and R. Giladi (Eds.)
IOS Press, 2006
© *2006 IOS Press. All rights reserved.*

Author Index